Leading the Historical Enterprise

AMERICAN ASSOCIATION FOR STATE AND LOCAL HISTORY BOOK SERIES

ABOUT THE SERIES

The American Association for State and Local History Book Series publishes technical and professional information for those who practice and support history, and addresses issues critical to the field of state and local history. To submit a proposal or manuscript to the series, please request proposal guidelines from AASLH headquarters: AASLH Editorial Board, 1717 Church St., Nashville, Tennessee 37203. Telephone: (615) 320-3203. Website: www.aaslh.org.

ABOUT THE ORGANIZATION

The American Association for State and Local History (AASLH) is a national history organization headquartered in Nashville, Tennessee. AASLH provides leadership and support for its members who preserve and interpret state and local history in order to make the past more meaningful to all Americans. AASLH is a membership association representing history organizations and the professionals who work in them. AASLH members are leaders in preserving, researching, and interpreting traces of the American past to connect the people, thoughts, and events of yesterday with the creative memories and abiding concerns of people, communities, and our nation today. In addition to sponsorship of this book series, AASLH publishes History News magazine, a newsletter, technical leaflets and reports, and other materials; confers prizes and awards in recognition of outstanding achievement in the field; and supports a broad education program and other activities designed to help members work more effectively. To join AASLH, go to www.aaslh.org or contact Membership Services, AASLH, 1717 Church St., Nashville, TN 37203.

Leading the Historical Enterprise

Strategic Creativity, Planning, and Advocacy for the Digital Age

Bruce W. Dearstyne

ROWMAN & LITTLEFIELD
Lanham • Boulder • New York • London

Published by Rowman & Littlefield
A wholly owned subsidiary of The Rowman & Littlefield Publishing Group, Inc.
4501 Forbes Boulevard, Suite 200, Lanham, Maryland 20706
www.rowman.com

Unit A, Whitacre Mews, 26-34 Stannary Street, London SE11 4AB

British Library Cataloguing in Publication Information Available

Library of Congress Cataloging-in-Publication Data Available

ISBN 978-0-7591-2398-4 (cloth : alk. paper) -- 978-0-7591-2399-1 (pbk. : alk. paper) -- 978-0-7591-2400-4 (electronic)

∞™ The paper used in this publication meets the minimum requirements of American
National Standard for Information Sciences Permanence of Paper for Printed Library
Materials, ANSI/NISO Z39.48-1992.

Printed in the United States of America

Contents

Introduction   1

1   The State of the Historical Enterprise   5

2   Leading Historical Programs   25

3   Creativity, Innovation, and the Historical Enterprise   45

4   Making Strategic Connections   67

5   Digital Engagement   85

6   Advocacy   107

7   Strategic Planning   131

8   The Historical Enterprise in Action   151

Bibliography   173

Index   179

About the Author   185

Introduction

Leading the Historical Enterprise is a book about the nation's "historical enterprise," broadly defined to include historical societies, history museums, historic houses, state historical agencies, archives, and similar programs. The term "enterprise" is meant to convey the notion of a big, bold, important, sometimes challenging undertaking requiring energy, initiative, and imagination. This is a book about leadership, aspirations, change, and taking our programs to new, higher levels. It assumes that, for most of our programs, the status quo is not something we should regard as a steady state and instead we should be aiming to keep innovating and strengthening our practices and services. The book is also based on the assumption that the work our programs are doing is of immense consequence. By preserving, organizing, and presenting historical sources and materials, we are the conduit between the past and the future. The work is essential in informing and enlightening the present by ensuring the availability of perspectives and insights from the past. There is a good deal at stake in what we do every day. *Leading the Historical Enterprise* tries to suggest optimal approaches to the work.

The book is organized in eight chapters.

Chapter 1, *The State of the Historical Enterprise*, describes pride in what we do, looks at some of the challenges history programs face, and also identifies some trends and developments that we can capitalize on to build into the future.

Chapter 2, *Leading Historical Programs*, discusses what leadership is and why it is so important and describes approaches to leading historical programs.

Chapter 3, *Creativity, Innovation, and the Historical Enterprise*, makes the case that creativity (imaginative new ideas) and innovation (putting the best ideas to work in historical programs) are the keys to the future.

1

Chapter 4, *Making Strategic Connections*, discusses the need for historical programs to connect with other groups and programs to help achieve their goals.

Chapter 5, *Digital Engagement*, analyzes the implications of providing history in digital form over the web and the application of modern information technology tools, particularly social media.

Chapter 6, *Advocacy*, explores strategies for programs in gaining recognition, support, and resources for their work.

Chapter 7, *Strategic Planning*, explains how programs can plan for their future and includes several examples.

Chapter 8, *The Historical Enterprise in Action*, the final chapter, profiles some of the strongest and most interesting historical programs, models of leadership and innovation.

This work is based heavily on research into issues, practices, and strategies exemplified by the best historical programs in the nation, and outstanding programs in other countries, as the footnotes indicate. But it also works in, interprets, and applies sources, lessons, and insights from business, management, and leadership literature. The *Bibliography* lists books that should be useful to leaders of historical programs.

I am very grateful to Charles Harmon, executive editor at Rowman and Littlefield Publishing Group, for his guidance in reviewing the proposal and shaping the book. I would also like to acknowledge the anonymous reviewers who went over the original book proposal and made a number of very helpful suggestions for revision which are reflected in the final version. Robert Beatty, vice president for programs at the American Association for State and Local History, provided his insights and perspectives as the book was taking shape, which were much appreciated.

Ms. Cyra Nealon, my sister-in-law, carried out the task of carefully reading the entire manuscript and identifying a number of corrections and changes which significantly improved the final product. I am grateful for that work.

I am most grateful to my wife, Susan, for her support and assistance during the two years that the book was under preparation. Susan identified many sources, obtained books through interlibrary loan, read through all the drafts, made many suggestions for strengthening the narrative, and also prepared the index. Her patience, wisdom, and insights have inspired and sustained my life and work for more than four decades. I can't thank her enough for all that she has done.

Historical insights and understanding are things that one generation passes on to the next, hopefully imparting wisdom that will enrich their lives. That is what makes the work described in *Leading the Historical Enterprise* so important. In that spirit, I dedicate this book to my four grandchildren, who are a constant delight and inspiration in all of my work. Their understanding of history will hopefully guide them as they become adults and begin making history of their own.

Abigail Gregory
Jack Gregory
Madeline Roberts
Stella Roberts

Bruce W. Dearstyne
Guilderland, New York
September 2014

Chapter One

The State of the Historical Enterprise

PRIDE IN SERVICE TO HISTORY

The nation's "historical enterprise"—broadly defined to include historical societies, history museums, historic houses, state historical agencies, archives, and similar programs—is facing unprecedented challenges alongside vast opportunities. There is much at stake in the future of these "public history" institutions, because they preserve, interpret, and present the histories of states and of thousands of communities across the nation and connect local events and individuals to larger national and international historical developments. They are animated by a deep sense of pride and mission and a tradition of service. "The real stuff of history is found in your community and your institutions such as the local archives, libraries, museums, and historic buildings and places," explains the Ohio Historical Society's *Citizen's Guide.* "These are where you find . . . original diaries, birth certificates, buried artifacts, buildings and histories. . . . History promotes educational achievement, stimulates our economy and contributes significantly to our quality of life."[1] "Newburgh [New York] is a fascinating place," says Johanna Porr, the director of the Historical Society of Newburgh Bay and the Highlands. "We call it 'History City' because you can take any major movement and tie it back here somehow; you can always find a way to understand the scope of American history through the narratives that are available in Newburgh."[2] "In Massachusetts, you find history under every rock and on every corner," boasts the website of a consortium of historic sites in that state.[3]

"History is not something obscure or unimportant," says historical novelist Steve Berry, whose lively works blend fictional accounts with historical evidence. "History plays a vital role in our everyday lives. We learn from our past in order to achieve greater influence over our future. History serves as a model not only of who and what we are to be; we [also] learn what to champion and what to avoid."[4] Historians have "a shared curiosity about the past," says the Canadian Historical Association, and "stitch together the threads of evidence" to "unveil the complexities of the large and small processes, community developments and personal choices which together combine to create the many strata of past human experiences."[5] Study of history is important for empowering people's analytical and other skills (See "History's Habits of Mind.")

"HISTORY'S HABITS OF MIND"

History is essential for our understanding of the past, ability to manage in the present, and planning for the future, all points that can be put forth in advocacy initiatives. But the study of history also strengthens our ability to understand cause and effect, complexity, individual motivations, and group dynamics. The National Council for History Education has issued a statement on "History's Habits of Mind" that suggests some of these benefits (http://www.nche.net/habitsofmind).

The National Council for History Education (NCHE) believes that historical thinking develops a unique capacity to comprehend human situations, challenges, and interactions. Thinking historically introduces students to the wonders of the past and fosters the ability to make judgments about the present. "History's Habits of Mind" articulates this distinctive approach, one that leads toward engaging with and understanding the contemporary world and serves as a foundation for life-long, productive learning and active citizenship.

History's habits of mind empower and enable individuals to:

- Grasp the significance of the past in shaping the present
- Perceive past events and issues as they might have been experienced by the people of the time, with historical empathy rather than present-mindedness
- Read critically, to discern differences between evidence and assertion and to frame useful and appropriate questions about the past
- Interrogate texts and artifacts, posing questions about the past that foster informed discussion, reasoned debate and evidence-based interpretation
- Recognize that history is an evolving narrative constructed from available sources, cogent inferences, and changing interpretations
- Appreciate the diversity of cultures and variety of historical contexts, as well as to distinguish elements of our shared humanity

- Understand the impact made by individuals, groups, and institutions at local, national, and global levels both in effecting change and in ensuring continuity
- Realize that all individuals are decision makers, but that personal and public choices are often restricted by time, place, and circumstance
- Negotiate a complex, often uncertain and ambiguous world, equipped with the appreciation for multiple perspectives
- Engage in patient reflection and constant reexamination of the past and present.

Public historian Darlene Roth notes that people have a deep desire to make sense of the human experience, broadly defined. She refers to "the functional past that consists of all the ways we do history or all the ways we communicate past images and ideas to each other" particularly through history programs. "We can learn from the past," and "narratives that serve the collective raise consciousness and provoke growth." She adds that "the future has use for the past" because people's understanding of the past colors how they understand the present and shape the future.[6]

When asked about whether they value history, people almost always respond positively. A 2009 survey by the University of Toledo for the Ohio Historical Society revealed that historic site visitors and social studies teachers overwhelmingly endorsed history programs. That was no surprise. But a random survey of residents in the state also showed an impressive appreciation for their state's history. For instance, 86 percent said Ohio history and historic places were important to them, 53 percent said history was important to their career, 76 percent said they thought about the past when making important decisions, and 72 percent look to historic figures as role models. Ohioans who said they valued Ohio's history scored much higher on an accompanying "Civic Participation Index," measuring levels of civic engagement, than those who did not value their state's history.[7] Historian David McCullough, speaking at the National Museum of American History in 2008, noted that "the thrill—the essential, never-ending fascination—of all to be found here within these walls—is that they are the real thing. There are no facsimiles here, no reproductions, no approximations."[8]

But the connection between programs that constitute the historical enterprise and the people whose lives and communities they document is more complex. Dan Spock of the Minnesota Historical Society has noted that "the traditional historical society is a parochial affair, more often than not dedicated to a particular city or state," based around artifacts that seem to have tenuous connections to contemporary individuals' lives or current affairs. But for most people, "the past . . . is a deeply personal and resonant place, a great well of feeling." Spock described a 2009 survey in the St. Paul region, where the Society is located, which revealed that less than 17 percent of the respondents had ever visited the Historical Society, but their perception of the institution nevertheless was very positive. "What people seemed to be telling us was that even though I don't really care to visit you, we're glad you're there."[9] People seem the most interested in history that enables them to make a personal connection. That accounts in part for the popularity of genealogy and family history and commercial services such as Ancestry.com.

It seems to be a near-universal pattern. "Australians are deeply interested in heritage issues, but primarily on a personal level," says a report from that nation, further evidence that connections to history need to be personal. "They are motivated to engage in heritage issues they find directly relevant to their own specific interests, culture, or history . . . heritage [is] a very individual thing."[10] A study by the British Museums Association found that "there is a strong, positive emotional attachment to museums by visitors and non-visitors" which has deepened as museums "shed their image of stuffiness and sterility and become more entertaining and interactive." Museums were perceived as highly trustworthy institutions that have "an active role in sharing new knowledge rather than as passive buildings simply storing objects." The poll showed that most people felt museums should "concern themselves with what they are good at first and foremost" rather than expanding their role to include providing forums for debating social justice, human rights, and other contemporary issues even if they are connected to the museum's mission. In Britain and elsewhere, though, this traditional view is being questioned. In its report based on the study, the Association did not endorse its own poll's conclusion that museums should stick to their historical curatorial and presentation missions. Instead, its report, entitled *Museums Change Lives*, advocated a broader and more interventionist and activist role for museums in the debate of contemporary issues.[11]

STRUGGLES AND CHALLENGES

State and local history are vital in defining and sustaining communities, revealing insights for and parallels with many contemporary issues and problems, supporting continuity of institutions and culture, and imparting civic awareness. They are, or at least can be, forums for drawing on historical insights to enlighten debate of contemporary issues and chart future directions. But many of our programs are struggling. Individuals who don't understand how history programs connect them with the past in a meaningful way may be indifferent. Members of the public say they value history, but their interest in and support for history programs often seems lukewarm or ambivalent. "You may have to search for it, but your hometown likely has a small building packed to the rafters with archives and artifacts. It's probably staffed by amateur historians and it tells the story of whatever made your town the unique place that it is," said a Buffalo news writer. "Depending on one's viewpoint of the past, [historical societies] are either isolated little outposts that traffic in memory or nostalgia and thus an acquired taste, or jewels in the crown of this remarkable part of America." The writer, who is also a local historian, described their mission as underappreciated keepers of the flame of local history. [12]

Leading a historical enterprise program sometimes seems like sailing in turbulent seas with crosscutting underlying currents of demographic changes and unpredictable customer expectations, irresistible winds propelling them toward an uncertain digital future, and a hard, steady rain of bad economic news and eroding budgets. The Oregon Heritage Commission, after a series of surveys and public hearings, summarized eight key issues in a 2011 report that it warned were putting the state's heritage at risk. In fact, they are common to most other states: [13]

> *Unstable and inadequate government and private funding.* Visitorship and requests for services from heritage organization was rising as the state began moving out of the recession, but state and county funding was declining and private funding becoming more competitive.
>
> *Little meaningful coordination and collaboration among heritage organizations and their communities.*
>
> *The inability to measure and articulate the economic value of Oregon heritage.* Heritage institutions generate "hundreds of millions of dollars of economic value annually" for the state, but the data to document it was incomplete or not recorded.
>
> *Changing educational requirements have reduced the time and respect given history instruction in primary, secondary, and higher education.* History education was being eclipsed by other demands on school spending and lack of public understanding of its importance.
>
> *Shortage of people with the skills and knowledge to address issues of preservation, fund raising, leadership, and technology.* Financial instability and other challenges have left many organizations "without the skills and knowledge to address their challenges."
>
> *Changing demographics and expectations, including developing new leadership.* "Connecting its heritage to newcomers" is a particularly critical challenge.
>
> *Limited use of 21st-century communications and advocacy strategies.*
>
> *Uneven development and use of technology.*

The executive director of the New England Museum Association noted that there are so many museums in his region that they "are so much of a landscape that they are often overlooked in terms of civic participation and support." Many are underfunded, suffer from the perception of being elite institutions, and have low visitation numbers. They need to collaborate, become more entrepreneurial, and deliver "deep authentic experiences that improve the quality of life of our audiences" to avoid "the slow drowning of the institution itself due to irrelevance." His association issued a white paper warning museums need an "image lift."[14]

Historical programs face at least eight inter-related challenges.

1. History Diminished in the Schools and Public Life

Public ambivalence toward history and history programs reflects inconsistency in broader areas. A report by the American Academy of Arts and Science noted that overemphasis on science and math education and a narrow focus on preparing students to be employable were leading to diminished study of history and the other humanities. "The humanities remind us where we have been and help us envision where we are going," it noted. "A thorough grounding in history, civics, and social studies allows citizens to participate meaningfully in the democratic process—as voters, informed consumers and productive customers." Study of history and other humanities also strengthens critical thinking, complex problem solving, and written and oral communication.[15]

A 2011 report on state US History educational standards concluded that "a majority of states' standards are mediocre to awful" and assigned an average grade of "D" across the nation. Only one state (South Carolina) merited an "A." Moreover, the report found that the state history standards, almost always part of broader social studies curricular documents, often "ignore chronology by separating related content into social studies themes and categories," "posit students' present, personal interpretation of historical events as the main arbiters of historical significance," and too often were "couched in abstruse and often meaningless edu-jargon, and presented in overly complex mazes of charts and tables."[16]

The "Common Core Standards," developed by a consortium of the nation's governors and state education commissioners mainly to strengthen math, science, and English language arts in 2011, relegated social studies to a subsidiary role in support of reading and composition until 2013, when a standard covering social studies was finally issued. But it was ponderously entitled "College, Career & Civic Life: C3 Framework for Social Studies State Standards." History received only a few pages in the 108 page document, which gave sustained attention to geography, economics, and literacy. The history standards described historical thinking and historical inquiry, insisted that "history is interpretative," discussed the nature of historical sources, and went into "causation and argumentation." But they provided little guidance on working solid historical content into state curricular guidelines and classrooms, and did not mention state and local history.[17] The status of social studies continued to slip as it was upstaged by science and math and other subjects with allegedly more direct usefulness in the work-place and more relevant to sustaining the nation's international competitive-ness. Within social studies curricula frameworks, history tended to be squeezed by other topics, including civics, which was, too often, disassociat-ed from study of history. Within history segments of the curricula frame-works, state and local history tended to be pushed out of high school into the earlier grades in favor of American and world history.

Given the limited coverage of history in the schools, it is no surprise that public knowledge of US history is limited. Recent public surveys revealed that most people could not identify Susan B. Anthony, two-thirds could not name Yorktown as the last major military action of the Revolution, 40 per-cent did not know whom we fought in World War II, and 40 percent believe Congress shares power over US foreign policy with the United Nations. *Newsweek* magazine gave the test that all immigrants applying for citizenship are required to take to a representative sample of Americans; 38 percent failed.[18] Dim awareness of history carries over to attitudes toward programs that make up the historical enterprise. A study by the North Carolina State Historic Preservation Office found limited public awareness of history pro-grams and confusion about which were private and which were public. "The primary threats to successful preservation within North Carolina are plainly evident: lack of funding, apathy/lack of interest, and lack of awareness."[19]

2. Dwindling Resources Intensify a Culture of Scarcity

Many history organizations got started in order to commemorate a commu-nity milestone, save a threatened house or other building, house an important person's papers, or serve as a gathering-place and forum for a group of people interested in the history of a certain region or topic. Pride and enthu-siasm often brought the programs quickly into existence. Strategic planning, provision for a reliable source of funding over the long term, and questions of how to serve a changing audience over time were often not considered in-depth when the program was established. State chartering or incorporation guidelines imposed limited requirements. Often volunteer led, programs op-erate on small budgets, mostly in isolation from each other. Sometimes, they compete for resources, collections, and audience. This has led to what Anne Ackerson, former director of the Museum Association of New York, has called "scarcity thinking":[20]

> Bottom of the pyramid . . . chronically under-resourced . . . pressure for change
> coming from history consumers and young generations of history profession-
> als . . . "culturally resistant"—this is a field that, despite the richness of collec-
> tions and the breadth and dominance of the state's [New York] historical

narrative, suffers greatly from real and imagined scarcity . . . scarcity thinking
permeates the history museum landscape . . . a mindset colored by the belief
that growth is difficult to achieve because there are never enough resources to
do the job.

The national recession, which began in 2008 and gradually relented several years later, further squeezed historical programs as attendance tapered
off, contributions diminished, endowments shrank, and government funding
dried up. Two-thirds of the museums covered in a 2012 report by the
American Alliance of Museums reported some degree of financial stress,
though attendance was slowly rising for many of them and budget prospects
were less daunting than a few years earlier. The museums reported resorting
to tactics of deferred maintenance, more reliance on volunteers to fill the gap
left by paid staff who had been laid off or left, and less frequently changing
exhibits. Museum leaders were said to be "mildly, not wildly, optimistic"
about the future.[21] The American Historical Association's public history specialist wrote in 2012 that many historical societies are "tiny, underfunded and
understaffed . . . many societies are run by people with little formal training
in history . . . many societies simply don't have the resources to update their
exhibits or conservation practices." Moreover, their core audience is "white,
older and middle class, a serious drawback in a country that is being radically
transformed in demographic (and ethnic) terms."[22]

3. History Scattered on (and by) the Web

The Internet and the Web are disrupting and transforming how people access,
study, and understand history. Authoritative sources such as libraries and
museums are being challenged by web-based information that anyone with a
computer and access to the Internet can create. Part of the issue is that
Google, *Wikipedia*, YouTube, and Flickr have established themselves as the
de facto "museums of the digital world that are actively trying to redefine the
idea of curating content," setting expectations for convenient "remote visits"
and easy-to-find information that museums and similar institutions are now
challenged to match.[23] "We are in a crisis of knowledge at the same time that
we are in an epochal exaltation of knowledge. We fear for institutions on
which we have relied for trustworthy knowledge, but there's also a joy we
can feel pulsing through our culture," says Internet expert David Weinberger.[24] "It comes from the *networking of knowledge*. Knowledge now lives
not just in libraries and museums and academic individuals. It lives not just
in the skulls of individuals. Our skulls and our institutions are simply not big
enough to contain knowledge. Knowledge is now a property of the network,
and the network embraces businesses, governments, media, museums, curated collections and minds in communication." Weinberger notes that information on the Net has five traits.

Abundance beyond anything we imagined back in the days of television and physical libraries.

Ideas and concepts can be hyperlinked, so you can go from one to another with just a click.

Permission free in the sense that people can post what they wish and everyone can access it unless the creator or the website imposes restrictions.

Public—"The Net is a vast public space within which the exclusion of visitors or content is the exception."

Unresolved, a place for continual disagreement and debate and for adding more and more information.

Recognized historical experts and venerable institutions in the historical enterprise are searching for new ways to retain their traditional status as authorities on historical facts and interpretations. "No forces of change are impacting cultural practice, including public history, faster, deeper, and wider than technological innovation," notes a book on sharing historical authority. "Virtually overnight it seems, the cultural power center has shifted from the wizened and experienced practitioner to a younger, more nimble collection of experts and non-experts, all communicating with each other constantly and sharing their individual/collective production with lightning speed. Attention spans are breaking down and expectations are growing that everyone could and should arrange, direct, produce, curate, comment, and upload on any and all means of cultural production."[25] "The ease in which digital information can be disseminated has fundamentally changed the pursuit and transmission of enduring knowledge," notes the Canadian government's library/archives program. "Physical boundaries become far less important as does geographic location. Controlled access to information resources gives way to unmediated electronic access; marshalling information resources to a physical location gives way to sharing information resources in multiple locations; and competition for scarce information resources gives way to collaboration to gain access to a superabundance of information."[26]

4. Perpetual Reinterpretation

Historical programs are challenged to balance the traditional ways in which they have presented history with new interpretations, some of them controversial and subject to continuing, spirited debate. Of course, historians are accustomed to "investigating and interpreting the past as a matter of disciplined learned practice" and "strive constantly to improve our collective understanding of the past through a complex process of critical dialog—with each other, with the wider public, and with the historical record . . . [and] contesting each other's interpretations."[27] A study of the National Park Service's (NPS) history programs by the Organization of American Historians recommended that the historic sites "acknowledge that history is dynamic and always unfinished."[28]

> History practice should be grounded in and incorporate the inherently dynamic processes of historical scholarship and recognize that meanings change over time, and respond to not only new information, but new audiences, new questions, new approaches and analytical techniques and new perspectives. Interpretations of the past are forever open and subject to reconsideration; history is never "done." . . . Historical narrative should acknowledge ways in which the past was always open-ended and contingent. . . . [The national parks should] forthrightly address conflict and controversy both in, and about, the past.

The NPS is a good example of the swirl of controversy that can precipitate, or accompany, change. For instance, the Washita Battlefield National Historic Site in Oklahoma, which once presented the 1868 battle as the glorious triumph of the US 7th Cavalry over hostile Indians, drew criticism for only telling one side of the story. It now takes a more balanced view that "the attack was an important event in the tragic clash of cultures in the Indian Wars era." Its planning document notes that it regularly involves Indian tribes in planning and education programs.[29] The NPS is committed to "focus on aspects of the American story that are absent or are inadequately or inaccurately covered at present," "preserve and interpret forgotten, overlooked or omitted stories," constantly "review for cultural bias," and accommodate "the needs and desires of different urban populations."[30]

Sometimes, the controversy just leads to more discussion and debate. *New York Times* museum critic Edward Rothstein decried the trend toward what he called "identity museums" highlighting particular ethnic and other groups and exaggerating their historical importance.[31]

> Me! Me! Me! That is the cry, now often heard, as history is retold. Tell my story, my way! Give me the attention I deserve! Haven't you neglected me, blinded by your own perspectives? Now let history be told not by the victors but by people over whom it has trampled. [Identity museums are] designed to affirm a particular group's claims, outline its accomplishments, boost its pride and proclaim "We must tell our own story!"

Nina Simon, a proponent of "participatory museums" that are broadly inclusive and invite the community to help shape exhibits and programs, responded to Rothstein that too often museums are seen as elitist bastions of white privilege. People don't find traditional museums relevant anymore, leading to the new sorts of museums that are more inclusive and appeal to America's growing ethnic and racial diversity. Museums bucking the trend of declining attendance and diminishing significance offer "an interactive, educational, social experience."[32]

Many historical programs lack the resources, or the interest, to keep up with cutting-edge historical scholarship, or do not have sufficient resources to change exhibits, publications, and staff presentations to visitors to reflect the latest interpretations. In other cases, they were established to document the history of a community or industry but the demographics of the community were transformed, the industry declined or left town, and the program seems isolated, elitist, and outdated to newcomers.

5. New Styles of Teaching and Learning

Historical programs, particularly history museums, have a long tradition of defining their own mission and developing exhibits, publications, and other materials to provide historical information in ways they deem appropriate. Visitors customarily are expected to visit and learn about history. But this simple model has been challenged and is waning. Learning styles are shifting to being learner-centered, self-directed, self-paced, cross-disciplinary, multi-dimensional, and more geared to appealing to learners' inquisitiveness and imaginations. They are moving away from the sort of one-way process represented by teachers lecturing at the front of a class while students studiously take notes or by people walking through history museums during appointed hours, reading the labels, and carefully heeding the "do not touch" signs. People expect to be more engaged, to apply critical thinking, integrating information, and reaching their own conclusions. Community members may even expect to be involved in planning for exhibits and programs, or at least to have their opinions solicited and considered.

Museums, libraries, and other non-school centers of information and expertise are well positioned to capitalize on the new style of learning and involvement, which is particularly popular with young people who are accustomed to getting information "on demand" from the Internet and the Web and to being connected and integrated via social media platforms like Facebook. An American Association of Museums report asserts that in the future "museum audiences are likely to expect to be part of the narrative experience of museums," a dramatic shift from traditional approaches, but one that "provides an opportunity to create deeper, more immersive experiences for visitors."[33] The Institute of Museum and Library Services, a federal agency that provides grants and support for libraries and museums, developed this chart for the shift that is occurring:[34]

Twentieth-Century Museum/Library	Twenty-First-Century Museum/Library
Primarily content-driven	Combination of audience-and-content driven
Mostly tangible objects (art, books)	Combination of tangible and digital objects

One-way information (institution presents information to audiences)	Multi-directional (co-created experiences involving institution, audiences, and others)
Focus on presentation and display	Focus on audience engagement and experiences
Emphasis on enhancing knowledge	Emphasis on enhancing knowledge and twenty-first-century skills
Acts independently	Acts in highly collaborative partnerships
Located in community (acts independently)	Embedded in community (aligned with and acts as a leader on community needs/issues)
Learning outcomes assumed, implied (content knowledge and skills like critical thinking tend to be byproducts of programming)	Learning outcomes purposeful (content knowledge and twenty-first-century skills like critical thinking are visible, intentional outcomes of audience experiences)
Institution leads content development (content tightly edited and controlled)	Content co-created among diverse partners and audiences; accessible in multiple ways

History museums and other historical programs need to develop creative approaches to align with the new learning trends: [35]

> From the passive to participative: learning that involves participation and hands-on activity rather than just being a receiver of knowledge.
> From standardized delivery to personalization: one size does not fit all and different learning programs are required that can be tailored to an individual's needs.
> From the didactic to co-learning: a shift from the transmission model of learning with a single expert/tutor, to shared learning that is guided in response to the needs of the users and shaped in collaboration *with* them.
> From knowledge acquisition to knowledge application: the movement away from learning information for the sake of doing so, to understanding how to use knowledge across different settings and in original ways for valued outcomes.
> From a single authorial voice to plural voices: the development of collaborative practices and production, giving rise to a wider range of perspectives and opportunity for the student's voice in formalized settings.
> From private knowledge to public access: best exemplified through the World Wide Web/open source, but [also] relating to the ways in which the private knowledge of individuals and institutions has been opened up, shifting power relationships away from closed knowledge workers.

6. Demographic Disarray

One other set of challenges and opportunities lies in the changing demographics of the nation, which is shifting from a majority of white people to a majority of minorities, including a diverse array of racial and ethnic groups. An American Association of Museums 2010 study found that the minority population was around 34 percent, but minorities made up only about 9 percent of core museum visitors. The underlying reasons apply to museums, but also to many other historical programs as well:[36]

"Historically-grounded cultural barriers to participation" that make museums feel unfriendly, intimidating, or exclusionary

Lack of specialized knowledge by visitors to understand and appreciate the significance of what is being presented

"No strong tradition of museum-going habits," often the result of visiting museums not being part of family traditions or experience while children were growing up

Influence of peers and social networks (i.e., "none of your friends go to museums [so] you don't go either")

In addition, history museums and historic sites have generally older visitor bases. A 2010 survey by the museum research firm Reach Advisors found that 65 percent of respondents for history museums were over the age of fifty (and 95 percent identified as being white).[37] A Washington State Historical Society 2012 membership survey found the average age was seventy, 95 percent identified as white/Caucasian, and 79 percent had annual incomes above $50,000. Asked what they valued most about membership, most responded by identifying *Columbia* magazine, the society's popular history publication, followed by "being a steward of Washington State History." On the question of what kinds of exhibits they enjoyed most, "high scholarly content" and "arts and cultural" were at the top of the list, "family friendly" and "contemporary topics" at the bottom.[38]

7. No Safety in Numbers

According to American Association for State and Local History (AASLH) figures, in 1936 there were 583 historical organizations in the nation. By 2013, that number was up to more than 15,000, averaging over 300 per state. New Hampshire had over 200; Ohio more than a thousand. Many are small, entirely volunteer-run, hold meetings with interesting speakers several times a year, produce informative newsletters, are featured at town festivals, and testify in favor of historic preservation at town board meetings. They help create a local identity, linking residents to a past that some residents remember but many, particularly newcomers and young people, never knew.[39]

But many others are located in aging historic houses where deferred maintenance is taking a toll; the economic, social, and ethnic makeup of the neighborhood has changed, making the aging structures seem like relics from a distant past; collections are marginally useful; and visitation is low and sporadic. Many have become

> financially strapped, struggling for visitors, and badly in need of repair. . . .
> [M]any if not most historic house museums need to rethink and expand their
> purpose if they hope to remain viable. Aside from places of exceptional histor-
> ic or architectural distinction, the old "velvet rope" strategy is necessarily
> deadly and ultimately bound to fail. Most sites need to find ways to become
> more relevant to the community by becoming gathering places for purposes
> other than the site itself.[40]

Museum consultant and writer Linda Norris has asked directly whether there are too many museums with unsustainable and unrealistic missions, under-documented and uncared for collections, inflated expectations for visitation, and no collecting strategy. Norris suggests that too many programs have an inability to say "no" to offers of artifacts that are unrelated to the program's mission, an inability to say "yes" to new ideas, and little sense of urgency about the need for change.[41] Moreover, there is limited cooperation and coordination among the programs in most states. Programs have their own separate charters or incorporation documents, reflect distinct community identity and pride, and have interests that are circumscribed by the borders of their communities. It is common to find historical societies in adjacent towns that never hold joint meetings or sponsor joint public events. This pattern at the community level reflects splintered authority at the state level, for instance, the state museum being separate from the state heritage council and the state historic preservation office, and, in turn, those state agencies having no formal relationship with the private, membership-based state historical society. It is also common for public history programs such as historical societies to have limited connections to local college or university history departments. Rugged individualism, which some historians regard as an inherent national trait, seems to be flourishing in the historical enterprise.

8. Individual-Centric Historical Engagement

This challenge is tied to number 5, above. "It is a common misconception that museums are designed to house objects," says a recent British report. "In actual fact they are designed to give visitors an experience." Making our programs individual visitor-centric is challenging because we are catering to increasingly disparate visitor groups, from tech-savvy young people through aging baby boomers. Demographic diversity will tend to stretch the capac-ities of museums and other history programs to connect with their extended audiences on a sustained basis. This report says we need to meet the chal-lenge, and in fact exceed expectations, by making it possible for every indi-vidual who is interested to experience our programs in a way that is consistent with their information-gathering and learning styles. The challenge is particularly pronounced for people who are immersed in digital information.

> Today's digital-native generation consumes such large quantities of media that people are constantly torn between simultaneously texting, posting information on social media networks, or watching video clips online. With shorter attention spans, and a growing tendency to be increasingly distracted by the thousands of 140 character news snippets, how will museums provide novel experiences to the Generation Twitter?

Through analyzing the experiential requirements of each demographic group, programs can shift their designs and investments. Museums and other historical programs need to diversify their content in response to a rising desire among audiences to shape their own cultural experiences and shifting cultural attitudes about what topics are important and relevant. "In the future, museums may employ new patterns of collaborative curation, allowing for individually curated experiences and giving the public greater control over both content and experience." "Nomad" or "pop-up" museums combined with broadened digital access to collections via mobile devices untether museums from fixed locations and permit reaching a broader demographic, changing the notion of where and how museums will exist in the future. With the shift to more digital content will come a blurring of distinctions among museums, libraries, and archival programs. "We are increasingly shifting to hybrid environments where digital technologies are used to enhance and enliven the physical experiences and offer new immersive experiences." The use of mobile devices and sensors and data generated by visitors will help programs shift and customize exhibits and programs. "In the museum of the future, data collection and analytics coupled with automation will provide a way for museums to deliver highly compelling, individually-curated experiences where users, exhibits, light, sound, and space interact to create a seamless environment. This will enable a more dynamic synergy between digital and analogue and help create more immersive experiences." Advances in modeling, 3D printing, and rapid prototyping will give curators the ability to accurately and quickly build high-resolution reproductions of rare or previously unavailable objects and may even offer the option for individual visitors to create their own facsimiles on-site and take them home. [42]

PROACTIVELY SHAPING THE FUTURE

We are engaged in a new set of challenges without a clear set of solutions or end states. When the future seems uncertain, it's time to take stock, try to find ways to sail with rather than against the currents, and to imaginatively shape the future of our programs and to some degree of the contexts in which they operate. Programs that comprise the historical enterprise need to maintain their proud traditions of dedicated service, trustworthiness, and historical accuracy and authenticity and at the same time proactively adapt to change. They need to retain and strengthen the bonds with traditional audiences and at the same time engage people representing the nation's growing diversity. They need to work toward improving public appreciation of the value of history, particularly state and local history, to lay the basis for progressive increases in resources that are needed to carry out their dynamic work.

The programs that constitute the historical enterprise seem ready for change. In some cases, financial exigencies have accelerated the process of revisiting missions, streamlining, and coming up with new approaches. The Ohio Historical Society, for instance, after sustaining a sizable cutback in state funding in 2009, was forced to reduce staffing and hours. But the Society also launched new approaches, such as "collections learning"—more direct public access to collections and more opportunities for hands-on experiences—and more exhibitions and programs traveling to OHS sites, libraries, historical societies, and community centers across the state. "We will be a museum with a presence all over the state—not just in Columbus," said a society news release.[43] Carol Kammen, summarizing selected themes in the entries in the revised edition of the *Encyclopedia of Local History*, published in 2013, noted:[44]

- Concern over the large number of small history organizations competing for resources and local interest.
- Initiatives to make available source material online.
- Efforts to make history more popular, including making history journals and magazines available online.
- Growing number of online history encyclopedias.
- Broadening the image of history programs (e.g., moving away from the word "society" and instead using terms like "museum" and "center").
- Growing recognition of the importance of ethnicity and indigenous peoples.
- Using state and national anniversaries (e.g., centennials and bicentennials) as a basis for historical celebrations.
- Securing adequate funding is a constant problem.

Kammen concluded that "historical organizations need to adapt and change, to entice as well as educate, to be modern even when we look back at the past lest all we hear at future gatherings is a clanking of canes." Another ongoing discussion has focused around the question of whether there are too many historical programs competing for limited resources and attention.

A 2007 conference on the sustainability of historic house museums and other sites pointed out that many were small, lacked "financial sustainability," needed to adopt business practices and focus on community needs, or, in some cases, merge with others or discontinue operations.[45] Some could not be sustained through the recession that began in 2008. But as Elizabeth Merritt, the director of the AAM's Center for the Future of Museums noted in 2013, the conference report "has not, unfortunately, been particularly influential." She observed that there is a "need for museums to collaborate, merge, share resources, create integrated strategies—instead of trying to carve out overlapping niches and do their own thing, on their own." On the other hand, "there is certainly plenty of room to weed out chronic underperformers and organizations that are serving very personal, rather than community, interests."[46]

A 2011 international conference on "Libraries and Museums in an Era of Participatory Culture" discussed several themes, including:[47]

Libraries and museums need to become "inclusive, accessible community participants."

An important question is "where do our programs fit into larger community needs and challenges?"

Museums "can and must collaborate to strengthen cultural diversity and social inclusion."

"Cultural institutions must communicate directly with their communities, asking what they want and in what format they want it."

The programs should "connect people who want to share, show, and above all discuss their own cultures and identities, allowing voices never before heard to be part of the conversation."

"A shared trait in all forward-looking spheres of communication and technology is that they encourage participation."

Our programs need to allow "decentralization of authority" but also avoid "the tyranny of the community."

Libraries and museums must "open our walls, break down boundaries, and orient ourselves culturally, becoming the modern equivalent of the agora as a hub of communication."

The conference reached a consensus that libraries and museums "must be repurposed, re-thought, and re-imagined as places of life-long learning, as responsible stewards of cultural heritage, and as community anchors that must invest in both programs and people."

John Durel and Anita Nowery Durel projected a potential "golden age for historic properties" if they shift focus away from visitors and more toward volunteers, retired baby boomers, and affinity groups with interest in particular historical topics and develop exhibits and programs to provide meaningful individual historical experiences through the "spiritual dimension" of historic sites.[48]

Strengthening history programs will require using analysis to probe our current situation but also reframing our view of the future from *predictive* (asking "What will happen?") to *prospective* (asking "What *can* or *should* happen?" and "What should I do about it?"). This chart contrasts the two styles of thinking about the future: [49]

	Predictive Thinking	Prospective Thinking
Mindset	Forecasting, "We expect . . . "	Preparing, "But what if . . . "
Goal	Reduce or even discard uncertainty, fight ambiguity	Live with uncertainty, embrace ambiguity, plan for set of contingencies
Level of uncertainty	Average	High
Method	Extrapolating from present and past	Open, imaginative
Approach	Categorical, assumes continuity	Global, systemic, anticipates disruptive events
Information inputs	Quantitative, objective, known	Qualitative (whether quantifiable or not), subjective, known or unknown
Relationships	Static, stable structures	Dynamic, evolving structures
Technique	Established quantitative models (economics, mathematics, data)	Developing scenarios using qualitative approaches (often building on megatrends)
Evaluation methods	Numbers	Criteria
Attitude toward the future	Positive or reactive (the future will be)	Proactive and creative (we create or shape the future)
Way of thinking	Generally deduction	Greater use of induction

NOTES

1. Ohio Historical Society, *2012–2013 Citizen's Guide* (2012), 5. http://www.ohiohistory.org/about-us/citizens-guide.

2. "Historical Society of Newburgh Bay and the Highlands Hires New Director, Johanna Porr" (March 30, 2012). http://newburghrestoration.com/blog/2012/03/30/historical-society-of-newburgh-bay-and-the-highlands-hires-new-director-johanna-porr.

3. The Trustees of Reservations, "History and Culture." http://www.thetrustees.org/what-we-care-about/history-culture.

4. Steve Berry, "Why Preserving History Matters" (April 23, 2012). http://www.huffingtonpost.com/steve-berry/why-preserving-history-matters_b_1446631.html.

5. Canadian Historical Association et al, *Becoming a Historian: A Canadian Manual* (ca. 2010), 9. http://www.chashcacommittees-comitesa.ca/becoming%20a%20historian/pdfs/becomingahistorian.pdf.

6. Darlene Roth, "Seven Reasons the Past Never Dies," *History News* (Summer 2013), 14–18.

7. Ohio Historical Society and University of Toledo, *Exploring the Public Value of Ohio's History* (2009), 1–6. http://ww2.ohiohistory.org/sn/022409-02l.html.

8. David McCullough, Keynote address, National Museum of American History re-opening ceremony, Nov. 19, 2008, quoted in G. Wayne Clough, *Best of Both Worlds: Museums, Libraries, and Archives in a Digital* Age (2013), 34. http://www.si.edu/bestofbothworlds.

9. Dan Spock, "In Defense of Nostalgia" (2009), http://historymuseums.wordpress.com/2009/08/03/dan-spock.

10. Don Garden, President, Federation of Australian Historical Societies, "Who Are the Players in Heritage and What Roles Do They Play?" *Australian Heritage Strategy* (2012) 1–15. http://www.environment.gov.au/heritage/strategy/pubs/essay-players.pdf

11. Museums Association, *Public Perceptions of—and Attitudes to—the Purpose of Museums in Society* (2013). http://www.museumsassociation.org/download?id=954916.; and *Museums Change Lives.* 2013. http://www.museumsassociation.org/museums-change-lives.

12. Ed Adamczyk, "Keepers of the Flame," *Buffalo Spree* (June 2012). http://www.buffalospree.com/Buffalo-Spree/June-2012/Keepers-of-the-flame/.; and "Our Historical Societies: Keepers of the Flame" (October 1, 2012). http://foreveryoungwny.com/news/2012/oct/01/our-historical-societies-keepers-flame.

13. Oregon Heritage Commission, *Oregon Heritage Vitality 2010: The Challenge of the Past for Oregonians Today and Tomorrow* (January 2011). http://www.oregon.gov/oprd/HCD/OHC/docs/hvreport2010.pdf.

14. Dan Yaeger, *Museum Futures: Place Your Bet* (2012); and New England Museum Association, *Mapping a Strategy for the Museum Field* (2013). http://www.nemanet.org.

15. American Academy of Arts and Sciences, *The Heart of the Matter: The Humanities and Social Sciences for a Vibrant, Competitive and Secure Nation* (2013). http://www.humanitiescommission.org/_pdf/hss_report.pdf.

16. Thomas B. Fordham Institute, *The State of State U.S. History Standards 2011* (2011), 1–8. http://www.edexcellence.net/sites/default/files/publication/pdfs/SOSS_History_FINAL_7.pdf.

17. National Council for the Social Studies, *College, Career & Civic Life: C3 Framework for Social Studies State Standards* (2013), 45–50. http://www.socialstudies.org/system/files/c3/C3-Framework-for-Social-Studies.pdf.

18. *American Heritage*, "Why Do We Need a National Nonprofit Membership Society for American History?" 2013. http://www.americanheritage.com/about/advertising.

19. North Carolina State Historic Preservation Office, *North Carolina 2013–2022 State Historic Preservation Plan* (2013), 18. http://www.hpo.ncdcr.gov/NorthCarolina_2013-2022_HistoricPreservationPlan.pdf.

20. Anne Ackerson, "The History Museum in New York State: A Growing Sector Built on Scarcity Thinking," *Public Historian* 33 (August 2011), 18–37.

21. American Alliance of Museums, *America's Museums Reflect Slow Economic Recovery in 2012* (2013). http://www.aam-us.org/docs/research/acme-2013-final.pdf.

22. Debbie Ann Doyle, "The Future of Local Historical Societies," American Historical Association, *Perspectives on History* (December 2012). http://www.historians.org/perspectives/issues/2012/1212/Future-of-Local-Historical-Societies.cfm.

23. American Association of Museums/Center for the Future of Museums, *Museums & Society 2034: Trends and Potential Futures* (2008), 15. http://www.aam-us.org/docs/center-for-the-future-of-museums/museumssociety2034.pdf.

24. David Weinberger, *Too Big to Know: Rethinking Knowledge Now That the Facts Aren't the Facts, Experts Are Everywhere, and the Smartest Person in the Room Is the Room* (New York: Basic Books, 2011), xii, 11, 60, 174.

25. Bill Adair et al, eds., *Letting Go: Sharing Historical Authority in a User-Generated World* (Philadelphia: Pew Center for Arts & Heritage, 2011), 17.

26. Library and Archives Canada, *Modernization* (2012). http://www.bac-lac.gc.ca/eng/about-us/modernization/Pages/default.aspx.

27. American Historical Association, *Statement on Standards of Professional Conduct* (2011). http://www.historians.org/pubs/free/ProfessionalStandards.cfm.

28. Organization of American Historians and National Park Service, *Imperiled Promise: The State of History in the National Park Service* (2011), 16-29. http://www.oah.org/site/assets/documents/Imperiled_Promse.pdf

29. "The morning was still and bitter cold when cultures clashed," (2013); and *Washita Battlefield National Historic Site First Annual Centennial Strategy* (2007), both at: http://www.nps.gov/waba/index.

30. National Park Service Second Century Commission, *Advancing the National Park Idea: Cultural Resource and Historic Preservation Committee Report* (2009), 7. http://www.npca.org/assets/pdf/Committee_Cultural_Resources.PDF.

31. Edward Rothstein, "To Each His Own Museum, as Identity Goes on Display," *New York Times*, December 15, 2010.

32. Nina Simon, "An Open Letter to Ariana Huffington, Edward Rothstein, and Many Other Museum Critics" (January 2, 2011); and "On White Privilege and Museums" (March 6, 2013), both at http://museumtwo.blogspot.com.

33. American Association of Museums/Center for the Future of Museums, *Museums & Society 2034: Trends and Potential* Futures (2008), 18. http://www.aam-us.org/docs/center-for-the-future-of-museums/museumssociety2034.pdf.

34. Institute of Museum and Library Services, *Museums, Libraries and 21st Century Skills* (2009), 7. http://www.imls.gov/assets/1/AssetManager/21stCenturySkills.pdf.

35. Quoted from Anna Cutler, "What Is to Be Done, Sandra? Learning in Cultural Institutions of the 21st Century," in Gail Anderson, ed. *Reinventing the Museum: The Evolving Conversation on the Paradigm Shift* (Revised edition, New York: Alta Mira, 2012), 354.

36. American Association of Museums/Center for the Future of Museums, *Demographic Transformation and the Future of Museums* (2010), 13–15. http://www.aam-us.org/docs/center-for-the-future-of-museums/demotransaam2010.pdf?sfvrsn=0.

37. "Demographic Realities in the 21st Century" (2010). http://reachadvisors.typepad.com/museum_audience_insight/2010/04/whos-coming-to-your-museum-demographics-by-museum-type.html.

38. Washington State Historical Society, *2012 Member Survey Results* (2012). http://www.washingtonhistory.org/about/performance.

39. Carol Kammen, "Too Much of a Good Thing?" *History News* (Autumn 2012), 3.

40. Richard Moe, "Are There Too Many House Museums?," National Trust for Historic Preservation, *Forum Journal* 17 (Fall 2012), 55–61.

41. Linda Norris, "Too Many Museums?" (March 10, 2010); and "Are County Historical Societies Dinosaurs?" (Sept. 19, 2010), both at *The Uncataloged Museum.* http://uncataloged-museum.blogspot.com.

42. ARUP, *Museums in the Digital Age* (2013). http://www.arup.com/Publications/Museums_in_the_Digital_Age.aspx.

43. Ohio Historical Society Reinvents Itself for Future Growth" (October 9, 2009). http://ww2.ohiohistory.org/about/pr/072109a.html.

44. Kammen, "Too Much of a Good Thing?" 3–4.

45. Jay D. Vogt, "The Kykuit Simmit: The Sustainability of Historic Sites," *History News* (Autumn 2007), 7–21.

46. Elizabeth Merritt comment on Nina Simon, "What Should Happen to Underperforming Nonprofit Organizations?," *Museum 2.0* (Oct. 23, 2013). http://museumtwo.blogspot.com/2013/10/what-should-happen-to-underperforming.html#disqus_thread.

47. Institute of Museum and Library Services and Salzburg Global Seminar, *Libraries and Museums in an Era of Participatory Culture* (2012). http://www.imls.gov/assets/1/assetmanager/sgs_report_2012.pdf.; Nancy E. Rogers et al., "From Quiet Havens to Modern Agoras: Libraries and Museums in an Era of Participatory Culture," *History News* (Autumn 2012), 7–9.

48. John Durel and Anita Nowery Durel, "A Golden Age for Historic Properties," *History News* (Summer 2007), also at http://www.qm2.org/files/EngagingAudiences/Golden_Age.pdf.

49. Luc de Brabandere and Alan Ivy, *Thinking in New Boxes: A New Paradigm for Business Creativity* (New York: Random House, 2013), 91–94.

Chapter Two

Leading Historical Programs

THE LEADERSHIP IMPERATIVE

Most historical programs are well *managed*—they have a defined mission and an appropriate structure and staff and program elements in place to meet defined goals. They perform an invaluable service to the people they serve and to history generally every day. Management is mostly about keeping the program going and ensuring that services are provided on a continuing basis. But in a context of rising and shifting expectations—the sea-change transformational developments outlined in chapter 1 and chronic resource challenges—just keeping programs going day-to-day is often not enough for them to thrive. Historical programs need to be both *well managed* and *well led.* Management and leadership are related but different. Managers may be known for such traits as *rational, consulting, persistent, problem solving, tough-minded, analytical, structured, deliberate, authoritative, stabilizing, influencing people through the power of their position.* Leaders, by contrast, are likely to be characterized by these qualities: *visionary, passionate, creative, flexible, inspiring, innovative, courageous, imaginative, experimental, initiate change, influencing people toward organizational goals through the power of their personalities and their convictions.* [1]

There is a good deal of literature in our field about how to *manage* well. [2] But there is less on the dynamics and successful practices of *leadership.* Anne Ackerson and Joan Baldwin's book *Leadership Matters* provides an excellent discussion of museum leadership, particularly leadership traits and what it takes to be a leader, based on extensive interviews with three dozen leaders in the field. [3] The American Association for State and Local History's (AASLH) annual *Developing History Leaders* seminar features sessions on developing a vision, strategic thinking, and leading programs through change. They are excellent, but more is needed because leadership is a critical but often under-developed trait in the programs that make up the historical enterprise.

Of course, particularly in small-to-modest sized programs, the director may function as both manager and leader, sometimes managing day-to-day, sometimes forging new directions for the program. But there is a distinction between management and leadership. Leadership is mostly about vision, inspiration, innovation, and transformation. Leadership can be uncomfortable. It is often about challenging, shaking up, or replacing the status quo. Leaders are restless. They have a heightened sense of what is possible and a determination to take their programs to new levels. Leadership expert Warren Bennis contends that leaders and managers have fundamentally different perspectives:[4]

The Leader	The Manager
Innovates	Administers
Is an original	Is a copy
Develops	Maintains
Focuses on people	Focuses on systems and structure
Inspires trust	Relies on control
Has a long-range perspective	Has a short-range view
Asks *what* and *why*	Asks *how* and *when*
Has his or her eye on the horizon	Has his or her eye on the bottom line
Originates	Imitates
Challenges the status quo	Accepts the status quo
Is his or her own person	Is the classic "good soldier"
Does the right thing	*Does things right*

Edie Hedlin, who directed a number of major archival programs, says that leaders are devoted to change, managers to stability. She explains:[5]

> Archival leaders assess their programs constantly, looking at current needs but also future trends. They make difficult decisions that are intended to provide a better foundation for the archival enterprise in the future. They change the direction of programs that need new approaches, altering job responsibilities and relationships. They set goals and measure progress in areas where previously none existed. They listen to both the staff and the program's multiple constituencies but in the end take decisive action even if it is unpopular. . . . They seek nontraditional partners and find ways to make the archival program applicable to nontraditional users. In short, they welcome change, encourage innovation, and embrace new ideas.

Several trends are complicating the work of leadership regardless of setting. Some examples:[6]

Erosion and blurring of the long-standing and often rigid barriers between work and home, public and private, men and women, boss and employee, teacher and student, product and service, service provider and advocate, and so on.

The spread of mobile technologies that enable people to work anywhere, at any time, and also to continuously access information.

Customers and clients are no longer just consumers of products and recipients of services; they may now be active partners in setting expectations and shaping those products and services.

People entering the workforce may have less interest in institutional mission and destiny than in the past. The operative questions in the work domain may become "What about me? What about my group, my community, my family? How does this opportunity support what I want to do or be in the world?"

Career paths become more individualized and distinctive, less predictable, more customized.

Workplaces encompass people from different generations, diverse backgrounds, and different values.

There is a need for inclusiveness in the workplace, particularly in soliciting input and ideas from those who execute or carry out the work—people who interact with the customers every day and understand their interests and needs.

The 24/7 environment puts organizations under pressure to focus on the short-term, responding to demands for immediate results and dealing with crises. In this climate, "the leader's job is to push back against unremitting urgency by balancing long-term vision and commitments with immediate concerns."

Despite the challenges and needs, leadership in historical programs may be underdeveloped for several reasons:

The need does not seem urgent. The status quo seems comfortable, no one seems to be demanding change, and expanding the program or moving it into uncharted new territory seems potentially risky and a lot of work.

Program directors may be simply too busy managing their programs, and, with small or modest sized staffs, often doing much of the work themselves. It is difficult to find time for leadership concerns like long-term strategic planning or continually updating the program's vision.

Leadership concepts may seem to be theoretical and difficult to grasp, while management seems more concrete, down-to-earth, and tangible.

Leadership implies change, and change is unsettling, may jar people who are complacent with the status quo, and may engender resistance or opposition.

The program director may have tried to lead a new initiative or major project in the past which turned out to be less-than-successful or even a setback for the program. A strategic planning effort may have ended in exhaustion with a document that was seldom consulted and had little real impact on the program. Chastened by these or similar experiences, the director is reluctant to take a chance with a new leadership initiative.

Leadership responsibility may be uncertain, blurred, or scattered (e.g., board of directors vs. director of the program).

People may be promoted into a leadership position before they are fully prepared. Once there, they are faced with issues, challenges, and opportunities and have little time to learn leadership skills.

Leading, while sometimes uncomfortable and stressful, is nevertheless necessary. There is much at stake—our programs are the guardians and perpetuators of the past, and most of our "customers" haven't been born yet. If we succeed at steady-state management but fall short at dynamic leadership, our programs can stagnate, and we miss filling our deepest obligations. Proactive, decisive leadership is particularly important when historical programs are:[7]

- Organizing for the first time, where vision, strategic planning, resources, hiring initial staff, and gaining initial traction and momentum are key challenges.
- Revisiting and significantly changing their mission and heading in new directions where leadership is needed to guide the organization into unexplored territory (e.g., after hiring a new director, embarking on strategic planning, or engaging a broader audience).
- Significantly expanding or adding a new dimension where leadership is required to integrate the new work with the program's historical mission (e.g., more connections with schools or integrating social networking applications).
- Experiencing serious challenges (e.g., fiscal constraints in hard times) where steadfast leadership is needed to keep the program going strong, make strategic reductions and retreats where necessary, and use the crisis to plan for a better, more robust future.
- Strengthening capacities and services as part of a determined effort to achieve a higher degree of excellence and recognition.
- Consolidating with other historical organizations to pool resources and strengthen common or similar missions.

- Joining other programs in advocacy and lobbying (e.g., for adequate funding for state historical agencies and programs).

Well-led programs are the type likely to be recognized and honored as models and inspiration for others. They are the sorts of programs that win the AASLH *Leadership in History*, American Alliance of Museums (AAM) *Excellence*, the Institute for Museum and Library Services' *National Medal for Museum and Library Service* awards, and comparable recognition by regional, state, and local associations. They exhibit traits of "high performance" and are distinguished from other programs in several ways:[8]

> Their strategies are more consistent, clearer, and well thought out. They have clear visions supported by flexible and achievable strategic plans. Their strategies align with and match the program's philosophy.
> They are more likely to go above and beyond for their customers. The organization exists primarily to serve customers, continually assesses and determines their future needs, and is determined to excel in meeting them.
> Everyone in the organization is clear about performance expectations.
> They are superior in terms of clarifying performance measures, training people to do their jobs, enabling employees to work well together, and supporting, recognizing, and rewarding innovation.
> Their employees feel empowered and use their skills, knowledge, and experience to create unique solutions for customers.
> People at the top "treat employees well so that employees will treat the organization well." Their employees are more likely to think the organization is a good place to work.

ELEMENTS OF LEADERSHIP

The rest of this chapter discusses several aspects of effective leadership.

Moving to Leadership Requires a Shift in Expectations

Transitioning or shifting from a management role to a leadership role requires a shift in outlook, expectations, and level and type of responsibility and accountability. The scope, complexity, and consequences of the work move up to a new level. The familiar, routine, and traditional give way to the novel, unprecedented, and innovative. Michael D. Watkins, author of *The First 90 Days*, a book to guide new leaders, explains that there are seven "seismic shifts" that need to occur when someone takes on a leadership position or moves to play a leadership role:[9]

Specialist to generalist. There is a shift from responsibility for a particular function or aspect of the program to responsibility for the entire enterprise. The leader needs to understand the entire program, its staff, audiences, opportunities, and challenges. He or she must evaluate the staff throughout the program and make decisions for the good of the program as a whole.

Analyst to integrator. The leader needs to manage and integrate the collective knowledge of experts in particular areas and functional teams to get everyone to see the big picture, understand where they fit in as individuals and teams, and encourage people to work across departments.

Tactician to strategist. The leader develops broad strategies. Leaders move fluidly among levels of analysis and know when to focus on details, when to focus on the big picture, and how the two relate. They discern causal relationships and other important patterns in the program and its environment. They predict how outside parties (e.g., funders, customers) will respond to what the program does.

Bricklayer to architect. The leader must "understand how to analyze and design organizational systems so that strategy, structure, operating models, and skill bases fit together effectively and efficiently and harness this understanding to make needed organizational changes."

Problem solver to agenda setter. Managers are adept at problem solving. Leaders need those skills too. but they function at a different level, perceiving the full range of opportunities and threats facing the program and focusing the attention of staff members on the most important ones. The leader also needs to identify "white spaces"—issues that don't fall neatly into any particular function but are still important to the program.

Warrior to diplomat. The leader needs to spend time trying to influence a host of external constituencies (i.e., community groups, potential funding sources, the news media and government agencies).

Supporting cast member to lead role. "Becoming an enterprise leader means moving to center stage under the bright lights." When people assume leadership positions, "their influence is magnified, as everyone looks to them for vision, inspiration, and cues about the 'right' behaviors and attitudes." In addition, they need to "define a compelling vision and share it in an inspirational way."

Leaders Are the Heart of the Enterprise

Leaders often symbolize their programs. If they are dynamic, upbeat, optimistic, determined, and expansive, the program will usually reflect those traits. If they are downcast, overly cautious, self-serving, intent on preserving the status quo for too long, or reluctant to champion change, their programs may be static and undistinguished. Leaders set the tone from the top, and people who work *for* them, and sometimes trustees and others who work *with* them, may emulate them.

"You *are* the enterprise," says leadership writer Liz Mellon, with some slight exaggeration. The person in charge is a highly visible representation of the program and primarily responsible for its welfare and its future. That person provides a model for caring, dedication, hard work, and strict adherence to legal and moral requirements of the work. There is no "safety net"— in the final analysis, it is up to the leader to make tough decisions in the face of uncertainty and ambiguous evidence when there is no clearly right or wrong answer. The leader brings clarity and certainty in the face of uncertainty and complexity. Leadership confidently moves the program forward, often into uncharted territory. In the traditional model of leadership, the leader used a deliberate, extensively consultative style, made sure all issues were clearly resolved, resources identified and aligned, stakeholders fully supportive, and a consensus in place before taking action. Newer literature, more attuned to the fast-changing world of demographic transformation and digital information, advises less consultation and deliberation and more accelerated decision making. This fits the style of most successful leaders these days, who have a bias for action. The data and evidence may not form a coherent pattern, and the leader may need to "eat the uncertainty" and make the call anyway, pushing the boundaries and leading toward a future that others cannot see even when critics and detractors urge hesitation or heap on criticism. They consult, weigh the evidence, consider the options, but move decisively. They are inclined toward action, always thinking about what can be done to achieve more and better results, aware that things may not work out the first time or may not work out exactly as expected. In fact, in general the more innovative the program, the less likely it is that the leader will have full, incontrovertible evidence before making key decisions. Leaders need to be resolute and assume responsibility:

> I act at the edge of uncertainty and I am willing to [make] decisions that move the enterprise into uncharted territory. At the point of the decision, there is no one else to look to for reassurance. I am alone. I am not waiting for permission and I am willing to lean into unknown risk. I am unafraid. [10]

Leaders are energetic people with high resolve, "a paradoxical blend of personal humility and professional will . . . their ambition is first and foremost for the institution, not themselves . . . seemingly ordinary people quietly producing extraordinary results." They push their programs toward greatness and demonstrate determination in doing whatever needs to be done to advance the program. But they also demonstrate personal modesty, tend toward being self-effacing, act with calm determination, and rely on vision and commitment rather than charisma or flashiness to motivate people. They credit other people with the program's triumphs but take responsibility themselves for poor results. They work hard on succession planning and set up their successors for even greater success.[11]

Leaders Make Decisions

The responsibility of a leader, above all, is to make decisions. Some have moderate impact on the organization, but others have fundamental, long-term, transformative consequences. Leaders need to adopt and hone their decision-making styles, particularly striking a balance between more or less unilateral decision making and decision making based on extensive consultation. Leaders' decision-making styles may fall into a number of categories, for instance:[12]

Decisive: Leaders using this style value action, speed, efficiency, and consistency. There is likely to be at most only a moderate amount of study and consultation. When seeking input from other people, they value directness, relevance, clarity, and above all conciseness. Leaders act when they feel they have enough information to make a reliable decision; they are wary of over-studying something or gathering so much information that they are bogged down getting through it. They trust their instincts, based on experience. Their decisions are fast and firm. They see issues, and the decisions needed to address them, as discrete rather than inter-related, and tackle one issue, and make one decision, at a time, and then move on to the next one.

Flexible: Faced with a problem, a leader with a flexible style sets out to gather just enough information to choose a line of attack. But they keep abreast of immediate, shifting situations and may revisit their decisions and change course quickly.

Hierarchic: People in this mode are not in a hurry to rush to judgment. Instead, they analyze a great deal of information, expect others to contribute, and are inclined to challenge others' views and analyses to draw out deeper insights. Once they make their decisions, though, they expect everyone to support them, and they expect the decisions to stand the test of time.

Integrative: Leaders using this style don't necessarily look for a single best solution. Their tendency is to frame any situation broadly, taking into account multiple factors and elements that may relate to or overlap with other, related situations. They like lots of input and welcome the chance to explore a wide range of viewpoints, including those that differ from their own. They are inclined toward openness, diversity of opinion, collaboration, and participative decision-making. Their decisions tend not to be narrow or focused but, instead, may set forth multiple courses of action that may evolve over time as circumstances change.

The style may vary over time, but research indicates that experienced leaders favor the integrative style for deciding on vision and mission for a strategic planning process and for major decisions affecting the future of the program.

Leaders Apply Personal Leadership Styles

Leadership styles are learned, personal, and distinct. No two program directors lead in exactly the same way. It depends on education, experience, personality, and the circumstances of the program. It may also evolve over time, as a leader gains more experience and learns from both successes and failures. A recent study suggests that there are at least seven leadership styles:[13]

The coach: The motto here is "to lead change, lead people, start with the heart." Leaders with a coaching style support and promote involvement, extensive discussion, active listening, feedback, consensus building, and an informal, almost relaxed participative culture. They encourage people to speak up and propose new projects and listen attentively to all viewpoints. Staff members see them as encouraging, supportive, positive, and tolerant of new ideas and of mistakes made in actively exploring and testing new ideas.

The visionary: "Onward and upward toward new horizons!" is the visionary leader's mantra. They are change-oriented, future-focused, big-picture leaders who give mission and vision sustained attention. They are particularly interested in emerging trends and excited by new possibilities. They are known for being forward looking, impatient with the status quo, eager to move on to new initiatives.

The executer: These leaders emphasize extensive, detailed planning that develops a well-thought-out plan, and then careful execution of the plan. They emphasize the process of change, laying out time frames and resources necessary to accomplish the objectives. They have practical, analytical mindsets, do their homework, push others to achieve high performance standards, and allocate resources wisely. Executers model reliability, dependability, steadiness, and predictability, even in times of rapid change.

The champion: These leaders excel at rallying people around major change goals and things that are new and different. They engage a wide variety of people and inspire them toward new possibilities. They combine an intuitive grasp of possibilities, a dynamic interpersonal style, and exceptional communication and persuasion skills. People see them as compelling, charismatic, and enlightening.

The driver: Drivers focus on results and are passionate about achieving the objectives of a change initiative. They push to accomplish immediate tasks along the way in their drive toward meeting the ultimate goal. Drivers are forceful, pragmatic, and analytical. Their communications are likely to be about strategy and execution. Staff members describe them as confident, intentional, and focused.

The facilitator: Their motto might be "I'm here to help. Lean on me." They emphasize both tasks and process, making change happen but also caring about how it happens. They foster change by encouraging involvement, use their listening and negotiating skills to resolve differences, and do all they can to make the change process smooth and help others through it. They are participative, involved, resourceful, and supportive.

The adapter: They are versatile and can utilize any or all of the other styles, depending on the circumstances. Adapters tend to be flexible and open to new ideas. They can be electric and magnetic, sparking creative ideas, appealing to workers from a wide variety of backgrounds. They tend to get personally involved and engage with a wide variety of stakeholders in the process of change. People see them as flexible, adaptable, and modeling the trait of being open to experimentation and new experience.

Key Personal Traits: Authentic, Trustworthy, Compelling

No matter what their style, the best and most effective leaders have certain deep-seated personal traits which give rise to their motivations and leadership strategies. They are fundamental and continuing and the basis for respect and confidence by employees, peers, executives above the leaders, and people who interact with the program. These leaders have core values that guide their behavior. To staff and outsiders alike, the traits of the leader help determine their feelings about the program. Anne Ackerson and Joan Baldwin, in their book on museum leadership, identify self-awareness, authenticity, courage, and vision as essential traits.[14] John Hamm, another leadership expert, emphasizes three characteristics:[15]

Authentic. Leaders are true to their core values. Their communications, decisions, and other actions seem natural rather than forced, showy, or insincere. They explain themselves in terms of their own background and experiences, and their stories include disappointments as well as successes. They make personal connections with their followers. They are personally modest, blending personal humility with strong professional will. They have the courage to listen and value honest feedback.

They're known for personal courage, including standing up for the program when it is threatened. "Authenticity is the first step of leadership greatness because it is the basis for the kinds of trusting relationships with followers that are critical for taking on demanding tasks that lead to notable accomplishments."

Trustworthy. Leaders are honest, fair, and known for their integrity. They recognize that behaving unethically, even on small matters, diminishes their credibility and undermines confidence people have in them. They have a bias toward openness and disclosure, promoting easy information flow within their programs, sharing information about critical developments, including bad news, and going out of their way to explain the basis for critical decisions. Being trustworthy extends to supporting staff who exhibit commitment, risk-taking, and innovation.

Compelling. Leaders are imaginative and articulate a compelling vision for the future. They exhibit an unwavering commitment to achieving the vision. "Followers are compelled by a cause. This starts with a vision that expresses a substantial commitment in tangible ways. Leaders must paint a picture for those they wish to enroll—a vision of what winning will look like and how participants can contribute their talents in pursuit of that vision and share in the ultimate success. . . . Great leaders evoke the emotion and energy of being involved in a crusade."

Leaders Create Strong Cultures

"Culture eats strategy for breakfast," famed management writer Peter Drucker once said. Particularly in difficult or challenging times, culture—the way people feel about their program, esprit d'corps, their working relationship with each other, their relationship with the boss, and the spirit of cooperation in getting work done and moving the program ahead—is what makes the difference. Leaders build strong cultures that encourage initiative from everyone in the program. Employees need to *believe* in the program and feel *engaged* (understand how their work benefits the organization and how they will be held accountable), *energized* (assignments are clear and people have plenty of leeway in how to approach them), and *enabled* (they have the tools they need and managers act as counselors and coaches to help people with challenges that they may encounter). This set of insights is particularly important for history programs where resources are likely to be modest, ability to promote people or provide monetary incentives is limited, and leaders need everyone's energy and talent fully engaged every day. People know the importance of history, and leaders need to explain how that cause connects with the work of their historical program.

"Leaders . . . must provide clarity around what the [program] does and why it does it, whom it does it for, and the ways their employees are going to collectively reach their goals—all the way down to each individual's job." Effective leaders keep talking about the larger cause—why we do what we do. "They motivate others by reminding them of the view of a better future and by providing the clear goals, values and expectations associated with their role in helping fulfill the bigger mission and, in turn, employees focus their energies on the tasks with the most impact." Leadership literature often cites a large sign over the door of a model company so that every employee saw it as they came to work every day: THE ACTUAL IS LIMITED. THE POSSIBLE IS IMMENSE. Leaders also identify and dramatize the critical issues the program faces and separate them from the routine challenges and day-to-day work. They galvanize people toward change, recognizing that "most people will change only when their survival anxiety is greater than the apprehension they face that about learning something new."[16]

Conventional leaders concentrate on the world as it is, while dynamic ones think about the world as it might be. Their expansive perspective cascades down through the organization; everyone is encouraged to find ways out of problems and past dilemmas. Outstanding leaders excel at "integrative thinking." They consider diverging or opposing viewpoints and can hold two opposing ideas in their minds simultaneously. Rather than settling for one or the other, they creatively resolve the tension by coming up with an innovative "third way" that contains elements of each but improves on both. They proceed by resisting the conventional "either-or" style of thinking that may reduce decisions to one of two less-than-desirable alternatives. They are comfortable with the messiness and complexity of confronting conflicting options and create multiple working hypotheses on the road to a decision. They tend to be skeptical about existing models or may regard them as the best that anyone has come up with so far, but believe that better models could be developed, and they are comfortable wading into complexity to find or create those models. They look beyond the decision in front of them to see the problem as a whole, examining how the parts fit together and discerning less obvious but potentially more important long-term considerations. They consider multidimensional and non-linear causal relationships. They see a problem as a whole even while working on its constituent parts, determining how its various aspects affect each other. Leaders give themselves plenty of time to make key decisions, including building in time to take walks, attending sporting events, or engage in other activities that take their attention off the issue at hand but give their subconscious time to work on it. The process may take time and look disorderly:

> The integrative thinker will always search for creative resolutions of tensions, rather than accept unpleasant tradeoffs. The behaviors associated with such a

search—delays, sending teams back to examine things more deeply, generating new options at the eleventh hour—can appear irresolute from the outside, but the results are choices that could only have been generated by an integrative thinker who won't settle for trade-offs and conventional options.

This is inherently a confident, optimistic stance. "Integrative thinkers understand that the world imposes constraints on them, but they share the belief that with hard thinking and patience, they can find a better outcome than the unsatisfying [options] they're presented with."[17]

Keep Attention on Core Purpose

Leaders build a sense of inclusiveness, connection, and common purpose. It should be distilled and expressed succinctly in the program's formal mission statement, but it is deeper than that. It is essentially a baked-in understanding of what the program does and why it does it—its reason for being. It is a solid foundation that endures no matter how the program changes to meet challenges and opportunities. Leaders need to ask "what do we stand for and why do we exist," noted Jim Collins and Jerry Porras in their book *Built to Last.* "Visionary companies distinguish their timeless core values and enduring purpose (which should never change) from their operating practices and business strategies (which should be constantly changing in response to a changing world)."[18] A sense of clear purpose appeals to people's imagination and hearts and engenders motivation and inspiration. Leadership expert Marcus Buckingham identifies it as the key leadership trait:

> Effective leaders don't have to be passionate. They don't have to be brilliant. They don't have to possess the common touch. They don't have to be great speakers. What they must be is clear. Above all else, they must never forget the truth that of all human universals—our need for security, for community, for clarity, for authority, and for respect—our need for clarity, when met, is most likely to engender in us confidence, persistence, resilience, and creativity.[19]

For history programs, the mission that everyone should understand and acknowledge is profound, perpetuating documentation and insights from the past through the present into the future. Leaders keep reminding staff of the mission, particularly in hard times. Leadership writer Joel Kurtzman observes that common purpose is an "almost palpable experience that happens when a leader coalesces a group, team or community into a creative, dynamic, brave and nearly invincible *we.*" Everyone in the organization feels invested in the mission and purpose, people at all levels act as leaders in their own areas of responsibility in moving the program ahead, and everyone is empowered to make decisions based on the common purpose, solve prob-

lems that are standing in the way of achieving it, and come up with imaginative, innovative tactics for getting things done. Leaders guide, coach, and
advise rather than issuing orders. They act to build up the confidence of
everyone in the organization to act on their own.[20]

Leaders keep talking about the big picture, link specific projects and
assignments to outcomes and impacts on the program's customers, explain to
individuals that their work counts, and help build up a willingness for them to
be accountable for results. They make ambiguity and uncertainty comfortable by turning everyone's attention to mission and purpose and encouraging
innovative approaches to keep things moving. They make it safe for people
to bring them bad news and make it acceptable to fail sometimes in the
earnest pursuit of the mission.[21]

Warren Bennis and Robert Thomas, in their book *Leading for a Lifetime,*
after studying leadership traits in both younger and older leaders to identify
consistently effective approaches, concluded that one of the most important
is the ability to inspire and develop what they called "shared meaning."
Leaders constantly talk about vision as a way to unify, inspire, and mobilize
employees. They engage in community-building storytelling to describe the
program's past triumphs, illustrate key points, and deepen understanding.
They spend a good deal of time on communication, including a lot of active
listening to understand what people really think. They welcome bad news
and hard truths as a way to bring problems out into the open before they can
get out of hand. "Effective leaders don't just impose their vision on others,
they recruit others to a shared vision. . . . Especially in our digital age, when
power tends to coalesce around ideas, not position, leadership is a partnership."[22]

At the same time, leaders recognize and explain that the mission will be
refined and evolve with the times and that innovation, as discussed elsewhere
in this book, is essential to keep the program vibrant. A study some years ago
of organizations that have survived for more than a century found three
themes: deeply held core purposes, conservative financial management, and
what the study called "tolerance at the margins"—sufficient flexibility to
allocate resources in the form of funding and staffing for unorthodox ideas,
processes, and initiatives, regardless of where they originated in the organization. Some of the activities were "experiments and eccentricities that
stretched their understanding" of possibilities and led them into new business
areas or motivated them to develop new products and markets. Practicing
tolerance at the margins enabled these enterprises to learn and adapt over
time by anticipating changes rather than being surprised by them. This enabled the organizations to organically self-renew, rather than becoming set in
their ways and overly conservative, a common trait in long-established institutions. "Once a company has adapted to a new environment, it is no longer

the organization it used to be; it has evolved. That is the essence of learning." That sort of learning is very useful for historical programs.[23]

Leaders Challenge the Status Quo

Leaders hold onto core purpose and values, but most tend to be dissatisfied with the status quo or to feel that it isn't likely to linger for long. In part, the perspective comes from their view that history is mostly the story of change. Even when things are going well, they are constantly vigilant, strengthening their ability to anticipate by scanning the environment for incipient signals of change. The most effective leaders "maintain hypervigilance in good times as well as bad . . . even in calm, clear, positive conditions." They always worry a little that "events could turn against them without warning, at some unpredictable point in time, at some highly inconvenient moment."[24]

Satisfaction and pride in delivering quality services and programs are not allowed to lapse into complacency. The leaders are active in professional history and museum associations, constantly seeking to learn more about emerging best practices and model programs. They read management and leadership literature and case studies from their own and other fields to glean insights that can be interpreted and applied at home. They challenge their own and other's assumptions, revisit longstanding practices, and encourage divergent viewpoints. They are able to consider multiple options for relatively long periods of time. They don't rule out possibilities prematurely, so they are often able to make better, more creative choices. "They can tolerate the nettle of ambiguity in situations where others long for closure. Most of [the best] leaders have the requisite hungry patience to seek untested paths. But they may also have the discipline necessary to achieve a desired goal."[25] They may reframe a problem from several perspectives to understand root causes and identify potential options for solution. They encourage dialogue and hold meetings where dissent and debate are welcome, encouraged, and expected. They are open-minded and careful not to let their own preconceptions get in the way of weighing new ideas. "Leaders who challenge in the right way invariably elicit complex and conflicting information. . . . Instead of reflexively seeing or hearing what you expect, you should synthesize all the input you have. You'll need to recognize patterns, push through ambiguity, and seek new insights." Leaders should also be proponents of organizational learning. "They promote a culture of inquiry, and they search for the lessons in both successful and unsuccessful outcomes. They study failures— their own and their teams'—in an open, constructive way to find the hidden lessons."[26]

Leaders Make Connections for the Program

Leaders are the program's ambassadors. They build and strengthen the program's connections with its own parent agency, funding sources, and the communities it serves. This role requires a high level of communication, interpretation, and negotiation skills. It necessitates being proactive, taking the initiative to start building relationships, and continuing to invest time, imagination, and effort into keeping connections strong. Part of the work is explaining to everyone associated with the program how important the connections are and what the program needs to do to preserve them.

"The success of any unit—including archives—in any organization will hinge on the ability of its managers to correctly identify and serve the needs and objectives of the parent agency," notes James Fogerty, a longtime program director at the Minnesota State Archives. Success also depends on the value placed on the program's work by a wide variety of constituencies for which they provide service.[27] "For an archives to flourish over a long period of time, the concept of maintaining a historical records collection must be communicated to all levels of the organization," notes Philip Mooney, who for many years served as the Director of the Archives Department of the Coca-Cola Company. "The archivist must creatively work to mainstream programs and make history a relevant tool in the corporate arsenal." This means, for instance, "marketing" the archives through use in special events and exhibits, publications, and media stories about the company and finding ways to report on the value and usefulness of archival records. The program director must be an "activist archivist," constantly looking for business applications that would benefit from the use of archival records.[28]

Special Leadership Skills for Hard Times

Our programs are constantly challenged—by changing user needs and expectations, shifting technology, and modest budgetary resources. We need to keep our programs moving ahead but at the same time keep staff engaged and forward-looking in uncertain and hard times and dealing with the inevitable problems that crop up to prevent them from turning into setbacks. Several skills are needed, including:[29]

> Realistic optimism: Leaders work to fully understand the challenges their organizations are facing, including seeking out people with dissenting viewpoints and insisting on honest feedback. They avoid overconfidence in their own abilities and keep their own weaknesses as well as strengths in mind always. But they have confidence in their own ability, and their program's capacity, to surmount any challenge.
> Subservience to purpose: The welfare of the program is what counts. Leaders focus their energies there rather than their own situation,

holding themselves as well as their staff members accountable for results and carrying the program through hard times. They get satisfaction from the progress of the program rather than from their own personal advancement.

Take responsibility when things go wrong: Blame for major problems and setbacks ascends to the top, but the leader directs praise and credit when things go right to others in the organization.

Find order in chaos: Leaders bring clarity and order to quandaries that puzzle others through active listening, deep understanding of cause-and-effect patterns, and their own experience. "Crises force leaders to boil things down to the essentials of what really needs to be done in order to succeed—and then to pursue those essentials with renewed clarity."

Hard times may also be opportune times for leaders to "hit the organization's reset button," enter an adaptive phase for the organization, change the rules of the game, reshape parts of the organization, and redefine the work people do. Old methods such as lengthy analysis and discussion may not work anymore, and program directors need to realize that "leadership is an improvisational and experimental art." It should be a time for leaders to create "a culture of courageous conversations" and "distribute leadership responsibility, replacing hierarchy and formal authority with organizational bandwidth which draws on collective intelligence." Leaders must lead discussions to distinguish the essential from the expendable, realizing that people in the organization will feel a natural loyalty to legacy practices. People need to feel the opportunity to ask difficult questions and make difficult choices. At the same time, if the pressure to change is too intense, people may hunker down or panic. Sometimes, the leader will say "here are the trends we don't know how to address" or "here is a space where we really haven't defined our approach." The leader needs to orchestrate the discussion process, which may involve conflicting ideas and proposals, in such a way that the organization moves from an emergency phase to an adaptive phase and creative new ideas emerge. As the leader builds the organization's adaptability, he or she may want to encourage numerous small projects and experiments. Some will succeed; some will fail and quick post-project reviews will transform them into learning experiences. But the seemingly zig-zagging path will be emblematic of the organization's ability and determination to stay resilient and develop better programs and services.[30]

DISCUSSIONS OF LEADERSHIP ISSUES

Here are some suggestions for keeping up with developments and discussions in the area of leadership:

American Management Association (http://www.amanet.org). Books, seminars, and other materials on leadership and management issues.

The Getty Leadership Institute (http://www.cgu.edu/pages/7214.asp). Educational programs and an online forum to promote leadership in the museum field.

Harvard Business Review, "HBR Blog Network" (http://blogs.hbr.org). Bloggers cover a broad range of business and leadership issues.

IBM Institute for Business Values (http://www-935.ibm.com/services/us/gbs/thoughtleadership). Covers CEO leadership issues and trends.

Frances Hesselbein Leadership Institute (http://www.hesselbeininstitute.org). Reflecting the ideas of pioneering management theory pioneer Peter F. Drucker, the Institute is particularly strong on issues related to leading dynamic nonprofit enterprises.

National Council of Nonprofits (http://www.councilofnonprofits.org). Information on issues, trends, and best practices in leadership and management in the nonprofit sector.

New York Times, "Corner Office: Conversations about Leadership and Management" (http://projects.nytimes.com/corner-office). Interviews on leadership and management issues.

NOTES

1. Richard L. Daft, *Management* (6th ed., Mason, OH: Thompson Southwestern, 2003), 515.

2. For example, Gerald George and Carol Maryan-George, *Starting Right: A Basic Guide to Museum Planning* (Lanham, MD: Alta Mira, 2012); and Hugh M. Genoways and Lynne M. Ireland, *Museum Administration: An Introduction* (Lanham, MD: Alta Mira, 2003).

3. Anne W. Ackerson and Joan H. Baldwin, *Leadership Matters* (Lanham, MD: Alta Mira, 2014).

4. Warren Bennis, *On Becoming a Leader* (Boston: Perseus Books, 1989), 45.

5. Edie Hedlin, "Meeting Leadership Challenges: Lessons from Experience," in Bruce W. Dearstyne, ed., *Leading and Managing Archives and Records Programs: Strategies for Success* (New York: Neal-Schuman Publishers, 2008), 178.

6. Sally Helgesen, "Leading in 24/7: What Is Required?" *Leader to Leader,* 65 (Summer 2012), 38–42. http://www.hesselbeininstitute.org/knowledgecenter/journal.aspx?IssueID=65.

7. Bruce W. Dearstyne, "The Nature of Leadership: Strategies for Leading Historical Programs," AASLH *Technical Leaflet* no. 258 (Spring 2012).

8. Jay Jamrog et al, "High-Performance Organizations: Finding the Elements of Excellence," *People & Strategy* 31 (2008), 29–38.

9. Michael D. Watkins, "How Managers Become Leaders: The Seven Seismic Shifts of Perspective and Responsibility," *Harvard Business Review* 90 (June 2012), 65–72.

10. Liz Mellon, *Inside the Leader's Mind: Five Ways to Think Like a Leader* (New York: Prentice Hall, 2011), 1–47, 196.

11. Jim Collins, *Good to Great* (New York: Harper Collins, 2001), 17–40.

12. Kenneth R. Brousseau et al, "The Seasoned Executive's Decision-Making Style," *Harvard Business Review* 84 (February 2006), 111–121.

13. Barbara A. Trautlein, *Change Intelligence: Using the Power of CQ to Lead Change That Sticks* (New York: Greenleaf Book Group Press, 2013), 55–181.

14. Ackerson and Baldwin, *Leadership Matters,* 47–165.

15. John Hamm, *Unusually Excellent: The Necessary Nine Skills Required for the Practice of Great Leadership* (New York: Jossey Bass, 2011), 1–77.

16. Adrian Gostick and Chester Elton, *All In: How the Best Managers Create a Culture of Belief and Drive Big Results.* (New York: Free Press, 2012), 42–87.

17. Roger Martin, "How Successful Leaders Think," *Harvard Business Review* 85 (June 2007), 60–67; Martin, *The Opposable Mind: Winning through Integrative Thinking* (Boston: Harvard Business Press, 2009), 43, 107, 113–167.

18. James C. Collins and Jerry I. Porras, *Built to Last: Successful Habits of Visionary Companies* (New York: Harper Business, 1994), xiv.

19. Marcus Buckingham, *The One Thing You Need to Know about Great Managing, Great Leading, and Sustained Individual Success* (New York: Free Press, 2005), 197.

20. Joel Kurtzman, *Common Purpose: How Great Leaders Get Organizations to Achieve the Extraordinary* (New York: Jossey Bass, 2010), xii, 1–120.

21. John Baldoni, *Lead with Purpose: Giving Your Organization a Reason to Believe in Itself* (New York: AMACOM, 2012), 1–100.

22. Warren Bennis and Robert Thomas, *Leading for a Lifetime: How Defining Moments Shape the Leaders of Today and Tomorrow* (Boston: Harvard Business School Press, 2007), 121–155.

23. Arie de Geus, "The Living Company," *Harvard Business Review* 75 (March/April 1997), 51–59.

24. Jim Collins and Morten T. Hansen, *Great by Choice: Uncertainty, Chaos and Luck—Why Some Thrive Despite Them All* (New York: Harper Collins, 2011), 29.

25. Bennis and Thomas, *Leading for a Lifetime,* 101–102.

26. Paul J. H. Schoemaker et al, "Strategic Leadership: The Essential Skills," *Harvard Business Review* 91 (January–February 2013), 131–134.

27. James E. Fogerty, "Competing for Relevance: Archives in a Multiprogram Organization," in Bruce W. Dearstyne, ed., *Leading and Managing Archives and Records Programs: Strategies for Success* (New York: Neal-Schuman, 2008), 115–135.

28. Philip F. Mooney, "Stranger in a Strange Land: The Archivist and the Corporation," in Ibid, 183–205.

29. Justin Menkes, *Better under Pressure: How Great Leaders Bring Out the Best in Themselves and Others* (Boston: Harvard Business Press, 2011), 48–175.

30. Ronald Heifetz et al, "Leadership in a (Permanent) Crisis," *Harvard Business Review* 87 (July–August 2009), 62–69; "Ron Heifetz: Adaptive Leadership," Creelman Research (2009). http://www.creelmanresearch.com/files/Creelman2009vol2_5.pdf.

Chapter Three

Creativity, Innovation, and the Historical Enterprise

CREATIVITY, INNOVATION, AND RENEWAL

Directors of historical programs need to maintain their programs' best traditions of dedication, integrity, and objectivity in preserving and presenting history. At the same time, programs need to introduce new ideas and apply them in developing innovative initiatives and services. Integrating creativity and innovation into the DNA of historical programs can be a challenge. It is a skill that many of our programs need to strengthen and improve. There are a number of reasons why historical programs may be reluctant to encourage creativity and embrace innovation:

- Their leaders are risk-averse, fearing making a mistake, being criticized, or imperiling their funding if things go wrong. Their cautious attitude cascades down through the organization.
- The budget is meager or moderate and already stretched thin. Allocating existing resources for something new can seem risky. Seeking funding for something new can seem like a daunting process.
- Fixed job roles and institutional structures can lead to static thinking, barriers to working across departments or fields, or apprehension about getting into someone else's turf.
- The organization's culture and traditions stress continuity and predictability, and innovation can be jarring, sending the program in new directions.
- The organization operates according to a detailed prescriptive plan, and there is little or no room for modifying objectives and activities or adding something new.

Traditional visitors, researchers, or other users seem satisfied or at least don't demand something new. If the program broadens its appeal, it is uncertain who will come in or what they might want.

The organization operates in a top-down mode—good ideas are presumed to originate at or near the top, directives for new directions if any emanate from there, and ideas from the middle or front-line ranks are not encouraged, invited, or expected.

But there are overbalancing reasons why they should be innovative:

The trends in demographics, technology, and user expectations described in chapter 1 surround our programs with a swirl of change. To stay relevant and viable, we have to change, too, and that is the essence of creativity and innovation.

Being seen as innovative will help programs retain and even increase support from their parent programs, government agencies, and other sources that regard innovation as the hallmark of a successful enterprise.

Innovations such as application of information technology and social media can increase efficiency and stretch available resources.

Innovations add new dimensions to the program, stake its claim to be recognized for excellence in new areas, and add to its customer base.

THE SPARK OF CREATIVITY

Creativity is the springboard to innovation. A 2012 global survey by the software company Adobe revealed that unlocking creativity is the key to economic and societal growth around the globe. One respondent defined the term broadly: "To make something that did not exist before one creates it is being creative. To take something that exists and use it to make something else is being creative. To solve a problem by means of unconventional thinking is being creative." But many Americans surveyed for the study expressed concern that they were not achieving their creative potential. Explanations included our educational system, which stresses memorization and concept mastery rather than creativity; lack of time, training, and tools; and growing pressure to be productive rather than creative at work.[1] A 2011 IBM study concluded that creative leaders who "embrace the dynamic tension between creative disruption and operational efficiency can create new models of extraordinary value." These leaders built a culture where challenging assumptions is not only encouraged, but also expected.

Creative leaders invite disruptive innovation and encourage others to drop outdated approaches and take balanced risk. They're open-minded and inventive in expanding their management and communication styles, particularly to engage with a new generation of employees, partners, and customers.

Creative leaders are dissatisfied with today's choices and trade-offs and instead "embark on transforming tomorrow into what was once never thought possible." Creative leadership "finds ways to test as many ideas as possible to better understand those that afford the best opportunity."[2] Linda Norris and Rainey Tisdale, in their book *Creativity in Museum Practice*, explain that creative museum workers and creative museums "produce new ideas and new ways of seeing things that add value either internally (to the staff and to operations behind the scenes) or externally (to a public audience)." Creativity is seldom manifested in a sudden, out-of-the-blue brilliant idea that can be instantly implemented and leads to transformational change. Instead, it is a learned behavior that can improve with training and experience. Key elements of creativity include:[3]

Leadership that encourages creativity by hiring people with varying backgrounds to create a diverse workforce, encouraging curiosity, learning, development, and experimentation, and institutes a process for the program to consider and evaluate creative proposals and support good ones.

Staff members have deep and broad expertise in their field, keep up with the literature, regularly attend conferences, identify model programs, and are self-directed learners who keep growing. Along with the deep expertise, they also have a breadth of knowledge, experience, and interests that they can draw on to put their expertise in perspective. They have strong intrinsic motivation and passion for the work. They are inherently curious, constantly seeking new information and asking probing questions.

There is a well-understood individual *creative process* that happens in stages: (1) preparation where people study the problem to understand all its features and ramifications; (2) incubation, a time when the mind sorts through information, discerns patterns, and makes connections; (3) insight—the stage "when your brain finds a new connection within all that information rattling around in your head and pops it into your conscious mind and you realize how much potential it has"; (4) evaluation, a stage when you decide whether the idea really has merit and warrants further effort; and (5) elaboration, the stage when you write up the idea and begin trying it out, sharing it with others and perhaps some preliminary testing.

Creative intelligence is social, writes Bruce Nussbaum in *Creative Intelligence.* "We increase our creative ability by learning from others, collaborating, and sharing." He discusses several "competencies" of creative intelligence including:[4]

> Knowledge mining: Go to the source, talk with and observe people, find out what is deeply meaningful, partner with people who have even more insight. Cast widely, including outside your field, for new ideas. Search back through history to see what has worked and why, but also what ideas and practices were abandoned along the way that might be revisited, revised, and reapplied to meet new challenges.
>
> Framing: Understand your frame of reference—your way of seeing the world as it compares to other people's viewpoints. Understand how your biases, preconceptions, or worldview might be limiting your ability to come up with new, more creative strategies. "What if?" framing means shifting from a static view of the program and its setting as they are to a broader view that tries to envision how demographics, technology, economy, and other changes will impact its setting and services over the long run.
>
> Making: People have a "maker instinct"—they want to build something and test it. Creativity involves moving an idea quickly from just a concept to something concrete that can be observed, tested, and evaluated.
>
> Pivoting: After testing, put the idea into production, make it part of the program. "Most disruptive innovations come from individuals who are leading a cause and who've inspired a loyal following to get involved . . . most creative individuals see their work as a calling; their belief in their work gives them the energy to move forward and inspire others to join them."

Creativity can be a solo effort, but usually, it is a collective endeavor involving divergent thinking, surfacing of discussion of multiple insights and perspectives. Steven Johnson, who writes about intellectual history, notes that few breakthrough ideas are sudden "Eureka!" moments. Individuals may have the beginnings of a good idea but take a long time to get them to the stage where they are coherent and concrete—a process he calls "slow hunches." Ideas are sharpened and enriched through people being part of "liquid networks" of individuals where lots of ideas are surfaced, discussed, and debated. People change their minds or shape their own emerging idea in a different direction, and then articulate it at an opportune time when it seems timely and appropriate for the program, its setting, and its circumstances. "Chance favors the connected mind," he asserts.[5] Even where the process is more structured and deliberate (e.g., a facilitated discussion specifically to identify new ideas) the process can be unsystematic and the end result unanticipated. Team members practice "creative abrasion" through bringing different experiences and intellectual styles to the discussion, confidently offering ideas even if they are unorthodox, asking tough questions, challenging each other, and advising everyone who presents an idea on what questions or issues need to be considered and addressed. The discussions are collegial but also lively and spirited. [6]

INNOVATION: PUTTING CREATIVITY TO WORK

Good ideas by themselves don't help programs to soar to new levels. *Innovation* is basically creativity applied and put to work. "Don't confuse innovation with 'creativity' (or 'ideas')," cautions Richard Evans, president of EmcArts, a company that encourages innovation in the arts and is partnering with the American Alliance of Museums to encourage museum innovation. "Creativity is a characteristic of individuals, where *innovation* is a group or corporate activity [that] requires people to work together to turn ideas into practical projects that can feasibly be implemented. Innovation changes things by applying ideas to practice." [7] Innovation in the historical enterprise community is difficult to track. The American Alliance of Museums' Center for the Future of Museums has established an "Innovation Lab for Museums"—a competitive grants program to "encourage museums to experiment and take risks." The director of the center has noted that "if the future is going to be significantly different from the present, museums are going to have to find new ways of operating." But encouraging innovation is still a novelty for the professional museum community, "somewhat at odds with our 100-year+ history of fostering consensus on standards and best practices and then nudging museums to comply. It's hard to shift from the message of 'emulate the best museums, which all behave this way' to a message of 'but feel free to try something else in case it works better!'" The initial projects funded through the Innovation Lab focused on innovating in markets (how to get different people to care about what we do), relationships (new ways of interacting with people and entirely new types of innovation), economies ("how to monetize our work in new ways"), and experience (delivering content in new ways). They explored what it means to be a participant (not just a visitor) at a museum, how to engage and bring in younger people, the role of the museum as change-agent and community representative. They studied the traditional role museum-as-expert vs. the advent of "participatory experiences" involving visitors in influencing exhibits. [8] One of the grants supports a "Re-Imagining Historic House Museums" initiative by the National Trust for Historic Preservation to "raise our sites to new levels of financial sustainability, structural integrity, and programmatic quality, while offering a visitor experience that is more critical, layered, and sensory." The project, when completed, is expected to yield insights for other historic house museums. [9]

MODELS OF INNOVATION

Leaders of innovative organizations exhibit a number of traits. They constantly seek new knowledge and have the ability of associating—connecting seemingly unrelated questions, problems, or ideas from different fields. Innovative entrepreneurs constantly ask questions that challenge common wisdom and spend a good deal of time thinking about how to change things. They are particularly adept at formulating questions of "Why?," "Why not?," and "What if?" They scrutinize common phenomena, particularly the behavior of customers and potential customers, acting like social scientists and anthropologists. They encourage and support experimenting. They "go out of their way to meet people with different kinds of ideas and perspectives to extend their own knowledge domains."[10] Innovative companies have a number of distinct traits:[11]

Consistency. Their strategies are consistent, clear, and well thought-out. They have an underlying philosophy, and their strategies are consistent with it.

Values. The organization values innovation and shows it by continual endorsement and support from the leader, spending on entrepreneurial projects, and encouraging continuous employee growth and learning.

Customer focus. They go "above and beyond" for their customers and are determined to provide customer value, assess and work to determine customers' future needs as well as their present ones, gather information on customer preferences, and aim to exceed customer expectations. They are more concerned with what is best for the customer than what is best for the organization.

Behaviors. Leaders and managers energize employees by providing vivid descriptions of the future and cutting through red tape. Employees show determination in overcoming technical roadblocks, "scrounging" resources when budgets are thin, and listening to customers.

Climate. This refers to the tenor of the workplace. An innovative climate fosters engagement and enthusiasm, challenges people to take reasonable risks in experimenting and supports them when they do, and encourages independent thinking and learning.

Resources. Funding is available to support innovation and the leadership designates selected staff as "innovation champions" to encourage original thinking and help transform good ideas to practical applications.

Processes. The organization has processes in place for discussion of creative new ideas and a review/approval process for prioritizing projects and prototyping.

Success. Innovation is celebrated internally, and the organization is recognized by its peers for being a model. Individuals who participate in development of innovation initiatives are rewarded, with financial resources if available and with recognition and promotion.

Innovation baked into the culture. Organizations that are highly innovative build on the momentum that comes with success. Customers think of them as responsive and leading edge institutions. They treat innovation as a long-term strategy rather than a short-time or one-time solution. Transformative projects help the organization develop new capacities, generate employee pride and optimism, and make it easier in the future to get resources for more experimentation.

The nation's leading companies are useful models of leadership and innovation. Of course, historical programs need to be selective when deciding which strategies to consider and to adapt them to fit their program's mission and circumstances. Some examples: [12]

Hard decisions, clear priorities. P&G leader A. G. Lafley, quoting management theorist Peter Drucker, often said that "the CEO decides on the balance between present activities and investment in an unknown, unknowable, and highly uncertain future." Lafley described the turnaround he led at P&G, which was foundering and running out of cash when he took over in 2000:

1. *We faced up to the reality.* We started seeing things as they are, not as we wanted them to be.
2. *We accepted change.* We stopped trying to ignore or resist it. We embraced change; we committed to lead change.
3. *We started making choices.* Clear choices, tough choices; what [the company] would do and not do. Choice making is the essence of strategy.
4. *We put together a strong, cohesive team.* We put the right players in the right seats on the same bus headed in the same direction. We shared a compelling vision of what we wanted to achieve, and we worked as a team on strategies and action plans.

Lafley had P&G staff interview customers and observe not only what they purchased but how they used it and what their unmet expectations and needs were. Through constant, intensive discussion of customer preferences, he led a process of selling off weak household and beauty brands and focusing the company's energies and resources on popular products that people really wanted and on research for the future. "Define the relevant outside"—the constituencies that matter most, where the results are most meaningful and the impact is the greatest—to help the program set direction and priorities, he advised.

Passion, intensity, focus. Steve Jobs, the inspirational, driven, and demanding CEO of Apple for several years, emphasized focus—"deciding what not to do is as important as deciding what to do." He simplified products and services, cut red tape and clutter, accelerated development when he sensed the company was falling behind customer needs, and was fanatical about quality. Listen to focus groups, he counseled, but don't be a slave to them because "customers don't know what they want until we've shown them . . . our task is to read things that are not yet on the page."

Keep services customer-centric, set new directions, disrupt the field. Jeff Bezos calls Amazon.com "the world's most customer-centric company" and says "we innovate by starting with the customer and working backwards." Tracking user purchase patterns and preferences helps Amazon customize its ads, offer what customers want, and keep customers coming back. Amazon keeps expanding, and Bezos has helped transform the book publishing industry. Amazon's Kindle portable computer enables people to read e-books, newspapers, magazines, blogs, and other digital media. New-device launches and new product or service offerings are carefully choreographed.

Keep strong principles and traditions, but bring them forward, refine them, and apply them to current needs. Lou Gerstner, who transformed IBM from a fading computer and software company to a leading provider of technology integration and consulting services, knew the proud history of the company, dating back to 1911, when he took over as CEO in 1993. IBM employees were known for being "very good, very relentless, very focused, and very individualistic" with a buttoned-up, by-the-book culture that had become "inbred and ingrown," given to "studying things to death" and "obsessive perfectionism." IBM had not changed with the times. Customer service had shrunk to peddling equipment rather than really probing customers' business needs. "Respect for the individual" had been corrupted to spawn a culture of entitlement and lack of accountability. Gertsner changed all that, reverting to the company's founding principles but giving them new meaning and applicability. He divested unprofitable product lines, consolidated operations, belatedly but successfully launched a new PC line, and restored the IBM brand to its historical greatness.

Elevated mission, hands-on leadership. When Howard Schultz returned to Starbucks as CEO in 2008 after a hiatus of nearly eight years, he found the company strategically adrift with an excess of new and unprofitable stores, too many product lines, dispirited employees, and unenthusiastic customers. Schultz made tough decisions to close underperforming stores, pulled back to the company's central upscale coffee business, intensely trained frontline staff in customer service, expanded ethical sourcing of coffee, and initiated a new style of carefully managed innovation to "create innovative growth platforms worthy of our coffee." He redefined and elevated Starbucks' mission from serving coffee to becoming a company "known for inspiring and nurturing the human spirit."

Starbucks continues to be a model for connecting with customers. The company's leadership aims for more than just providing satisfying coffee. Its frontline staff manifest a genuine interest in customers and provide personalized service; the "Starbucks Experience" is designed to "inspire, nurture, and uplift." Customers are invited to make suggestions for services and products through an online website, "MyStarbucksIdea.com," where they can interact with subject-matter moderators. Employee training, incentive, and rewards programs help reinforce the customer-centric focus. Leading edge technology, including a mobile app for on-site payments, helps maintain the company's progressive image. Customers can stay connected with the company and each other through its Facebook site. The company has a philosophy of "honor the past but don't be trapped in it" and balances adhering to solid principles like individual customer focus with willingness to make "potentially game-changing big bets."

SEARCHING FOR NEW IDEAS

In most cases, the best creative ideas that can be transformed into innovations may come from the people most familiar with the historical program—its trustees, its director, and its staff members. But leaders of historical programs need to be imaginative and expansive in where they look for new ideas. Some come from within their program; some, from our professional associations and colleagues; and still others from sources beyond our field. Some examples:

- American Alliance of Museums, Center for the Future of Museums (http://www.aam-us.org/resources/center-for-the-future-of-museums). Monitors cultural, economic, and technological trends.
- American Association for State and Local History (http://www.aaslh.org). Books; articles on innovative programs in its journal, *History News*; winners of its Award of Merit, Albert B. Corey Award, HIP Award; sessions at its leadership institute, Developing History Leaders@SHA (http://historyleadership.org)
- Ash Center for Democratic Governance and Innovation, Kennedy School of Government, Harvard University (http://www.ash.harvard.edu). Recognizes and promotes innovations in government.

- The D School at Stanford (http://dschool.stanford.edu). Formally named the Hasso Plattner Institute of Design at Stanford, the school is a leading proponent of design thinking to address a variety of problems.
- EmcArts (http://www.emcarts.org). Innovative practices in the area of arts, including collaboration and audience engagement.
- Fast Company (http://www.fastcompany.com). Information on innovative leaders, developing companies, and imaginative design.
- Foundation Center (http://foundationcenter.org). Information on philanthropy, foundations, fundraising, and nonprofit management.
- IBM Center for the Business of Government (http://www.businessofgovernment.org). Original research and practical ideas for managing in government.
- IBM Institute for Business Value (http://www-935.ibm.com/services/us/gbs/thoughtleadership). Reports on emerging trends and business innovations.
- IDEO (http://www.ideo.com). Design firm known for its innovation and pioneering in design thinking.
- Inc. (http://www.inc.com). Innovative ideas from the nation's fastest growing companies.
- *Museum 2.0* (http://museumtwo.blogspot.com). The blog of Nina Simon, discussed below, is a constant source of new ideas about reinventing museums and customer engagement.
- National Council for Nonprofits (http://www.councilofnonprofits.org). Information on issues, trends, and the best practices in leadership and management in the nonprofit sector.
- TED—Ideas Worth Spreading (http://www.ted.com/talks). Videos and transcripts of talks on innovation, media, technology, entertainment, and other topics.

Another approach is to systematically and proactively draw on users, such as visitors to our sites and programs, as innovation partners. There are multiple potential benefits: widening the circle of involvement, engagement, and support; bringing in new ideas to keep the program on the move and responsive; and building a dedicated advocacy alliance. The concept needs to be applied carefully and judiciously, with the program director retaining ultimate control over program makeup and content. Consumer-oriented companies have long prided themselves on their ability to understand the insights and experiences of their customers and integrate the best ideas into future products and services. Years of use of "crowdsourcing" has demonstrated that for certain types of problems, thoughtful, informed individuals can often come up with new ideas and solutions to problems that may not have occurred to program staff. Companies have cracked some of the toughest technological and scientific problems in history through contests where people on the outside suggest solutions. IBM and Apple have used it to develop and refine products and services. Wikipedia, the Internet-based encyclopedia, in less than a decade disrupted the reference world and demonstrated the value of large-scale, highly diverse collaboration in a new organizational model. National Geographic recently drew on an online crowd of about 28,000 people to sift through satellite imagery of Mongolia in search of Genghis Kahn's tomb. Lego, the manufacturer of the popular toy line of interlocking plastic bricks, solicits user-generated creative ideas to revise products and create new ones. Potential customers also pretest innovations to eliminate problems and reduce risk. [13]

Nina Simon, a former museum consultant and now director of the Santa Cruz Museum of Art and History, applied the model of systematic user involvement to museums in her book, *The Participatory Museum*, in 2010 and elaborates it in her blog, *Museum 2.0.* She advanced several ideas:

Museums should be places for community engagement, conversations about important issues, and catalysts for social change. Artifacts and objects such as paintings can form the centerpiece for conversations about the events depicted or represented and about modern issues in the same topical areas.

We should treat in-person and online visitors as partners—creators, re-mixers, and redistributors of content. Regard every visitor who walks in the door or logs onto the website as a potential contributor who can make the program better. Design a way for people to contribute ideas and suggestions. At her museum, for instance, visitors can write on white boards and use post-it notes to leave reactions and suggestions. She calls it "multidirectional content experiences."

Part of our work should be providing personally relevant experiences and relationships with users and visitors.

We should encourage conversations and relationships among our visitors and members (e.g., through multi-platform engagement tools and mechanisms such as online blogs and wikis).

We should engage interested outsiders as collaborators and co-producers (e.g., brainstorming new exhibits and public programs). This can be done online, for instance, in regularly-scheduled on-site meetings or online by sharing your programming goals on your website and solic-iting collaboration in general and for specific events and projects. Be prepared to listen and respectfully consider even what seem like wild ideas and after discussion scale back and zero in on the most viable and exciting ones.

"I want to offer the most desirable experience possible—even if it's not what people walked in thinking they were seeking," says Simon. Rather than say-ing we meet user needs, we should say something like "our job is to connect the familiar to the unfamiliar, and in doing so, ignite a passion for how diverse, exciting, and essential art (or history, or science) can be."[14]

Simon suggests several tactics for application by "participatory" programs might include:

> Carefully observe how people walk through the facilities, where they stop, what takes most of their time, where their conversations seem more engaged and animated.
>
> Generate maps or directions to the most popular or provocative exhibits, based on comments by visitors.
>
> Provide for responsiveness and feedback, including telling visitors and people who log on and make suggestions how their suggestions will be reviewed and evaluated, to let them know that their insights and work will be used.
>
> In visitor surveys, or post-visit surveys online, structure questions to elicit responses about what people liked best and why, what they liked least (or did not like at all) and why, and their suggestions for future exhibits and programs.
>
> Provide public forums for visitors and staff to discuss current and possible future exhibits and programs, and ask and answer each other's questions.
>
> Help visitors find other people (staff members or visitors) with shared or similar interests with whom they can engage in content-specific activities or discussions.

In a participatory institution, as Nina Simon suggests, "staff would continually seek out opportunities to improve the institution via contributions by and with visitors. When planning every new exhibition, program, or fundraising campaign, staff would ask themselves: how can visitors help? What can they provide to make this project better?" Of course, this does not mean turning over control to visitors or making program decisions based only on their preferences. It does mean finding a way to convert their recommendations and contributions into action. It celebrates diverse voices, makes the institution feel more dynamic, provides alternative contexts for the content presented, introduces new opportunity for learning around cultural artifacts, and "makes the museum feel like a creative and social place."[15] The textbox "Participatory Historical Program Initiatives" provides some examples.

PARTICIPATORY HISTORICAL PROGRAM INITIATIVES

"Participatory" program exhibits and events are growing in popularity. A few examples:

- The Brooklyn Historical Society has for several years held a "Public Perspectives Exhibition Series" to provide a forum for Brooklyn residents to present community-curated exhibits. Topics have included Italian Catholic culture, storefront facades, affordable housing, and other issues related to changes in Brooklyn. "I think it has definitely served to bring new people to the Historical Society who have not been here, hadn't known about the place," said the Society's director Deborah Schwartz (Deborah Schwartz and Bill Adair, "Community as Curator: A Case Study at the Brooklyn Historical Society," in Adair et al, eds., *Letting Go: Sharing Historical Authority in a User-Generated World.* (Philadelphia: Pew Center for Arts and Heritage, 2011), 112–123).
- The Detroit Historical Museum is concerned with building community spirit and ensuring preservation of historic structures in a city that has experienced urban decline and downsizing. Its *Detroit Decides: Our Most Celebrated Building* invited visitors (in-person or online) to nominate "any past or present building that best embodies the spirit of Detroit." Planners had originally intended to select the top three for coverage in an exhibit, but they received so many nominations that they decided to mount a series of exhibits (http://detroithistorical.org/detroit-historical-museum/exhibitions/special-exhibitions/detroit-decides).
- The Oakland Museum of California calls itself "the people's museum" and has a long tradition of reaching out to intended audiences. As part of its work to demonstrate diversity, it recruited participants for its "Forces of Change" exhibit by asking "What was your life like in California during the '60s and early '70s? How did you participate in and react to the social changes of the time?" Participants attended a workshop and worked with staff to curate their own display case as part of the exhibit (http://museumca.org/forces-of-change).
- The Minnesota Historical Society's *If These Walls Could Talk* exhibit profiles the histories of families that lived in one modest house in St. Paul from the first German immigrants through the Italians, African Americans, and Hmong who succeeded them and how the neighborhood changed over the years. The exhibit drew on recollections of occupants and their descendants but also extensively on interviews and collaboration with neighborhood residents. "Sometimes people would tell us they had nothing important to say, but then the memories would start flowing, and we would hear such wonderful, revealing anecdotes," said the exhibit's curator, Benja-

min Filene. "It really does show how everyone has a story to tell. That's what history is all about" ("Open House: If These Walls Could Talk," 2013. http://www.mnhs.org/exhibits/openhouse/exhibit.htm).

- The Historical Society of Pennsylvania's PhilaPlace interactive website includes text, photos, and audio and video clips documenting the history of Philadelphia's neighborhoods. It includes a "My Phila-Place" feature where people can share their own recollections about living in a particular neighborhood by uploading their own stories and including a photo and video or audio file if they wish (http://www.philaplace.org/myphilaplace).
- Some programs have initiated "citizen history" projects. The National Maritime Museum in Britain has solicited volunteers to transcribe Royal Navy logbooks from the World War I era to aid scientists searching weather patterns. The University of Iowa invited the public to help transcribe Civil War diaries in its collection. Several documentary editing projects are using crowdsourcing to transcribe and keyboard documents. Some of the projects are in-house, but others are online, using digital materials made available on the sponsoring program's website. The projects require significant staff time to ensure accuracy and completeness. "Democratizing history through crowdsourcing is offering public historians another meaningful route to create a sense of community around content," said Sharon Leon, director of one of the documentary projects (Tom Grove, "Citizen History Projects," *History News*, Autumn 2011, 5–6).
- One of the goals of the British *Moving Here* project on immigration, organized by a consortium of libraries, archives, and museums led by the National Archives of Great Britain, was to encourage minority and ethnic groups to document their own history of migration. The site provided an opportunity for visitors to publish their own experience of migration (http://www.movinghere.org.uk/default.htm).

INNOVATION ON FAST FORWARD

Traditional project management often involved lengthy, substantial projects, extensive planning, intensive management, and strict definitions of success: on time, within specified budget, and delivering a product that met the specifications laid out in the plan. Newer approaches, more geared to creativity and innovation, are likely to be more pragmatic, improvisational, iterative, and faster. Rather than beginning with a lengthy business plan, they start out with the search for a viable model. Quick rounds of experimentation and feedback reveal what works and what does not. The approach emphasizes breaking large projects into smaller ones, bringing in lots of new ideas, experimenting, quickly adapting, using what works, and learning quickly from initiatives that are less than successful.

Eric Ries's book, *The Lean Startup*, focused on creating something new under conditions of extreme uncertainty. The idea has been adapted and applied to evolving existing enterprises as well as starting up new ones. Rather than relying on elaborate strategic plans, Ries advocates experimentation, continually testing goals and strategies, and adapting and adjusting as you go. He emphasizes shortened development cycles and extensive customer engagement and continual feedback in the development of new services and products. The book advances the concepts of "validated learning"—try an initial idea and quickly measure it to see if it moves toward the goal of building a sustainable program and "pivot"—"structured course correction designed to test a new fundamental hypothesis about the product [or] strategy." If a small experimental initiative works, scale it up and stick with it; if it fails, learn from the failure and pivot, moving on to something else. [16]

Organizations that emulate "startup" strategies probe for new possibilities and think aspirationally about change. They accelerate exploration of needs and development of solutions. They believe that "good enough"—the idea is feasible and adds value—is a sufficient basis for starting. Too much assessment will stall the transition from creativity to innovation. "Launching a good idea is always better than not launching an awesome one . . . distill the concept into raw form and go with it. Get it into others' hands and see what happens. If you are too hung up on creating policies and procedures, workflows and logistics, wordsmithing and committee debates, then . . . the project will stall out before you can even find out if it's worth the effort." Rely on iteration—developing and improving incrementally, step-by-step—to keep developments on track and moving in the right direction. [17] Innovation expert Peter Sims recommends "little bets"—discrete "concrete actions taken to discover, test, and develop ideas that are achievable and affordable." These can result in "small wins" which you can build on and extend, or "failing quickly to learn fast" from small experimental, low-resource projects and using the insights to refine, modify, or try something entirely different. [18]

Organizations that follow the "lean startup" or "little bets" approaches take a view of things that differs from traditional approaches. The chart below illustrates these changes. [19]

A related concept called "design thinking" takes a similar approach. It is based on a penchant for experimenting and doing rather than analyzing and talking. It has a flavor of optimism and confidence—you want to tackle problems and feel you will succeed. It observes customers and end-users carefully and involves them in design of new products and services. In the

Feature	Traditional	Lean
Strategy	Business plan Implementation-driven	Business model Hypothesis-driven
New-product process	Product management Prepare offering for market following a linear, step-by-step plan	Customer development Get out of the office and test hypotheses
Engineering	Agile or waterfall development Build the product iteratively or fully specify the product before building it	Agile development Build the product iteratively and incrementally
Organization	Departments by function Hire for experience and ability to execute	Customers and agile development teams Hire for learning, nimbleness, and speed
Financial management	Accounting Income statement, balance sheet, cash flow statement	Metrics that matter Customer acquisition cost, lifetime customer value, churn, viralness
Failure	Exception Fix by firing executives	Expected Fix by iterating on ideas and pivoting away from those that don't work
Speed	Measured Operates on complete data	Rapid Operates on good-enough data

world of business, it includes something akin to anthropological research—observing people interacting with products and services, dialoging with them about their interests and needs, seeking to build an empathy with customers. It has a "do something" mindset that minimizes extensive planning and maximizes action, moving quickly from thought to deed via experimentation and prototypes. The process is imprecise and fast-moving, involving quick invention, experimentation, and iteration. The goal is not the absolutely definitive answer but rather "satisfying authenticity." Institutions need

> design's enthusiasm for the experiment and its patience with failure in service to learning. Design teaches us to let go and allow more chaos into our lives; designers lean into uncertainty, while managers often deny or fight it. When the world is in flux, acceptance is superior to denial. And designers have real tools—like experience mapping and hypothesis generation and testing—that can add structure (and comfort) to an unpredictable environment.

The next chart contrasts traditional and design approaches.[20]

From another perspective, using design thinking requires answering four questions:[21]

	Traditional	Design
Underlying assumptions	Rationality, objectivity; reality as fixed and quantifiable	Subjective experience; reality as socially constructed
Method	Analysis aimed at proving one "best" answer	Experimentation aimed at iterating toward a "better" answer
Process	Planning	Doing
Decision drivers	Logic; numeric models	Emotion; experimental models
Values	Pursuit of control and stability; discomfort with uncertainty	Pursuit of novelty; dislike of status quo
Level of focus	Abstract or particular	Movement between abstract and particular

What is? This stage develops an accurate assessment of the current reality. The key here is to study users whose experience you want to understand more fully to determine just who they are, why they visit our museum or use our services, and what their experiences are, a deep understanding of their motivations and reactions. Try to assess the experience through the customers' eyes, for instance noting the steps a visitor has to take to get at research materials in an archives or how constrained they feel by restrictions against touching materials in a historic house. This stage involves data such as statistics on visitors, users, budgets and other resources; questionnaires; talking with visitors and users and if possible assembling focus groups for more sustained discussions; checking professional standards and literature to determine how the program stacks up against models in the field. The process may produce an overabundance of data, opinions, and other information, but design strategists are patient in the face of uncertainty and inconsistent evidence. Discussion will show patterns and help differentiate people, for instance, by demographics, areas of interest, and personal goals, when they engage with a history program.

What if? This stage envisions a new future; it is generative and creative. It begins with discussions about possibilities, trends, and uncertainties. This can be done through brainstorming discussions, but it needs to focus on new possibilities, not constraints which can dampen down breakthrough thinking. It needs to elicit new ideas and build them up and above all avoid the pattern of breaking them down and finding flaws before they have been fully explored. Insights generate more insights. Ignoring constraints, or at least pushing them off stage for a while, fosters creativity. After brainstorming ideas, return to the constraints and begin discussing how to get rid of or around them. After brainstorming ends, select a small, diverse group to identify the strongest proposals, which may involve combining some that were proposed, and developing them into a modest number of descriptions for new approaches or initiatives.

What wows? This stage makes some choices—what are the ideas that really *wow* people? For each of the proposed new ideas, ask "what are the features that make this concept so engaging," "what are the assumptions underlying this concept," and "what would need to be true for this concept to be a good one?" Test the assumptions through further discussion. Focus on how to describe and express new concepts in ways that showcase their strongest elements. Try the emerging concept out on a group other than the one that developed it. You should also consider developing prototypes—the idea in tangible form, for exploration, testing, and refinement—something small that can be tested with key stakeholders or sample groups of users.

What works? This fourth stage takes the idea in the form of a prototype into the "marketplace," in the case of historical programs, visitors, researchers, and other end users. Try out a prototype on customers, particularly those whom you most want your program to serve (which may be different from the current customer base). Invite the customers into the conversation in a direct, hands-on, lots-of-discussion way, in effect, involving customers in design of the final product. In effect, you are asking customers to take a walk with you into possible futures with the understanding that their reactions, input, and advice will be critical in the decision about which future the program chooses, and exactly what it will look like. This is learning-in-action, a form of customer co-creation that involves lots of asking, listening, and discussing. You are trying to find out how it actually works in the program and make adjustments on the fly. If the initiative is not a success, the sooner it fails, the better, and the sooner you can debrief and move on to something else, based on what you learned in the process. "Fail early to succeed sooner" is a common motto.

PUTTING CREATIVITY AND INNOVATION INTO ACTION

The authors of the book *Creative Confidence* summarized themes behind successful innovative practices:[22]

"Innovation catalysts"—people in the organization who advocated, initiated, and supported change.

Broad executive support for experimentation, including providing "cover" for experiments that do not work out.

Small actions that require only modest commitment of employees' time.

Avoid big complex projects.

Management willing to take a "leap of faith"—recognition of the value of design thinking, putting his or her resources behind it.

Minimize hierarchy.

Value team camaraderie and trust—"mindset of working together toward a shared solution. No one person is responsible for the final outcome. It is the result of everyone's contribution. Instead of individuals protecting or promoting 'my idea,' colleagues become comfortable with group ownership."

In discussion, avoid introducing phrases such as "we can't," "we've tried that already," and "that will never work." Instead, use questions like "how might we . . . " to get people to elaborate on their initial proposals and seek out new possibilities.

"Great groups believe they are on a mission . . . great groups are more optimistic than realistic . . . great groups *ship*," notes leadership expert Warren Bennis. They are "places of action not think tanks or retreat centers devoted solely to the generation of ideas . . . dreamers with deadlines."

How can you tell if a new idea or proposal is good enough to try out in your program? Taking the discussion in this chapter into account, it is useful to endorse and begin implementing an idea that:

Is consistent with the program's mission and values.

Has been tried out, perhaps with some variation, in another history or museum program or in some other setting where the results are clear and you can draw on them for your program.

It was developed through a process that included frank discussion and respected dissent.

It can succeed with the program's current people, resources, and assets, or with additional resources that can be obtained.

It can be applied in a way that you can learn and refine it as it is rolled out.

You can develop measures to gauge its impact.

It has potential as a learning experience especially in areas where you would like to expand and need to learn more how to do it.

It has the potential to garner new support (e.g., from a funding source that is interested in the approach that will be taken).

If it fails or is less-than-successful, the negative consequences to the program will be minimal and the process can be used as a learning experience.

NOTES

1. Adobe, *State of Create Study* (2012). http://www.adobe.com/aboutadobe/pressroom/pdfs/Adobe_State_of_Create_Global_Benchmark_Study.pdf.

2. IBM Institute for Business Value, *Cultivating Organizational Creativity in an Age of Complexity* (2011), 1–6. http://www-935.ibm.com/services/us/gbs/thoughtleadership/ibv-organizational-creativity.htm.

3. Linda Norris and Rainey Tisdale, *Creativity in Museum Practice* (Walnut Creek, CA: Left Coast Press, 2014), 10, 40–43, 69–87, 102–104.

4. Bruce Nussbaum, *Creative Intelligence: Harnessing the Power to Create, Connect, and Inspire* (New York: Harper Business, 2013), 12–115, 146–220.

5. Steven Johnson, "Where Good Ideas Come From," TED video (July 2010). http://www.ted.com/talks/steven_johnson_where_good_ideas_come_from.html.

6. Dorothy Leonard and Walter Swap, *When Sparks Fly: Igniting Creativity in Groups* (Boston: Harvard University Press, 1999), 19–50.

7. Richard Evans, "The Transformative Power of Innovation," Center for the Future of Museums Blog (September 20, 2011). http://futureofmuseums.blogspot.com/2011/09/transformative-power-of-innovation.html.

8. Elizabeth Merritt, "Fostering Innovation: Part I." Center for the Future of Museums Blog (September 26, 2013). http://futureofmuseums.blogspot.com/2013/09/one-of-cfms-assignments-is-to-encourage.html.; EmcArts, *Innovation Lab for Museums* (2013). http://www.emcarts.org/index.cfm?PAGEPATH=Programs_Services/Innovation_Lab_for_Museums&ID=38130.

9. National Trust for Historic Preservation, "National Trust Initiative to Innovate House Museum Model" (July 9, 2012). http://www.preservationnation.org/who-we-are/press-center/press-releases/2012/national-trust-initiative-to.html.

10. Jeffrey H. Dyer et al, "The Innovator's DNA," *Harvard Business Review* 87 (December 2009), 61–67.

11. Jay Rao and Joseph Weintraub, "How Innovative Is Your Company's Culture?," *MIT Sloan Management Review* 54 (July 2013), 29–37; John J. Jamrog and Miles H. Overholt, "High Performance Organizations: Finding the Elements of Excellence," *People and Strategy* 31 (2008), 29–38.

12. A. G. Lafley, "What Only the CEO Can Do," *Harvard Business Review* (May 2009), 54–62; Noel Tichy, "Lafley's Legacy: From Crisis to Customer-Driven," *BusinessWeek Online* (June 11, 2009). http://www.businessweek.com/managing/content/jun2009/ca20090610_248094.htm; A. G. Lafley and Ram Charan, *The Game Changer: How Every Leader Can Drive Everyday Innovation* (New York: Profile Books, 2008), 177–178; Walter Isaacson, "The Real Leadership Lessons of Steve Jobs," *Harvard Business* Review (April 2012), 93–102; "Amazon's Jeff Bezos: The Ultimate Disrupter," *Fortune* (September 16, 2012). http://management.fortune.cnn.com/2012/11/16/jeff-bezos-amazon; Louis V. Gerstner, *Who Says Elephants Can't Dance? Leading a Great Enterprise through Dramatic Change* (New York: Harper Business, 2002), 181–198; Howard Schultz, *Onward: How Starbucks Fought for Its Life without Losing Its Soul* (New York: Rodale, 2011), 102–115; Joseph A. Michelli, *Leading the Starbucks Way: 5 Principles for Connecting with Your Customers, Your Products and Your People* (New York McGraw-Hill 2014), 1–278.

13. Kevin J. Bourdeau and Karim R. Lakhani, "Using the Crowd as an Innovation Partner," *Harvard Business Review* 91 (April 2013), 61–69; Yun Mi Antorini et al, "Collaborating with Customer Communities: Lessons from the Lego Group," *MIT Sloan Management Review* 53 (Spring 2012), 73–79.

14. Nina Simon, *The Participatory Museum* (2010); "Making a Participatory Exhibit at Santa Cruz" (September 12, 2012), "Broad Questions about Audience Participation" (September 18, 2013) at *Museum 2.0*. http://museumtwo.blogspot.com; "Opening Up the Museum" (November 6, 2012), http://www.youtube.com/watch?v=aIcwIH1vZ9w; and "Let's stop talking about what people want and need . . ." (November 20, 2013). http://museumtwo.blogspot.com.

15. Nina Simon, "Participatory Design and the Future of Museums," in Bill Adair et al, eds, *Letting Go? Sharing Historical Authority in a User-Generated World.* (Philadelphia: Pew Center for Arts and Heritage, 2011), 18–32.

16. Eric Ries, *The Lean Startup: How Today's Entrepreneurs Use Continuous Innovation to Create Radically Successful Businesses* (New York: Crown Business, 2011).

17. Brian Mathews, *Facing the Future: Think Like a Startup* (April 2012). http://vtech-works.lib.vt.edu/bitstream/handle/10919/18649/Think%20like%20a%20STARTUP.pdf.

18. Peter Sims, *Little Bets: How Breakthrough Ideas Emerge from Small Discoveries* (New York: Free Press, 2011).

19. Steve Blank, "Why the Lean Start-Up Changes Everything," *Harvard Business Review* 91 (May 2013), 69.

20. Jeanne Liedtka, "Business Strategy and Design: Can This Marriage Be Saved," *Design Management Review* 21 (June 2010), 6–11.

21. Jeanne Liedtka and Tim Ogilvie, *Designing for Growth: A Design Thinking Tool for Managers* (New York: Columbia Business School, 2011), 39–178.

22. Tom Kelley and David Kelley, *Creative Confidence: Unleashing the Creative Potential within All of Us* (New York: Crown Business, 2014), 175–209.

Chapter Four

Making Strategic Connections

This chapter explores several ways of strengthening programs by connecting them with professional associations, users, and other programs, and using the appeal of heritage tourism and historic preservation to boost their visibility and appeal for resources. It suggests the possibility of strategic connections with groups at the two ends of the age spectrum—students in public schools who need to learn history if they are to become customers of historical programs as adults; and retired professionals who can support program capacity building.

ADVISORY SERVICES TO STRENGTHEN PROGRAMS

One approach to stronger programs is seeking support and advice from professional associations, state historical agencies, and large, well-established historical programs. The AASLH's Standards and Excellence Program for History Organizations (StEPs) is an outstanding national example. It helps small- and mid-sized history museums, historic sites, and houses, including all-volunteer ones, assess their policies and practices, strengthen the management of daily operations, improve their stewardship practices, and plan for the future, including developing or revising their mission and vision statements. StEPs is self-paced and uses a workbook, an online community with hundreds of resources, and certificates to help organizations identify their strengths and opportunities for improvement. It uses self-assessment questions and performance indicators and makes the work less daunting by providing for gradual improvement, getting programs first to the basic level, then to good, and then to better. The emphasis is on continuing improvement. The assessment-and-improvement process raises the program's visibility, elevates its credibility and stature, and positions it to garner more resources because it can demonstrate adherence to professional practices and a deliberate approach to management.[1]

The American Alliance of Museums' Museum Assessment Program helps small and mid-sized museums plan for the future, strengthen operations, and improve communications with staff, board, and other constituents through self-study and a site visit from a peer reviewer.[2] The Minnesota Historical Society provides workshops, onsite consultation, and networking forums to history programs in that state. The New York State Archives' Documentary Heritage Program offers advisory services and grants to strengthen historical records programs. The Historical Society of Pennsylvania created the Historical Affiliates program to aid small programs in southeastern Pennsylvania with funding and marketing. The Indiana Historical Society's Local History Services Team consults with organizations in that state on management challenges and provides informal assessments of collections care, facilities, and exhibits.

Advisory services should aim to do more than just help programs fix problems or operate at a minimally acceptable level. They should explore underlying trends and developments that are changing the contexts in which historical programs operate. They need to help programs confront rather than avoid hard questions, including whether the program's best course of action is to proceed unilaterally or whether it should consider merging with some other group, cooperating on major ventures, or even discontinuing operations. The Bridgespan Group, which advises and supports the work of nonprofit organizations, suggests that there are five areas for assessing programs and strengthening capacity:[3]

- Leadership

    1. Clear vision and priorities
    2. Cohesive leadership team

- Decision-making and structure

    1. Clear roles and accountabilities for decision
    2. Organizational structure that supports objectives

- People

    1. Organization and individual talent necessary for success
    2. Performance measures and incentives aligned to objectives

- Work processes and systems

1. Superior execution of programmatic work processes
2. Effective and efficient support processes and systems

- Culture

    1. "High performance" values and behaviors
    2. Capacity to change

EXPERIENCED PROFESSIONALS TO HELP BUILD PROGRAM CAPACITY

Historical programs should consider new ways to get people to invest time and talent to ensure the welfare of the program. For instance, about ten thousand people reach the age of sixty-five in the United States each day. Many of these retiring "baby boomers" have time, retirement savings and pensions, relatively good health, and health insurance and Medicare. They are seeking opportunities to:

Stay engaged. Studies by AARP have shown that older workers some-times stay on at their jobs past retirement age primarily for the social networking and feeling of being part of something worthwhile. New retirees are also seeking opportunities for meaningful engagement.

Give back. There is an upsurge in interest in finding ways to contribute to society, leave a legacy, and give back something that helps the common good.

Make a difference. Many retiring baby boomers like challenges and believe they can make a real difference through applying their skills and experience.

Historic sites and other historic programs "can give retiring boomers a place to pursue interests and friendships [and] make it possible for someone to make a lasting difference. Becoming involved and attached to a [historic] site can make one's last decades of life especially rewarding, fulfilling a basic human need to honor one's ancestors and to leave something of enduring value for those who follow."[4] Retirees can serve as volunteers, in some cases taking up the slack when programs lack funds for paid staff. They are at work in processing archival records, serving as docents, and leading tours. Their dedicated services are often one of the most substantive resources that the program has. But our conceptualization of the possibilities needs to be much broader than that. Many history programs need a different sort of assistance from getting hands-on work done. They need support in planning, capacity building, advocacy, and other strategic areas.

Organizations such as the Retired Public Employees Association, the Service Core of Retired Executives, and Civic Ventures suggest ways of enlisting retirees with leadership and management experience for good causes, but history programs are not often on their radar. History programs could recruit retired executives, attorneys, teachers, government officials, and other professionals for building program capacity. Working at the direction of the history programs' managers, this new corps of retired professionals might carry out some or all of the following:

Provide guidance on provisional and permanent chartering, particularly meeting expectations for program achievement

Work with the board of trustees or directors on succession planning and defining the knowledge, skills, and abilities needed for the next program director

Advise on, and where appropriate partially carry out, training and development activities for program staff

Offer seminars and workshops on topics identified by the program director (e.g., dealing with digital materials, getting the program on the Web)

Prepare reports on best or model practices, professional standards, and the like.

Support the development of strategic plans (e.g., through research to identify potential models and best practices, facilitating discussions, and drafting materials for the director and/or the board)

Develop publicity and outreach programs

Develop advocacy initiatives

Assist with fundraising and development

Develop volunteer programs

Develop liaisons with the public schools and help initiate such things as tours, document packets, and historical agency personnel speaking in classes

Help prepare grant applications

Work for two or more historical programs, serving as the coming-together point for cooperative ventures

ENGAGEMENT

Much of the discussion of connections revolves around the concept of "engagement" of groups and individuals (e.g., members of the community in the geographically surrounding area, representatives of groups whose histories are under-represented in the history program's collections and exhibits, people whom the program is trying to attract and retain as regular visitors). Chapter 3 introduced it in the context of "participatory" initiatives to involve users in conceptualizing new exhibits and programs. "Engagement" is broader than that and more than just an appeal for advice or advertising to increase visitation. It involves a two-way dialogue, lots of discussion, and an ability to impart the program's perspective and at the same time understand how others see and feel about history and exhibit a receptivity to new points of view. It is particularly useful and timely when a program is undertaking strategic planning, evaluating its services, or seeking to evaluate and shift or expand its customer and user base. The National Park Service developed an interlocking set of strategies for discussion and collaboration in various challenging situations (e.g., the need to engage people whose histories the Service was trying to portray in a sensitive, accurate, responsive manner). The NPS uses several strategies:[5]

Be an effective, collaborative leader. This includes managing staff and partner expectations appropriately; listening carefully to interests, needs, and concerns without preconceptions about outcomes; always being honest and transparent and demonstrating respect; and "articulat[ing] a clear and compelling vision that speaks to shared values and hopes for the future in order to build buy-in and bring people on board."

Build team capacity for engagement and collaboration. One of the keys to engagement is to ensure that the program's staff have well-developed "people skills" and understand that gaining deep understanding and building relationships is an art that takes time and energy. Involving people from the program's staff with diverse perspectives often helps. It may be helpful to develop staff capacity to mentor, work collaboratively, appreciate diversity, be willing to experiment, and the like.

Prepare in advance before launching an engagement process. "Gather the necessary information to understand the background, issues, and history of relationships that have shaped the current situation." It is helpful to look for individuals and groups who are open to engagement. It is often useful to seek advice and/or support from people in other programs who have dealt with similar situations.

Embrace diversity as a prerequisite to dialogue and discussion, recognizing that diverse viewpoints can produce creative new approaches that participants would not have come up with on their own.

Share leadership, responsibility, credit, and success.

Communicate openly, effectively, extensively, and continually.

Treat each other with dignity and respect; work in an atmosphere of trust, transparence, and accountability.

Look for opportunities for "deep engagement"—beyond short-term outreach, building richer relationships and pathways for program-community relationships (e.g., broadening the diversity of the program's workforce, opportunities for volunteers, internships, summer work opportunities, opportunities for volunteers).

Build and maintain relationships. Successful efforts require commitment
of sufficient time and resources to engage/collaborate successfully.
Sustain the effort.

Engaging a community (e.g., appealing to and convincing a particular
group to visit a history museum and support its work) requires a sensitivity to
people's feelings and learning styles. As noted earlier in this book, people
see "the past" in personal terms. They want to make personal connections, to
feel as well as learn something when they visit a historic site or view an
artifact or exhibit.[6] People visit museums and other history programs to see
real objects and experience history first-hand, a plus in a world of information noise and superficial experiences. Closeness to artifacts and the sources
of history "hit their emotional core and create meaning and response in
them." Visitors to museums want to feel as well as learn something. Museums "have the capacity to create truly meaningful, even transformative
experiences for our visitors."[7] That may happen when a visitor feels trans-
ported back to a time when an artifact was used or where an event happened;
have memories and associations that are triggered by objects, ideas, or
themes; feel empathy with the lives or experiences of other people; experience a sense of awe or reverence when being on hallowed ground; experience a sense of nostalgia; or are part of a social experience with family
members or friends where there is conversation about the significance of the
historical object or exhibit.[8] We need to deliver *more* than visitors expect by
making our programs exceptionally user friendly, telling engaging stories
that connect and reveal, holding people's attention, getting them so excited
that they talk about their experience to family members and friends and urge
them to visit and get involved. Those are all marks of successful engagement.[9]

Engaging a community requires highly developed communications skills.
This is particularly true when the institution has few existing connections to
the community or communities it is trying to engage. A good example would
be a historical society in a historic mansion that was once owned by one of
the most prominent families in a city and is situated in what was once the
most affluent area of the city. The historical society's exhibits depict the life
of the family that owned the mansion. In its heyday, the family was prominent, influential, a pillar of the community. Over the years, though, as one
generation succeeded the next, the family faded from prominence. Eventual-
ly a descendant sold, gave, or willed the mansion to a local government,
which decided to make it into a museum, or to a historical society. Over the
years, too, the demographic makeup of the surrounding neighborhood
changed and became more diverse, and the neighborhood became an area of
middle- and working-class families. The society wants to retain its building
and its core mission of documentation but needs to engage its new neighbors

both to find out their interests and needs and, possibly, to take up the challenge and opportunity of documenting their history. That requires building relationships and listening. Organized dialogue sessions with representatives of the community can accomplish that, but the questions for discussion need to be carefully formulated. For instance: [10]

> What do you believe is the current mission and role of our historical program?
>
> How often do you visit our exhibits, attend public events, and the like, and what is your impression of them?
>
> What issues need to be addressed in your community, and how might the historical program have relevance to those issues and add value to community conversations and decision making?
>
> How can the historical program broaden and deepen its connections with the community in other ways, particularly through its exhibits and programs?
>
> What are some ways that the community might become more integrally involved with the program (e.g., through serving on the board of directors, advising on development of strategic plans, serving on committees to develop programs, jointly developing school programs)?

Engagement implies a receptivity to new ideas, heeding other people's perspectives, and being open to sharing responsibility and work on new initiatives that are mutually beneficial. It supersedes the old idea that museums and similar history programs are the definitive and final authority in collecting, preserving, and presenting history. It can be unsettling and the source of some discomfort, but, managed appropriately, the prospects for new ideas and new audiences can outweigh the apprehension about ceding control. Final decisions on what to pursue, when to postpone, and when to proceed with a test-the-waters prototype, remain with the program director. Engagement is an art and a learning experience; the more the program does it, the more comfortable and adept the trustees, director, and staff become at managing it.

COOPERATIVE VENTURES

Every historical program has its own origins, charter or authorizing legislation, history, mission, and funding streams. Most proceed on their own course, more or less unilaterally, with their own discrete programs based around their holdings and focused on their identified audiences. That is a challenging model to sustain in an era of limited resources and people seeking historical information via the Web regardless of its physical setting. Programs can sometimes accomplish unprecedented things if they join forces with other programs that complement theirs and focus on common goals. Cooperative projects can evolve into continuing alliances between programs that keep working together on initiatives that serve their missions and customers. The key is identifying your own program's exceptional strengths, recognizing its weaknesses, and understanding how another program's strengths can complement it. Successful partnerships are built around several elements: [11]

> Common mission. The cooperating programs need a common agenda and agreed-on set of goals, in writing and clearly understood by all parties. A consensus on a common vision will encourage people in the cooperating programs to work together and go the extra distance to make things work.
> Committed leaders: Individuals who possess the skill, creativity, dedication, and tenacity to move an alliance forward even when it hits the inevitable rough patches.
> Communication. It is important to write a plan indicating who is going to do what by when, and for the directors of the participating programs to keep closely in touch or for there to be a joint administration and monitoring team including people from all the participating programs.
> Complementary strengths. One of the most powerful incentives for programs teaming up is that they have strengths that match each other.
> Fairness. The cooperative venture needs to be perceived as fair to all the programs involved—all contribute, all benefit; they share the resources, work, and responsibility; and they realize benefits.
> Trust. Working with another program means relinquishing some control, taking risks, and trying something unprecedented. That requires trust, something that can be built up during the first project and then grows after that, with more successful cooperating experience.
> Learning from experience. A post-project review, to discuss what went right, what went wrong, and why, can help build the relationship and lay the basis for subsequent joint efforts.

It is often easiest to start out with something modest. For instance, cooperation between a few historical programs in the same region on a history lecture series is relatively easy to organize. Jointly hiring a technical expert (e.g., someone with social media expertise to set up websites for several programs) may be a way of securing a service that no individual program could afford on its own. Many historical programs collect archives, artifacts, and other cultural materials without carefully written collections strategies and in competition with others in the same region or specializing in the same topical area. Well-considered, cooperative geographic or subject-based collection policies, worked out by networking with like-minded organizations, forming relationships with colleagues across institutional boundaries who may have subject-area expertise, and welcoming the diverse views of non-professionals, can result in more systematic, efficient, economical collecting. The public can help here; for instance, the views of current and past residents of a geographical area can be invaluable when two historical societies are working on a joint documentation program. The archives community has developed a "community documentation strategy" that defines communities; identifies the people, places, and events that are the most important to historical representation of the community; and defines how participating programs will cooperate to collect and preserve the documentation. "It makes sense for diverse community organizations that are collecting multiple, overlapping cultural resources, using diverse support systems, and attracting similar audiences, to look towards this approach."[12] Traveling history exhibits, developed jointly by several programs, are another way of pooling resources and sharing benefits. Several history groups in a county might cooperate on a county-wide history or a celebration commemorating the county's settlement.

Some public history programs have internships or field study placements with local historical programs and museums. But others have gone much further, for instance, conducting oral history interviews for histories of businesses or cultural institutions, co-developing exhibits on particular topics, and carrying out studies of topics where the historical program has a special interest but needs more in-depth historical analysis. A public history professor who has developed a number of successful partnerships notes that good planning is the key to success—universities need to determine which local museums or cultural institutions are considering projects that could easily involve students, and the institutions need to fully understand faculty members' interest and expertise, their expectations for students, and students' backgrounds and experiences. She also advises: think big; work out a detailed plan; consider how the partnership will help your institution with public relations and development opportunities; and carry out a project assessment to make it a learning opportunity for both institutions.[13]

Cooperation works at the state level as well. For instance, the New York State Archives partnered with the governor's office on a government efficiency and paperwork reduction initiative and with the state's court system on the bicentennial of the state's Court of Appeals. The Pennsylvania Historical and Museum Commission joined with the Pennsylvania Federation of Museums and Historical Organizations on an internship program that encourages minority students to consider museum careers; with the State Humanities Council on a historical speakers' series; with the Pennsylvania Historical Association on publication of *Pennsylvania History* and an annual conference on state history; and with the state Department of Community and Economic Development's tourism office to promote "Pennsylvania's Trails of History."[14]

HERITAGE TOURISM

Heritage tourism is defined as people traveling to experience places and events with historical significance. It can involve a short trip to a historic site but also longer trips where people spend considerable money both in reaching the destination and while they are there. Visitors to historic sites and related cultural attractions stay longer and spend more money than other categories of tourists. These tourists have goals of both learning and having experiences of personal identification and meaning. They are likely to seek a range of experiences and explore in their destinations of choice, particularly fairs, festivals, and other local celebrations and commemorations.[15]

Local, regional, and state history programs can build on heritage tourism to make connections and promote history. They can also demonstrate how history aids the economy because tourists spend money during their travels. Iowa museums are "exciting, educational, unique historic resources . . . employers, economic engines, tourism attractions . . . family-friendly, life-enhancing, community builders," said the Iowa Museum Association's 2013 *Museum Week* flyer. The previous year, Iowa museums attracted almost five million visitors, offered nearly sixty thousand public programs, employed more than twenty-three hundred state residents, and were supported by over thirty thousand volunteers. The flyer reinforced the theme of museums' importance by noting that nationally visitors to historic sites and cultural attractions stay 53 percent longer and spend 36 percent more money than other kinds of tourists.[16] A report on the 2007 celebration of the 400th anniversary of the founding of Jamestown concluded that the statewide celebration had generated $1.2 billion in sales, $22 million in state tax revenues, and $6.4 million in local tax revenues.[17] New York State's "Path through History" initiative features a website where visitors can access historic sites, museums, and heritage events by themes, regions, and dates. Its governor, Andrew Cuomo, launching it in 2012, emphasized the connection with economic development and the importance of heritage tourism, which he said has a $5 billion impact on the state's economy each year.[18]

Connecting with heritage tourism initiatives has a number of advantages for historical programs. It brings in visitors, some of whom may stay for a significant period of time or return later, boosting the use of the museum or historic site. It gives programs a basis for appealing to local governments and other funding sources because it is convincing to cite studies and reports that show how heritage tourism boosts the local economy, which, in turn, attests to the economic contribution of local historical programs. It enables state museums and historical associations to ally with state tourism, economic development, and budget offices to demonstrate the business value of historical and similar programs, a benefit at a time when public resources are tight and getting government support for history programs is an uphill battle.

HISTORIC PRESERVATION

Like heritage tourism, historic preservation is good for history and good for the economy. The National Trust for Historic Preservation makes a persuasive case that historic preservation helps preserve cities and communities. Officially designated historic districts, which require preservation of historical houses and other properties, protect the investment of owners and residents in the districts. Property values within historic districts appreciate at higher rates than values of properties outside the district in the local markets where they are situated. They encourage better quality design, a greater sense of cohesiveness, and greater public appeal. They help the environment and urban areas by encouraging communities to retain and use existing resources in established neighborhoods, cutting back on pollution and congestion and landfill waste from buildings that are preserved rather than demolished. Many older buildings were designed and constructed with energy conservation in mind, taking advantage of natural light, cross-ventilation, and climate-appropriate building materials. Aesthetically attractive, well-promoted districts encourage visitation and tourism. They attract businesses and residents who value the opportunity to live and work in attractive surroundings in recognizable and walkable neighborhoods.[19]

Historic buildings provide authenticity, sense of community, and sense of identity. "The truth is that historic preservation offers cities a major tool in working toward or maintaining livability," says the book *Historic Preservation and the Livable City*. Historic preservation is a natural partner of such objectives as diversity, greenspace, and walkability. "It can contribute to sustainability. It makes people want to live in cities where it is practiced. It fosters tourism and contributes to economic development. . . . Some people might prefer to live in sleek, modern dwellings but they like having the historic buildings and neighborhoods nearby."[20]

State reports provide more localized examples. A South Carolina report in 2005 showed that historic preservation increases property values, spurs heritage tourism, supports downtown revitalization, and is an economic force, with historic preservation work adding about $74 million annually to the state's economy.[21] A 2011 study of historic districts in selected Connecticut towns and cities showed that properties in the districts were worth more, on a per-square-foot comparison based on age and style, than other properties in the towns, and that housing values increased faster within the districts than outside them. During the recession that began in 2008, the foreclosure rate of properties inside the districts was half the rate outside them. Local historic districts have proven their value, socially, culturally, and economically, the study concluded.[22]

Another report the same year, focusing on tax credit programs to encourage investment in historic properties, documented $450 million in private sector investment in historic buildings in the years 2000–2010, $242 million in direct salary and wages from rehabilitating historic structures, and $7.8 million in increased property taxes to local governments each year.[23] A 2013 Utah report made the case for heritage tourism, downtown revitalization, and environmental responsibility associated with preserving rather than replacing historic buildings. But it went further, documenting that $1 million invested in rehabilitating a historic building in Utah meant $536,894 in direct salary and wages, $310,660 in indirect salary and wages, $998,000 economic activity elsewhere in the economy, and benefits in local taxes and state business and sales taxes. Overall, historic preservation efforts are "providing a broad, significant contribution to the economic health of this state."[24]

History programs can build on reports like these to make broader, deeper connections with historic preservation and indirectly demonstrate the importance of preserving the past. There are at least four other potential ways of making connections by building on the multiple attractions of historic preservation:

Historic preservation has measurable economic benefits. The case studies and tools developed by Donovan Rypkema can be applied to calculate values in any community. http://www.placeeconomics.com

Historic preservation is tied to "smart growth" policies that create walkable neighborhoods, foster distinctive communities with a strong sense of place, and strengthen and direct development toward existing communities. A good source is Smart Growth America. http://www.smartfrowthamerica.org

Historic preservation is tied to "placemaking," a planning method that capitalizes on a local community's assets, inspiration, and potential to create public spaces that promote community well-being. Project for Public Spaces is a useful source. http://www.pps.org

Historic preservation perspectives are invaluable when cities plan for "right-sizing" after losing industry and population by proposing creative, flexible approaches to the reuse of historic structures and the preservation of neighborhoods. A good example is found at Michigan Historic Preservation Network and National Trust for Historic Preservation, *Putting the Right in Rightsizing: A Historic Preservation Case Study.* 2012. http://www.mhpn.org/wp-content/uploads/2012/11/RightsizingCaseStudy11.12.pdf

HISTORY AND PUBLIC EDUCATION

What students learn about history in the public schools is important to historical programs, in part because it is essential preparation for the visitors, researchers, and users of the future. As noted in chapter 1, history and social studies courses are not being accorded a high priority in American education these days, and state and local history may be upstaged or pushed aside by US or international history. Every student should have the right, and the requirement, to learn the history of his or her state in public schools. Historical programs and state historical organizations should work with state social studies organizations to lobby state education departments to retain, or restore, substantial study of state and local history. The Fordham Foundation, cited in chapter 1 for its report on the status of US history in the nation's schools, awarded the grade of "A" to only one state, South Carolina. That state gives plenty of coverage to US and world history. But third grade is devoted to "South Carolina Studies," which introduces the fundamentals of the state's history. Eighth grade, a more appropriate time for teaching state history in depth because students are more mature, is devoted to "South Carolina: One of the United States." It is focused on "the history of South Carolina and the role that the state and its people have played in the development of the United States as a nation." It presents the full story of state history under seven standards:[25]

- The student will demonstrate an understanding of the settlement of South Carolina and the United States by Native Americans, Europeans, and Africans.
- The student will demonstrate an understanding of the causes of the American Revolution and the beginnings of the new nation, with an emphasis on South Carolina's role in the development of that nation.
- The student will demonstrate an understanding of South Carolina's role in the development of the new national government.
- The student will demonstrate an understanding of the multiple events that led to the Civil War.
- The student will understand the impact of Reconstruction, industrialization, and Progressivism on society and politics in South Carolina in the late nineteenth and early twentieth centuries.
- The student will demonstrate an understanding of the role of South Carolina in the nation in the early twentieth century.
- The student will demonstrate an understanding of the impact on South Carolina of significant events of the late twentieth and early twenty-first centuries.

For each standard, there is a description of the "enduring understanding" that students should take away from the unit, and a list of indicators.

Study of state and local history integrated into social studies curriculums can help reach a widely held goal of preparing students for active, engaged citizenship. Students who leave high school with civic competencies achieved through high quality learning that includes solid history courses are likely to be informed and thoughtful and participate in their communities. They will have the basic skills, knowledge, and commitment to be effective in accomplishing public purposes, for instance organizing people to address social issues, petitioning or protesting to influence public policy, and casting well-informed votes at election time. They have skills to address complex challenges, work with diverse colleagues, and creatively solve problems that defy easy solutions.[26]

The new "Common Core" standards, adopted by state education departments in most states, while not strong on history per se, emphasize the use of original source material, exploration of multiple perspectives, and student-centered, inquiry-based learning, fostering development of information literacy skills. Museums and other historical programs are curators of source material that students could study to develop those skills, and they are experienced at guiding people to original sources. This may provide an indirect way to interject historical facts and sources.[27]

A few additional strategies to connect with state social studies standards:

Mount an interactive exhibit on state history. Some history programs are dealing with the new world of high tech and Common Core with imaginative new exhibits that have user engagement and interactive features. The Minnesota Historical Society's *Then, Now, Wow!* exhibit, opened in November 2012 at the Minnesota History Center in St. Paul, was designed particularly for children. Visitors can "explode dynamite in an Iron Range mine; explore a 1870s replica sod house"; ride "a Soo Line boxcar through southwestern Minnesota . . . and hear and see stories from people across the world who now call Minnesota home." The Society introduced and tested a new feature, "History in Our Hands." Teachers could make arrangements for students entering the exhibit to receive handheld computers with a pre-installed application to promote interaction with the exhibit by encouraging them to answer questions, solve problems, and collect "digital artifacts" that could be accessed back at school, promoting more classroom study and post-visit projects ("you will be able to see if you can earn a day's wage in a historic iron mine, make trades at a fur trading post, and see if you can make it living in a sod house!") (http://www.minnesotahistorycenter.org/exhibits/then-now-wow).

Develop new strategies to align with the Common Core. The Common Core curriculum emphasizes literacy and interpretation of source materials. Some history programs are repackaging and revamping presentations to align with those priorities. The *California History-Social Science Project*, a consortium of universities and public school educators, has developed a new "History Blueprint" that combines innovative curriculum, assessment tools, student literacy support, and teacher professional development, aligned with the Common Core Standards. There is heavy emphasis on guiding students through sources and discussing critical questions and issues. Units have been developed and tested for the Civil War and the Cold War, and a unit for California state history is being developed (http://chssp.ucdavis.edu).

Issue a textbook for use in the schools. Some state historical programs are continuing and expanding traditional student field visits, holding seminars for teachers, but also providing guidance by issuing their own textbooks on state history. The Minnesota Historical Society has issued *Northern Lights*, which "delivers our state's story with primary resources, vibrant images, personal narratives, activities, and more." It meets all state standards, is available as an e-book, includes a website with downloadable digital worksheets and other online resources, and is supported by professional development seminars offered by the Society (http://education.mnhs.org/northern-lights).

Teach historical thinking. Students should leave school with more than an accumulation of memorized facts. They should learn, and strengthen through application, historical thinking concepts—basically, how to think like a historian. The Canadian Centre for the Study of Historical Consciousness' *Historical Thinking Project* has defined six key concepts. (1) Establish historical significance—"significant events include those that resulted in great change over long periods of time for large numbers of people." (2) Use primary source evidence—setting documents and other primary sources in their historical context and interpreting sources as evidence. (3) Identify continuity and change—"understand history as a complex mix of continuity and change." (4) Analyze cause and consequence—understanding "how and why" things happened. (5) Take historical perspectives—"understanding the social, cultural, intellectual and emotional settings that shaped people's lives and actions in the past." (6) Understand the ethical dimensions of historical interpretations—"we should expect to learn something from the past that helps us to face the ethical issues of today" (http://historicalthinking.ca).

Make source material available electronically. History programs have long assembled document packets and in recent years have posted them on their websites to make them easily available. The New York State Archives, in partnership with its fundraising and development office the Archives Partnership Trust, is developing an online resource for teachers called *Consider the Source: Historical Records in the Classroom*, an update of a publication originally issued in 1995. The new version will have a search function that allows users to locate documents on specific topics, an online tutorial for teachers on how to use historical records in the classroom, videos that provide educators with ideas on how to use specific documents, lessons aligned with the state's curriculum standards, customizable lesson worksheets for each document to allow teachers to edit and adapt lessons online to meet the particular needs of students, and case studies aligned with the curriculum that allow students to analyze topics in depth using the records (http://www.archives.nysed.gov/education/ed_web.shtml).

Emphasize analysis of historical documents. Other initiatives focus on how historians analyze documents and work with historical evidence that is often fragmented, incomplete, and contradictory, emphasizing strategies historians use to discern patterns and make sense out of this evidence. The *Historical Thinking Matters* project, jointly sponsored by the Roy Rosenzweig Center for History and the New Media at George Mason University and the School of Education at Stanford University, guides students through analysis of key historical events, including the Battle of Lexington in 1775, the Scopes "Monkey Trial" in 1925, and Rosa Parks and the Montgomery bus boycott of 1955. Students are encouraged to closely read and analyze historical sources and reach their own conclusions about what really happened and what its significance is (http://historicalthinkingmatters.org). The Stanford History Education Group offers lesson plans and document-based inquiries based around the theme of "Reading Like a Historian" (http://sheg.stanford.edu/home_page).

Encourage students to analyze historical sources and use social media in projects. The National History Education Clearinghouse's website presents helpful information on best practices and links to teaching materials (http://teachinghistory.org).

HISTORY BACKSTORIES ON PUBLIC RADIO

There are lots of imaginative ways to make connections between history and the public. Cooperation between historical experts and public broadcasting, which exists to educate and enlighten as well as to entertain the public, should be a natural venue. For instance, a historical program might host a weekly session on a local radio or TV station to discuss historical events, historical perspectives on current topics, or attractions at the historical program such as exhibits or speakers. Historical programs could benefit from the no-cost broadcast facilities; public radio in particular is always looking for solid, informative programming.

One partial model, sponsored by the Virginia Foundation for the Humanities, is *Backstory with the American History Guys*, a weekly broadcast from Charlottesville, Virginia, that airs on more than one hundred public radio stations in thirty-eight states. Its podcasts are also available for download from its website. In each broadcast, three historians take a topic from the headlines and plumb its historical depths, illuminating parallels with similar previous events and insights from the past. The broadcasts are timely and relevant since they relate to topics on people's minds because they are in the news. Over the course of an hour, the three historians are joined by other historians, people in the news, and people who call in with questions and comments. A parallel Facebook page publicizes the broadcasts, provides more in-depth commentary, and lets listeners pitch their own ideas for shows.

Topics in 2014 included: *Legislation Impossible: The Civil Rights Act of 1964*; *Tapped Out: Searching for Fresh Water*; *On the Take: Corruption in America*; and *America Incorporated: A History of Corporations* (*Backstory with the American History Guys*, http://backstory-radio.org).

NOTES

1. *Stronger Organizations Don't Happen Overnight.* http://tools.aaslh.org/steps.

2. American Alliance of Museums, *Museum Assessment Program.* http://www.aam-us.org/resources/assessment-programs/MAP.

3. The Bridgespan Group, *The Effective Organization: Five Questions to Translate Leadership into Strong Management.* http://www.bridgespan.org/getattachment/099fa836-b185-4107-92b3-4a87d4590c67/The-Effective-Organization-Five-Questions-to-Trans.aspx.

4. John Durel and Anita Nowery Durel, "A Golden Age for Historic Properties," *History News* (Summer 2007), 7–13.

5. National Park Service, *Leading in a Collaborative Environment,* (2010). http://www.nps.gov/civic/resources/Lead-ing%20in%20a%20Collaborative%20Environment%20FINAL%202010-27-10.pdf.; and *Beyond Outreach Handbook,* 2011. http://www.nps.gov/civic/resources/Be-yond%20Outreach%20Handbook.pdf.

6. Benjamin Filene, "Passionate Histories: 'Outsider' History-Makers and What They Teach Us," *Public Historian* 34 (February 2012), 11–33.

7. Reach Associates, "Meaningful Museum Experiences: It's the Cool Stuff!" (September 25, 2012), "Finding Meaning in Museums: Exhibitions or Programs and Events?" (October 9, 2012), "The Lens of Historical Experience" (October 25, 2012). http://reachadvis-ors.typepad.com.

8. Dale Jones, "Personal Connections and the Great Cosmic Soup," *History News* (Spring 2008), 14–18.

9. Bill Tramposch, "That Would Be Good Both *Going* and *Coming Back*," *History News* (Winter 2013), 16–20.

10. Janeen Bryant and Kamille Bostick, "What's the Big Idea? Using Listening Sessions to Build Relationships and Relevance," AASLH *Technical Leaflet* no, 263 (2013) provides helpful advice on conducting discussion sessions.

11. Rod Wagner and Gale Muller, "Why Partners Need Complementary Strengths," *Gallup Business Journal* (August 13, 2009). http://businessjournal.gallup.com/content/122237/why-

partners-need-complementary-strengths.aspx.; Mike Leavitt and Rich McKeown in *Finding Allies, Building Alliances* (San Francisco: Jossey-Bass, 2013), 4.

12. Melissa Mannon, "Cultural Heritage Collaboration," *History News* (Autumn 2010), 17–21.

13. Catherine M. Lewis, "Building Successful Partnerships between Museums and Universities," American Historical Association *Perspectives* (December 2007). http://www.historians.org/publications-and-directories/perspectives-on-history/december-2007/building-successful-partnerships-between-museums-and-universities.

14. Barbara Franco, "Partnerships for the Future," *Pennsylvania History*, 74 (Autumn 2007), 542–550; *Pennsylvania's Trails of History.* http://www.portal.state.pa.us/portal/server.pt/community/trails_of_history_sites/1800.

15. Ontario Ministry of Tourism, Culture, and Sport, *Ontario Cultural and Heritage Tourism Product Research Paper* (2009). https://www.google.com/#q=ontario+cultural+and+heritage+tourism+product+research+paper.

16. Iowa Museums Association, *Museums Matter* (2013). http://www.iowamuseums.org/UserDocs/Pages/2013_Iowa_Museum_Week_Flier.pdf.

17. Jamestown-Yorktown Foundation, "Measuring America's 400th Anniversary" (August 19, 2008). http://historyisfun.org/pdf/planning-a-commemoration/Economic%20Impact%20PR.pdf.

18. New York State *Path through History.* http://www.paththroughhistory.ny.gov/about.; "Governor Cuomo Unveils New York's 'Path through History'" (August 28, 2012). http://www.governor.ny.gov/press/08282012-Path-Through-History.

19. Julia Rocchi, "10 Benefits of Establishing a Local Historic District," *Preservation Nation* (Jan. 15, 2013). http://blog.preservationnation.org/2013/01/15/10-on-tuesday-10-benefits-of-establishing-a-local-historic-district/#.UvA710CA0qQ.

20. Eric Allison and Lauren Peters, *Historic Preservation and the Livable City* (New York: Wiley, 2011), 1–9.

21. Chad Lennox and Jennifer Revels, *Smiling Faces, Historic Places: The Economic Benefits of Historic Preservation in South Carolina* (2004). http://shpo.sc.gov/pubs/Documents/hpEconomicsbooklet.pdf.

22. Connecticut Trust for Historic Preservation, *Connecticut Local Historic Districts and Property Values* (2011). http://www.placeeconomics.com/wp-content/uploads/2011/03/ct_report_2011.pdf.

23. State Historic Preservation Office, *Investment in Connecticut: The Economic Benefits of Historic Preservation* (2011). http://www.ct.gov/cct/lib/cct/Economic_Impact_Study_%28Final_6-2011%29.pdf.

24. Utah Heritage Foundation, *Profits through Preservation: The Economic Impact of Historic Preservation in Utah* (2011). http://www.utahheritagefoundation.com/preservation-resources/econstudy#.UvBSb0CA0qQ.

25. South Carolina Department of Education, *South Carolina Social Studies Academic Standards* (2011). https://ed.sc.gov/agency/se/Instructional-Practices-and-Evaluations/documents/FINALAPPROVEDSSStandardsAugust182011.pdf.

26. National Council for the Social Studies, *Revitalizing Civic Learning in Our Schools* (2013). http://www.socialstudies.org/positions/revitalizing_civic_learning.

27. "Museums in a Common Core World," Center for the Future of Museums Blog (July 30, 2013). http://futureofmuseums.blogspot.com/2013/07/museums-in-common-core-world.html.

Chapter Five

Digital Engagement

A CHALLENGE AND AN OPPORTUNITY

Most historical programs hold—and present programs based around—two- or three-dimensional items (e.g., archives, artifacts, and historic houses). They count on people coming to their physical facilities during public hours for tours, exhibits, lectures, and other events. Visitors value the genuine, authentic, and sometimes moving experiences that only direct contact with the actual sources of history affords. On the other hand, a growing number of people who are their current and future "customers" also want the opportunity to access digital versions of historical information from anywhere, anytime. They also want opportunities to engage, interact, and participate—digitally and remotely—with the history programs themselves. This new, and growing, style of connection might be called *digital engagement*. In this arena, historical programs are following broad-scale trends that have for some time been transforming the way business is conducted and enterprises are administered. Companies are increasingly using social media for marketing, customer solicitation, and building and strengthening customer relationships "in which the aim is to start a conversation with customers and increase the richness and depth of those conversations over time."[1]

Young people in particular are interested in experiences that are relevant and authentic and that involve the digital "audience" in a way that makes them feel invested, lets them share ideas and contribute to discussions, and generally makes them feel they are "part of the action." A 2014 report by the Pew Research Center on the "Millennial Generation" (defined as Americans ages 18–23) identified three traits of particular interest to history programs. One, these young people are "digital natives"—they grew up with digital technologies and use them continually for work, professional contacts, and social networking. Some 81 percent are active on the most important social media network, Facebook. Two, they are indifferent to or mistrustful of institutions and less likely than previous generations to join them or be affiliated with them. There is a clear implication here that young people might be less than likely to join traditional historical societies with static historic houses and unexciting on-site presentations. Three, they like to put themselves at the center of things. For instance, fully 55 percent of the young people surveyed had posted a "selfie" (a photo taken of oneself) on a social media site.[2]

Social media and other digital technologies appeal to our future customers. "Younger generations especially expect to contribute to the conversation. They don't just want to receive content, they want to help generate it."[3] History programs need to find ways to put digital technology to work without at the same time neglecting traditional programs or stretching their usually modest resources to the breaking point. Excitement and anticipation about the possibilities of the new media need to be tempered by prudence and caution about taking on too much. Some of the visions for the application of digital technology are vast, almost breathtaking. "Today, digital technology is pervasive," writes G. Wayne Clough, the secretary of the Smithsonian Institution. "Its use, particularly by the world's youth, is universal; its possibilities are vast; everyone in our educational and cultural institutions is trying to figure out what to do with it. It is mandatory that museums, libraries, and archives join with educational institutions in embracing it." He suggests several guiding principles, including:[4]

Digital technology should enhance and reinforce the in-person visitor experience.

Digitization of collections should be a primary institutional goal.

Digital technologies should be used to connect to audiences not served today.

The public should have opportunities to be active participants in the creative processes of the institution.

A systematic approach should be taken to understanding and responding to consumer expectations.

Collaborations and partnerships should be the rule, not the exception, and best practices should be widely shared both within the institutional walls and with other institutions.

Digital activities should have aspirational goals and specific performance metrics that are evaluated on a regular basis.

In the meantime, many programs are finding their own way through experimentation and improvisation which, as noted earlier in this book, are good approaches generally when advancing into uncharted territory. The 2013 *Horizon Report*, which tracks emerging technologies for teaching, learning, and research, identified two key trends on the "near term horizon" for museums. One is BYOD ("Bring Your Own Device") where people bring their laptops or mobile phones with them, and museums are responding by offering mobile apps for way finding and providing additional information on artifacts and exhibits. The other is "crowdsourcing," where museums promote community engagement through social media (e.g., visitors submit observations and media to add an interactive dimension to exhibits). That is consistent with trends toward "participatory" museums and systematic engagement of audiences discussed earlier in the book.[5]

THE FIRST WAVE: DIGITAL INFORMATION, ONE-WAY COMMUNICATION

Historical programs have been working on what might be called the first wave of digital engagement for some time. These efforts include well-designed, content-rich, engaging websites with rich historical information and sometimes digital renditions of key exhibits. Others have gone further, digitizing key documents and making them available with interpretive information and links to other documents or materials. These information-packed websites not only inform, they also act as marketing and promotional tools, inviting and stimulating visits for people to further explore the rich, interesting sources that are typified by what they see on the website. A few programs have gone further yet, developing virtual recreations of historical sites and settings. The sites provide access to digitized sources and encourage explorations and questions. Many have special links and materials for educators and students. The sites are packed with information, but, like the history program websites, they are mostly one-way transmitters—people can access and download their information but cannot react, engage, or make suggestions. Some examples:

> *Crisis at Fort Sumter* (http://www.tulane.edu/~sumter). Project sponsored by Tulane University to present information available to President Lincoln from the time of his election to the attack on the fort. The viewer gets to see the crisis unfold more or less as Lincoln saw it, one piece of evidence at a time, which provides insight into the President's understanding of what was happening and his decision-making processes.
>
> *London Lives 1690 to 1800: Crime, Poverty, and Social Policy in the Metropolis* (http://www.londonlives.org). Cooperative project of the University of Sheffield and other organizations that presents archival sources on the lives of average Londoners with emphasis on criminal justice, medical care, and poor relief. The site conveys a sense of the

gritty day-to-day existence of average people in the eighteenth century.

The Lost Museum (http://www.lostmuseum.cuny.edu/home.html). A collaborative effort of the City University of New York and the Center for History and the New Media at George Mason University, the site has a three-dimensional recreation of P. T. Barnum's American Museum (1841–1865), a leading tourist attraction of the era. The visitor can "walk" through the rooms and see digital renditions of the exhibit, access primary documents relating to museum exhibits and subjects, and visit the "classroom" with teaching and learning materials.

Maine Memory Network (http://www.mainememory.net). This project of the Maine Historical Society provides access to thousands of documents, photos, and other items in over 260 historical societies, museums, and other repositories across the state.

Minnesota's Greatest Generation (http://www.mnhs.org/people/mngg). This Minnesota Historical Society site presents oral histories and digital information about the experiences of the people of the state before, during, and after World War II.

Raid on Deerfield: The Many Stories of 1704 (http://1704.deerfield.history.museum).The Pocumtuck Valley Memorial Association/ Memorial Hall Museum in Deerfield, Massachusetts, uses documents and recollections to reconstruct a colonial-era raid from the perspective of British, French, and Indian cultures.

Toledo's Attic (http://www.toledosattic.org). A multi-sponsored site with historical essays, photos, video, interactive media, and other resources.

The Valley of the Shadow: Two Communities in the Civil War (http://valley.lib.virginia.edu). A project organized by the Virginia Center for Digital History at the University of Virginia that explores the impact of the war in Augusta County, Virginia, and Franklin County, Pennsylvania, through original letters, diaries, speeches, census records, church records, newspapers, and other sources.

Wisconsin Historical Society (http://www.wisconsinhistory.org). This website, completely redesigned in 2014, is a model of user-centered design, simplified browsing, and streamlined search.

Websites are also very handy and useful for posting information about new accessions and public events and for online newsletters. Many also host blogs, mostly in the form of information posted by the director or staff members. Some blogs also provide for responses from readers. All of these applications are helpful in making information about history available and providing links to actual historical sources. But even the best blogs are not at the level of engagement and involvement of Facebook and other new social media tools. These "first wave" applications are somewhat like going to a history lecture—the information may be engaging, exciting, informative, even provocative. But the audience, who may be attentive and appreciative recipients, can't get involved much in the discussion.

THE SECOND WAVE: INTERACTIVE, CONTINUALLY ENGAGING, MULTIPLE CONVERSATIONS

Companies have for several years made increasing use of the Web to create interest in their products and services, engage customers, solicit feedback from customers, get customers talking with each other, and even get customers to respond to and advise on each other's problems.[6] This might be called the second wave of digital engagement—two-way, interactive, and robust, with lots of information continually created and accessed, and much more audience-centric than the first wave. Much of the interest is on "social media"—basically, tools and platforms for online social interaction among people in which they create, share, or exchange information and ideas in networks and virtual communities. Several applications were particularly popular as this book was nearing completion in late 2014. They are all free of charge:

Facebook, a robust, popular online social networking service where individual users or institutions (including history programs) can create a profile, add users as "friends," post updates and photos, receive and post comments (for instance, suggestions for programs or reactions by visitors to history exhibits), and host user-based discussions. Facebook claimed over a billion active users and continued to grow, but mounting concerns about privacy and the tendency of young people to move on to new, emerging technologies, were slowing its momentum. It is, however, the most popular and important social networking tool for historical programs.

Flickr, an image hosting and video hosting site, popular for users to share personal photographs and videos.

Instagram, an online photo-sharing, video-sharing, and social networking service that enables users to take pictures and videos and share them on a variety of social networking services.

LinkedIn, a networking site for professionals which allows users to create profiles and connections to each other in an online social network.

Pinterest, an online service that its proprietors describe as a "virtual discovery tool" that people use to collect ideas for interests and projects, create and share collections of visual bookmarks, exchange documents, and do things like develop projects.

Twitter, an online microblogging and social networking service that enables users to send and read short (140 character) text messages called "tweets."

YouTube, a video-sharing website that allows users to upload, view, and share videos, including educational videos, TV clips, and videos of such things as lectures and public presentations.

Wikipedia, an online encyclopedia where anyone can contribute content and edit entries, with a great deal of information about historical events and individuals in history.

Three trends have converged to raise the stakes for effectiveness of digital business models, all with implications for the world of history programs: (1) "The continuing march toward the digitization of ever-increasing aspects of business—incorporating more of your customers' experience, executing more of your business processes, and working together with partners in your value chain." (2) The rise of "digital natives"—young and future customers "who expect a brilliant digital experience with all of their interactions with you." (3) "The dawning age of the customer voice," in which customers have a much stronger impact on enterprises via ratings of companies' services and products and online comments through social media and customer-generated content, becomes much more important.[7] The growing use of mobile devices means people can access your content, provide their reactions, and share information about your program with anyone from just about anywhere, 24/7, every day of the year.

Expanding engagement via social media has great potential for museums and other history programs. "Museums are a meeting ground for both official versions of the past, their histories offered through exhibitions, and the individual or collective accounts of reflective personal experience known as memories. Social media can enable informal ways of drawing together this knowledge by providing tools for participatory engagement which have the potential to distribute new forms of learning."[8] Museum director Maxwell Anderson has contended that technology can enable visitors to go "behind the scenes" and permit museums and other historical programs to show a side of themselves that is "more sensuous and personal and behind the velvet rope." For exhibits, for example, Anderson urged museums to "take visitors to the movies instead of showing them the credits" by telling stories behind the objects, their context in history, how they fit into the museum's programs, and how people might relate them to their own lives. The stories, well presented, are "tactile, sensual, and visceral," engaging the digital visitors. Those visitors, in turn, can add to the conversation through their comments not only on the exhibit but on the processes that produced it.[9] Visitors can link with each other and urge their friends and colleagues to also link to the social media site. This sort of connectedness, replicated over and over, is a way of linking the historical program with large numbers of people.

Digital engagement enables museums to scale up participation, extend their influence, and draw on a vast array of talent and expertise beyond their staff. "User generated content" and "crowdsourcing" initiatives are dissolving the boundaries between the historical programs experts and outside contributors. The technology is elevating and empowering—it gives everyone with an opinion a chance to express it. History programs need to work that capacity to their advantage. "It's less about the technology and more about what the visitor can bring to the equation," says Shelley Bernstein, chief technology officer for the Brooklyn Museum. "In the end, we want people to feel ownership of this museum. We ask them to tell us what they think. They can give us a bad review; when we make a mistake they can come to our rescue. We want to engage with our community."[10]

Through the use of social media, a different kind of relationship emerges between the institution and its audience or customers. People who are particularly interested in the program or the topics it presents follow it closely and constantly offer feedback, advice, reactions, praise, and sometimes criticism. The historical programs can establish online forums for audience members to have discussions with other people with similar interests, for instance, on a historical topic documented in the historical program's holdings. Of course, reaction and engagement via social media has limits. Programs need to plan carefully and employ social media selectively lest the maintenance and interaction absorb too much staff time. The program must have ultimate decision-making power about blocking posts that are offensive or in bad taste. No matter what the public's reactions or suggestions via social media, the program retains final decisions about the content and interpretations of its exhibits, presentations, and other offerings.

The active, carefully planned use of Facebook and other social media can have several applications:[11]

Connect with visitors (actual and potential).
Connect with the media and the press. Many journalists and other writers use social media tools like Twitter and Facebook for sources. The more people who read you online, the more visible you become via search engines.
Push the program's events, such as an exhibit opening, with your online community and urge them to "like" it and share it with others, significantly expanding reach and audience.
Update people on new developments such as changes in hours, programs, or staffing. Keep putting out news items that draw attention to the holdings and services; this constant flow of information helps keep your program "top of mind" among its followers.

Share copies of documents, photos, artifacts from the collections (e.g., "Item of the Day"), with a story about their provenance and significance as a way of sparking a discussion and encouraging visitors to see the item first-hand.

Conduct market research, ask for help or advice.

Recruit donors, volunteers, and advocates.

Make "followers" (e.g., those who "friend" you on Facebook) feel like privileged insiders.

Direct people to new entries on the organization's website or in its blog or new YouTube videos.

Post reactions by visitors to your facility.

Establish forums for discussion of historical topics (e.g., subjects documented in your collection or public issues of the day where the debate could be enlightened by references to history and historical perspective).

SUCCESS IN THE SOCIAL MEDIA ENVIRONMENT

The social media environment is constantly evolving. Few standards have yet emerged. A good deal of the progress being made is through trial and error, experimentation, and testing. Some suggestions are provided in the following sections.

Borrow and Adapt

There are few standards for the use of social media, but there are numerous useful models in our field—programs that have used social media for some time, constantly assess their applications, make strategic changes to their approaches, and report at professional conference, in history and museum profession publications, and on their own social media sites, about what is working and what needs to be changed. A useful way to approach social media and other forms of digital engagement is to begin with listening and observing what other programs are doing and decide which features you like and do not like. Some useful examples:

- *American Alliance of Museums' Facebook page* (https://www.facebook.com/americanmuseums). Information about the association and issues of concern, and links to museums with model practices.
- *The American Museum of Natural History* (http://www.amnh.org). Multiple apps for mobile devices, including "Explorer" ("part custom navigation system, part personal tour guide for the Museum's world-famous halls") and several apps to photos of its collections of dinosaurs and other information.

- *The Brooklyn Museum* (http://www.brooklynmuseum.org/home.php). Multiple ways to interact with the museum, including blogs, suggesting tags for objects in their collections, uploading photos, and "First Fans," a networked community.
- *Colonial Williamsburg* (http://www.history.org). An exceptionally rich and engaging Web page which lets the online visitor quickly connect with history, education, publications, research, the several museums included in the enterprise, multimedia, and "about us." The multimedia section includes a webcam, slideshows, videos, games and puzzles, and apps for mobile devices. There are a number of topical blogs and one devoted to "what's new." There are several Facebook pages, and Colonial Williamsburg also has its own YouTube channel.
- *Historical Society of Pennsylvania's PhilaPlace* (http://www.philaplace.org). This was also mentioned in chapter 3. Using an interactive map, visitors can access documents, photos, videoclips, and other materials on Philadelphia neighborhoods. Visitors can also tag locations on the maps with their own short descriptions or memories and also add photos and audio or visual files. PhilaPlace also has a blog and resources for researchers.
- *Historypin* (http://www.historypin.com). Calling itself "a global community collaborating around history," Historypin collates images gathered via crowdsourcing and provides metadata for geographical location and time, attaching stories and anecdotes. For instance, the University of Arkansas at Little Rock's Center for Arkansas History and Culture uses Historypin to showcase a large number of digitized photographs as well as digitized audio and video.
- *Minnesota Historical Society*. A model progressive program in many areas. Its Facebook page—https://www.facebook.com/minnesotahistoricalsociety—is a model of blending information, program promotion, and user engagement.
- *Mount Vernon* (http://www.mountvernon.org). Anne Lindsay's article "Virtual Tourist" in *Public Historian*, February 2013, noted this site's hierarchical arrangement with each tier—information, mission, purchase tickets, and other materials, and connections via Facebook and other social media—providing opportunities for visitor interaction.
- *National Archives and Records Administration* (http://www.archives.gov). NARA invites "Citizen Archivists" to expand descriptions in the online catalog, share research tips, store information discovered during research, and make comments and suggestions about NARA programs and services.
- *National Park Service's Network to Freedom* (http://www.nps.gov/subjects/ugrr/index.htm). The site includes documents on the Underground Railroad, an interactive map, and a cooperatively developed app for mo-

bile devices for accessing the sites in New York (http://
www.jimapco.com/eriecanalway/ugrr).

- *San Francisco Museum of Modern Art* (http://www.sfmoma.org). Extensive use of Facebook, Twitter, Flickr (for sharing photographs), and
"Open Space"—"lively platform for critical and personal responses to art,
visual culture, and issues specific to the Bay Area, and beyond."
- *Santa Cruz Museum of Art and History* (http://www.santacruzmah.org).
Extensive, imaginative use of Facebook and other social media to promote
exhibits and programs and elicit audience reactions and suggestions. Nina
Simon, the museum's director, is an advocate of the "participatory museum," and author of the influential *Museum 2.0* blog (http://museumt-
wo.blogspot.com); the museum's social media programs reflect her activist approach.
- *Smithsonian Institution* (http://www.si.edu/Connect). Multiple social media options, including one for "virtual world." A "Seriously Amazing"
section poses and answers interesting questions. "The Smithsonian Fan
Forum is an online place where people all over the world can weigh in on
our upcoming plans. We want your guidance, advice, opinions, and feedback on the small and big things that make the Smithsonian special. We
value your frank opinion." The Smithsonian's National Museum of
American History (http://americanhistory.si.edu) has a very active blog by
several educational specialists that explains exhibits and the history associated with them and offers behind-the-scenes insights. It also includes
online exhibits, Facebook, Twitter, and YouTube, including opportunities
for visitors to ask questions and post comments.
- *Te Papa, the National Museum of New Zealand* (http://
www.ourspace.tepapa.com/home). In the Museum's "Our Space" area,
people can post images of themselves, families, groups, and localities, and
they are displayed on a large digital map of the nation.

The Right Set of Skills

Proficiency in use of social media requires a well-developed set of communication skills to originate content, monitor reactions and conversations, and
respond to (and converse with) people online, most of whom the history
program staff members have not met. Practitioners need to be versatile, shifting from one format or platform to another quickly and transitioning among
topics that the program wants to publicize or where audiences have something to say that warrants monitoring and, possibly, response. Lynda Kelly,
manager of online services at the Australian Museum, has identified skills
needed in environments characterized by mobility, shared authority, and audience participation:[12]

Continually researching and collaborating using a range of tools to understand and connect with our many and varied audiences. This means an inclination to constantly learn through experience, improvise, and evolve.

Content producers across a range of platforms, not just technological ones. People with expertise in the holdings and services, and people with public relations and writing experience, are very helpful.

Experts in their field, but not the sole experts. The idea is to offer expertise and insights but not to come across as having all the understanding or all the answers. One of the objectives is to provoke thoughtful consideration, reaction, and response.

Facilitators, not teachers. Social media is more like a facilitated discussion than a traditional classroom presentation.

Storytellers, using the tools of narrative to weave a range of stories around content from a range of perspectives. An essential skill on Facebook and other social media is to be able to tell interesting stories, using actual historical examples, working in documents and other evidence, bringing out "human interest" angles, adding photos and videos where available and appropriate, and presenting the story in a way that makes people want to read, seek out more, and comment.

Sharing policies and practices online. Facebook is an excellent platform for sharing some behind-the-scenes information, including how curators and historians go about doing their work. This de-mystifies the work and at the same time gives staff a chance to discuss with pride the work they do and for audiences to sense the real human beings behind the program's work.

Nimble and flexible, while being rigorous. Social media requires people to be agile and versatile, particularly if they are involved with more than one platform (e.g., short bursts on Twitter and also longer, more thoughtful pieces on Facebook). At the same time, everything has to be written carefully, accurately, and in line with the organization's policies.

Facebook's guide for causes and nonprofits advises: know your *story* (your unique voice, the story you can bring to life in a compelling and authentic way); know your *audience* (your constituents, how they want to connect with you, what content will be important to them); and know your *goals* (what kind of relationship you want to have with the people who connect with your Facebook page).[13]

It is important to remember that social media (e.g., maintaining an active Facebook page) is a demanding and time-consuming assignment. It has to be done continually in order to be timely, relevant, and accessed by people who want constantly fresh information. Time spent on this work may be a good investment, but it is time that cannot be spent on something else (e.g., other worthwhile work that the program needs to get done). Expectations for magnitude of effort need to be clearly established (e.g., in individuals' workplans), and the work needs to be monitored by supervisors.

Select the Best Platform (or Platforms)

Facebook is very popular these days, but technology does not stand still and history shows that the creation of social media platforms is a never-ending process. It is helpful to ask a few questions when evaluating platforms, or when deciding where to place the institution's priorities:[14]

Does it enable people to connect with each other in new ways? Social media is all about making connections. "If a tool makes those connections more interesting, more varied, or more frequent, it has good potential for adoption." Good applications spread virally as existing participants invite new people to join them. For instance, Facebook, opened in 2006 to anyone who wished to join, has grown rapidly ever since then. YouTube pioneered a new form of communication, universally available video. Twitter permits people to broadcast and subscribe to a constant stream of information, including on mobile devices.

Is it effortless to sign up for? The most popular social technologies are free, can be readily accessed over the Web, or require simple registration, such as a username, password, and e-mail address.

Does it shift power from institutions to people? Social media technologies open up channels of communication and invite very broad participation. Facebook gives people the power to connect without institutional approval or supervision; *Wikipedia* allows people to create online content, including accounts of historical events, without institutional approval and bypassing recognized experts including history professors and museum professionals. Individuals feel empowered and therefore motivated to engage and create. Of course, sites like this have their own issues, particularly reliability and accuracy.

Does the community generate enough content to sustain itself? The institution may be at the center of the picture, but the best applications "make it easy for people to create content and to benefit from each other's content." Use it, and "you create value for your followers" by sharing information but also by giving your followers a platform for sharing with each other.

Is it an open platform that invites partnerships? This determines whether an application will flourish or fail. Open platforms like Facebook continually get new functionality without much work on the part of their founders; their users are in effect the enthusiastic (and unpaid) developers.

Develop a Strategy

"A digital strategy is a gameplan, a course of action, for how you will prioritize projects and investments in information and communications technologies. Without a plan, you won't know where you're headed, how much it will cost you to get there, and what it will cost to maintain your technology environment," advises Rose Sherman, director of enterprise technology at the Minnesota Historical Society. "A digital strategy does not have to be an all-encompassing document that describes everything," notes Nik Honeysett, head of administration at the J. Paul Getty Museum. "But it should be detailed enough to provide a framework of where the institution is heading and maybe state some pre-agreed guidelines for technology adoption, containment, development or response."[15]

Developing a social media strategy should be tied to and support the program's mission rather than being something that is separate from it. Whenever possible, it should be developed as part of the strategic planning process for the entire program, described in chapter 7. "Digital engagement is as much about designing activities that engage as about finding an audience that is willing to engage" notes Jasper Visser, who advises museums and other organizations on digital strategies to keep them relevant for the future.[16] He and a colleague, Jim Richardson, have developed a "Digital Engagement Framework" and a workbook for using it, available from their website, http://www.digitalengagementframework.com. They define a "social institution" as one that has put in place "all the strategies, technologies and processes that are needed to systematically involve all stakeholders to maximize co-created effort."[17] The book describes key building blocks of digital engagement:

The organizational basis. The place to begin is revisiting the program's vision and goals, focusing on *why* the program exists and objectives that involve or promise change—your "bold and daring vision" for the future. "Your vision is always about bigger things than your organization, things bigger than today and bigger than the bottom line." How can you use digital media to more intensively engage your current audience and expand that audience to include individuals and groups you have defined as priorities?

Assets and audiences. This part of the analysis involves discussion of the program's assets—people, expertise, holdings, exhibits, tours, public programs—and deciding which ones might be transferable to digital media. For instance, the talent friendly front office staff and tour guides might be turned into videos and Facebook and blog posts. The stories that tour guides tell can be digitized. At public programs, "take pictures, make videos, interview visitors and turn the press releases into lively social media updates."

Engagement strategies. Engagement in a digital arena "is about strengthening existing relationships and entering into a valuable exchange with your audience." Engagement aims to take people through four stages: (1) Reach—study your audience, how they get information, what they say interests them, what others are doing to reach them. (2) Interest—get people interested by providing high-quality, relevant content on a reliable and continuing basis. (3) Involve—invite participation, facilitate connections (e.g., invite responses to blog posts). (4) Activate—get people to become advocates, get them involved with each other. It all depends on making the "assets" available—they form the magnet for participation. Possibilities might include an expert blog with in-depth information; an online newsletter with exclusive content; questions, a puzzle, or quest based on interaction with an asset; a social media channel with extensive audience contributions; or on ongoing behind-the-scenes video series. You need to invite, inspire, and thank people for their participation. The objective is a cooperative "co-creation" relationship, which may include such things as reactions to your blog, a "like" on Facebook, a positive review on Tripadvisor, even a complaint (which the authors liken to a free audit). Encourage your digital audiences to become members. Define the benefits associated with "liking" your Facebook page.

Develop Policies

Historical programs also need guidelines and policies to help shape and direct their digital engagement initiatives, particularly the use of social media. Policies may be short or detailed, but they need to be clear and should be reviewed periodically to ensure their continuing relevance. Some suggested guidelines:

Start with principles. The policy document should express an expansive view of digital engagement and embrace the notion of broadscale participation. "The Museum's web spaces are visitor and audience focused," says the National Museum of Australia. "The Museum values and supports online engagement with communities of interest; it supports and facilitates user-generated content, online consultation with stakeholders and online programs." The policy statement endorses key values—trust, diversity, inclusion, and transparency, and innovation. These principles form the basis for more precise guidance based on them.[18]

The Digital Engagement Framework

Assets

Assets are the valuable or special things, people or qualities you own or do. We distinguish tangible and intangible assets.

- What makes you stand out?
- Why do people choose you?
- What do you sell?
- What are your values?
- What can you give away?
- What experience do you offer?
- How are you different from your competitors?

Reach

Reach is about making a first connection with new audiences or existing audiences for a new activity or channel.

- Where can you find your new audience (online)?
- What communities are they part of?
- How do you relate to these communities?
- Which assets can you offer your new audiences?
- How can you connect with them?

Audience

Audiences are the people you exist for; both those you reach and those you don't reach yet. We like to make them specific.

- Who do you reach?
- Who visits you frequently?
- Who have a formalised relationship with your organisation?
- Who only knows about you?
- Who knows about you, but doesn't visit you?
- What new groups would you like to reach?
- What are the specifics of each group

Metrics

Metrics help you measure success and monitor progress

- What are your KPIs?
- What is success?
- How will you report?

Channels

Channels are where you share your content, reach and engage people.

- Which technologies, media and tools will you use?
- What content will you share

Guidelines

Guidelines tell you how we will work.

- What are your core values?
- Who is responsible for what?
- How do you respond to unexpected developments?

Objectives

Objectives are the measurable and specific things you want to achieve with digital engagement

- What do you want to achieve with digital engagement?
- What are your organisation-wide goals and objectives?
- What do you need to achieve to make the entire organisation more social?

Engagement

Engagement means developing the relationship between you and your audience. Only reached audiences will engage.

- What can you offer your audience to stay interested?
- How can you involve your audience in what you do?
- How can you activate them to become an active advocate for your organisation?
- How can you work together to co-create value?
- How can you build your communities?

Vision

Vision tells you what your future looks like

- Why does your organisation exist?
- How will your organisation be different in 15 years time because of digital media?
- How will you make the world a better place?
- What will people say about you in the future?

Trends

Trends describe developments that affect your organisation, its audiences, assets and vision.

- What are important developments in your industry, locality, organisation and market segments
- What new technologies and media do you see coming?
- How will society be different in 5 years time?

Tie it to the program's mission. Social media policies need to indicate that the work should be tied to, and reinforce, the institution's mission. "Social media accounts should be used as part of a strategy for supplementing and enhancing content available on Smithsonian websites, reaching and engaging existing and new audiences, and carrying out the Institution's strategic plan," say the Smithsonian's guidelines. Activity should "add value to the name and reputation of the Smithsonian," be accurate and reliable, "professional, dignified, respectful," and "conversational and friendly in tone." [19]

Include administrative guidelines. Policy documents should include administrative issues, such as permission to represent the program in social media in an official capacity, mechanisms for internal collaboration and review, standards for monitoring and responding to user feedback, and guidelines for preventing the release of confidential information. [20]

Encourage application of good judgment. Some policies are succinct, basically setting general parameters and urging staff to exercise common sense and good judgment in what they post and how they respond to others. The Virginia Association of Museums recommends including several guidelines in social media policy documents, including: Follow behavior protocol that applies "offline." Be smart. Be respectful. Distinguish between social media activity as a representative of the organization vs. social media activity as a private individual. Avoid disclosing confidential or proprietary information. [21]

Clarify what will not be tolerated. The policy should draw the line, indicating what is not acceptable and stating that the program will not post, or will remove, offensive content. The Institute of Museum and Library Services' policy indicates that "we will remove content that contains abusive, vulgar, offensive, threatening or harassing language, personal attacks of any kind, or offensive terms that target specific individuals or groups." The IMLS also reserves the right to delete spam, content with personal information, and "content that is clearly off topic." [22]

Customize for your program. Policies will vary from one program to another, depending on their settings, goals, and resources. The Minnesota Historical Society's Local History Services Office provides general suggestions but offers a "Social Media Strategy Worksheet" for self-assessment and the development of digital tools and guidance for their use. [23]

Experiment/Learn/Refine

Planning is important, but with a counterbalancing caveat: don't over-ana-lyze or over-plan. Historical programs can learn from each other, but there are few standards or rules in this area. Don't aim to be on the cutting edge or even an early adopter. It is almost always better to wait until a technology becomes mainstream. Improvisation, experimentation, finding something that is a good fit for your program, and launching without a 100 percent assurance of success is a useful strategy. Three questions that can kill a proposed project in the area of digital engagement, notes Tom Scheinfeldt, managing director of the Center for History and the New Media at George Mason University, are:

> (1) Haven't X, Y, and Z already done this? We shouldn't be supporting dupli-cation of effort. (2) Are all the stakeholders on board? (3) What about sustain-ability? . . . Sometimes, X, Y, and Z's project stinks, or nobody uses it, or their code is lousy. Sometimes stakeholders can't see through the fog of current practice and imagine the possible fruits of innovation. Sometimes experimen-tal projects can't be sustained. Sometimes they fail altogether. . . . Sometimes, we have to be ready to accept "I don't know, this is an experiment" as a valid answer to the sustainability question.[24]

It is essential to experiment with applications such as Facebook (e.g., frequency of posts, use of photos). A good approach is to try lots of things, remembering that some things will fail but you will learn from the process and the experience, and zero in on the things that work best. Dana Allen-Greil, who manages data outreach initiatives at the National Gallery of Art, notes that there are four possible ratings for social media efforts—*We're great! We're good! We're learning! We stink!*—and that the third one is where we should aim.[25] Getting reactions from the audience is always useful. One very important measure is the number of followers (e.g., "friends" on Facebook). The platforms may have measurement tools that can provide additional insights. For instance, Facebook uses Facebook Insights, available to page administrators. For 28 days after any content is posted, the Insights tool collects data on the number of unique users who saw it and how many engaged it by "liking" it, posting a comment about it, or re-sharing it on their own Facebook pages. Insights also measures the "virality" of each post based on how many times it was shared on someone else's page. Most social media applications have some way to tell how many people are visiting, where they are from, and what they are clicking on. A service from Google, called Google Analytics (http://www.google.com/analytics) may be helpful in tracking this information. It is free and fairly easily installed onto most websites and blogs.

Make It Fun and Interesting

In the social media arena, particularly Facebook, history programs are competing for time and attention. A basic question to ask is: why should people
decide to spend time engaging with your institution via social media? The
relationship is a reciprocal one—the program is committing time and resources to make information available, but it also asking people to invest
some of their time and share insights and vision. Participation should be
easy. Social media communication is more conversational, less formal and
structured, than much of the style we use when discussing historical topics.
"Use an informal, first-person voice. You are engaging in a conversation
with your audience—not lecturing them."[26]

Writing like a journalist, with vivid descriptions, dramatic touches, and a
keen eye for the current and timely, is appropriate for social media. It is
important to post frequently and regularly; social media platforms such as
Facebook and Twitter need a continuing flow of fresh information or else
people will lose interest and tune out. Generally, briefer posts are preferable
to longer ones—more likely to be read and to be forwarded or disseminated
(e.g., "liked" on Facebook). Posts focused on single, discrete topics are likely
to generate more attention than longer, more diffuse ones covering multiple
topics. Posing questions or asking people for reactions to particular topics or
to an opinion expressed in a post are good ways of sparking conversation and
drawing the audience into the discussion. Responding to questions shares
information and also lets everyone see that the program's staff really is
paying attention to what people are saying.

Using compelling content, such as photos from the collection that people
cannot find anywhere else, attracts attention and also provides a base for a
narrative built around the photo. Sharing exclusive content and providing
behind-the-scenes coverage (e.g., of how an exhibit is being developed) is
often of interest to people and makes them feel a bit like "insiders." On-site
photos of staff at work, volunteers, or visitors (with their permission) adds a
"human interest" dimension to the material on the social media site by reminding people that history work is about the people who preserve and
present history and those who encounter, enjoy, and study it. Some programs
schedule regular posts on specific topics and thereby create something of an
audience of people who are interested in that subject. Others have tried
"chat" sessions where a staff member answers questions. Providing information about ongoing or upcoming events usually trumps information on past
events; people want fresh information, and this gives them another reason to
keep coming back to your site.

Posts that generate multiple responses and comments garner attention.
"The added-value parts (the replies, the links to external content, and so on)
are what give your social media presences personality, and the personality is

what draws in more followers."[27] Addressing negative comments and criticisms quickly and appropriately is a way of fostering a favorable opinion by everyone who views the site. From another perspective, the American Alliance of Museums recommends that museums consider following the "rule of thirds": a third on the museum as an institution (e.g., events, exhibits, and the like); a third on the individuals on staff (e.g., personal ideas, commentaries, perspectives, opinions); and a third on establishing goodwill (e.g., linking to other sites, commenting on other institution's social media pages).

Heather Mansfield, in her book *Social Media for Social Good*, emphasizes the need for constant updates and fresh news. "Ninety percent of the power of a Facebook Page is in the status updates. Most fans don't hang out on your Facebook Page, browsing through photos, videos, and past posts on your wall." People get status updates in their news feeds and visit the organization's page for new information.

> Never waste an opportunity to drive traffic from Facebook to your website, blog, YouTube Channel, or somewhere else. Always share a link, photo, or video in a status update. It makes your status updates richer and more visually appealing because people will attach thumbnail images to them, and thus you're much more likely to earn comments and thumbs up. . . . Mix it up! Share breaking news related to your organization's mission, trending posts from the blogosphere, popular videos from YouTube, or striking photos from Flickr.[28]

The textbox "How to Create Brand Engagement on Facebook" offers some additional insights.

HOW TO CREATE BRAND ENGAGEMENT ON FACEBOOK

There are not many studies of how to increase the number of "likes" and "shares" a Facebook post on a history program's site receives, but there are studies of how to do it for business. With some creative interpretation and application, these provide insights for using Facebook and other social media for our history programs. Arvind Malhotra et al, "How to Increase Brand Engagement on Facebook," *MIT Sloan Management Review*, Winter 2013, suggested eight ways brand managers can increase the number of "likes" a post receives. Through Facebook connections, those endorsements are shared with others who are "friends" with the individuals making the posts, thus publicizing the post.

1. *Express yourself through photos.* "Every picture tells a story. A photo is personal, and it can communicate quickly and easily." Even photos that seem like "blatant product promotion" elicited a high number of "likes."

2. *Be topical.* "Keep up with the times. Messages considered topical are those referring to holidays, festivals, important events, etc." Even when they refer to brand or products, such messages "are perceived to be more personable, rather than scripted promotions."

3. *Don't hesitate to be in your face.* "When customers visit the brand's wall, promotional messages are expected." Customers visit the walls of brands they are interested in and want to engage with.

4. *Share the validation.* "Take a bow. Everyone wants to align themselves with a winner." Share success stories and news of achievements, awards, and praise. Customers are inclined to "like" these posts in part because it shows them aligned with the organization's achievements.

5. *Educate the fans.* "Create informational value. Brands that generated or passed along information through wall posts also garnered a high number of 'likes,' especially information designed for fans' enrichment and education."

6. *Humanize the brand.* "Inject emotions. . . . Fans like messages that paint the brand as a living object. . . . Sharing posts that contain emotions helps fans convey their own emotions to their network of friends."

7. *Humor is the best social medicine.* "Laugh and everyone laughs with you . . . posts that generate a chuckle receive a significant boost in the number of 'likes'."

8. *Ask to be "liked."* "We found that if you directly ask to be "liked" on Facebook, you tend to receive more 'likes'."

NOTES

1. Accenture, *Executive Summary: The Social Media Management Handbook* (2011). http://www.accenture.com/SiteCollectionDocuments/microsites/social-media-management/Accenture_Executive_Summary_Social_Media_Handbook.pdf.

2. Pew Research, *Millennials in Adulthood* (March 2014). http://www.pewsocialtrends.org/2014/03/07/millennials-in-adulthood.

3. Tim Grove, "Reflections on the Past Decade," *History News* (Summer 2013), 6.

4. G. Wayne Clough, *Best of Both Worlds: Museums, Libraries, and Archives in a Digital Age* (Washington: Smithsonian Institution, 2013), 1–10, 63. http://www.si.edu/content/gwc/BestofBothWorldsSmithsonian.pdf.

5. *NMC Horizon Report -2013 Museum Edition.* http://www.nmc.org/publications/2013-horizon-report-museum.

6. Josh Bernoff and Charlene Li, "Harnessing the Power of the Oh-So-Social Web," *MIT Sloan Management Review* 49 (Spring 2008), 36–42.

7. Peter Weill and Stephanie L. Woerner, "Optimizing Your Digital Business Model," *MIT Sloan Management Review* 54 (Spring 2013), 72.

8. Angelina Russo et al, "The Impact of Social Media on Informal Learning in Museums," *Educational Media International* 46 (June 2009), 161.

9. Maxwell L. Anderson, "Moving from Virtual to Visceral," plenary address at Museums and the Web conference (2009). http://thedigitalmuseum.tumblr.com/post/30523745271/moving-from-virtual-to-visceral-maxwell-l.

10. Carol Vogel, "The Spirit of Sharing," *New York Times,* March 16, 2011.

11. Dana Allen-Greil, "Evaluating Social Media," presentation to American Association of Museums (2010). http://www.slideshare.net/danagreil/evaluating-social-media-american-association-of-museums-aam-2010.; MuseumNext, "What Do People Want from Museums on Facebook?" (2011). http://www.museumnext.org/2010/blog/what-do-people-want-from-museums-on-facebook.

12. Lynda Kelly, "The Connected Museum in the World of Social Media," in Kirsten Drotner and Kim Christian Schroder, eds., *Museum Communication and Social Media: The Connected Museum* (New York: Routledge, 2013), 65–66.

13. Facebook, *Building Your Presence with Facebook Pages: A Guide for Causes and Nonprofits*, 4. Undated. https://www.facebook.com/nonprofits.

14. Charlene Li and Josh Bernoff, *Groundswell: Winning in a World Transformed by Social Technologies* (Boston: Harvard Business Press, 2008), 36–37.

15. Tim Grove, "The Importance of a Digital Strategy: Interview with Rose Sherman and Nik Honeysett," Parts I and II, *History News* (Autumn 2012), 5–6, and (Winter 2013), 5–6.

16. Jasper Visser, "Perspectives on Digital Engagement with Culture and Heritage," *History News* (Summer 2013), 9.

17. Jasper Visser and Jim Richardson, *Digital Engagement in Culture, Heritage and the Arts* (2013). http://www.digitalengagementframework.com/#book.

18. National Museum of Australia, *Online Content and Participation Policy* (2010). http://www.nma.gov.au/__data/assets/pdf_file/0014/1463/NMA_Onlinepolicyv1_24May2010.pdf.

19. Smithsonian Institution, *Social Media Handbook* (2011). http://www.si.edu/content/pdf/about/sd/SD-814.pdf.

20. Matthew MacArthur, *Do We Need a Social Media Policy?* American Alliance of Museums (2010). American Association of Museums, "Sample Social Media Policy," in *Social Media Handbook*, 12 (2011). Both available at http://www.aam-us.org.

21. Virginia Association of Museums, *How to Create a Social Media Policy for Your Museum* (2012). http://issuu.com/vamuseums/docs/vamsocialmediapolicywhitepaper/1.

22. Institute of Museum and Library Services, *IMLS Commenting and Posting Policy* (Undated). http://www.imls.gov/news/imls_commenting_policy.aspx.

23. Minnesota Historical Society, *Social Media Guidelines* (Undated). http://discussions.mnhs.org/mnlocalhistory/blog/2010/09/10/social-mediaweb-guidelines-and-strategy-worksheets.

24. Tom Scheinfeldt, "3 Innovation Killers in Digital Humanities" (Oct. 16, 2009). *Found History.* http://www.foundhistory.org/2009/10/16/3-innovation-killers-in-digital-humanities.

25. Allen-Greil, "Evaluating Social Media," American Association of Museums, 2010.

26. American Association of Museums, *Social Media Handbook* (2011).

27. Ned Potter, *The Library Marketing Toolkit* (London: Facet, 2012), 93.

28. Heather Mansfield, *Social Media for Social Good* (New York: McGraw Hill, 2012), 75–76.

Chapter Six

Advocacy

Historical programs that are dynamic, aspirational, and always seeking to climb to new levels of service and achievement need to constantly build and expand their relationships among influential policy makers, decision makers, resource allocators, and users. *Advocacy* refers to actions by the program to garner public attention and persuade individuals and organizations to provide support. Advocacy is sometimes relegated to secondary status in program planning and management, something that is ramped up once a year at budget time, or developed in haste in reaction to a crisis when the program's budget is threatened. That is too narrow, limited, and reactive. Advocacy should be a continuing, dynamic, energetic effort that tirelessly seeks support and resources. It is an essential responsibility of leadership.

INTEGRATE ADVOCACY INTO PROGRAM PLANNING AND SERVICES AND MAKE IT EVERYONE'S JOB

Advocacy is much more than an add-on or an occasional ad hoc intensive activity. It is continuing core work, connected to everything the program does, and is essential to sustain and build up support and resources for continually taking the program to new levels. Advocacy strategies need to be discussed and developed as part of strategic planning processes discussed in chapter 7. Boards of directors need to spell them out in their own plans and in the job descriptions and goals they lay out for program heads. Expectations for advocacy-related work should be included in the annual work plans for staff members, including volunteers where appropriate. It should be part of the creativity/innovation work discussed in chapter 3; staff members are likely to come up with multiple creative ways to boost the program's visibility and luster. "Think of advocacy as a cumulative building process that takes a lot of work," advises Lewis Bellardo, whose long career included positions as state archivist and records administrator of Kentucky, director of the Georgia Historical Society, and deputy archivist of the United States. His suggestions include:[1]

Excellent service is the fundamental basis for appealing for support. Programs that demonstrate exceptional dedication and effectiveness in their missions to collect, preserve, and make available history have a natural basis for seeking support to continue, and if possible expand, their work. Satisfied customers make good advocates. Resource allocators and decision makers are impressed by effective programs and satisfied customers. People like to support and get others to support successful programs because that makes their job as advocates easier.

Advocacy is about program building. "The purpose of advocacy is to develop, build, revitalize, redesign, and protect your program. We must shake every hand and write every report with that in mind. . . . Advocacy is mostly about offense not defense."

Advocacy means listening to others as well as making your case to them. It is about influencing others but also about being influenced by them. This includes seeking out the deep motivations of people who might want to donate artifacts or make sizeable financial donations, carrying out a dialogue with potential supporters and advocates to see which messages really resonate with them. It also means being realistic about the complicated motivations and views of political leaders who may understand the value of history but not be fully aware of the role of a particular program in preserving it.

Be persistent. "Never assume that your advocacy efforts are sufficient. . . . Expect the unexpected and make the most of it." Bellardo relates examples that are familiar to many program directors: they seem on the brink of success with a new initiative (e.g., a boost in their budget or authorization of a new building) when something unexpected intervenes (e.g., new questions about plans or unforeseen opposition). Build a solid network of advocates, ask them to be alert for unexpected bumps in the road, move quickly to put out small fires of opposition, and keep the work going until the goal is achieved.

Advocate effectively with key internal and external groups. It is important to build rapport and support with key internal offices in the parent organization (e.g., the library, budget office, facilities office, and public relations office). It is also essential to build support with key outside groups. One useful strategy is to appoint oversight and advisory committees or boards and consult with them on program development and priorities, but also get them to double as advocates for the program.

Follow the 80/20 rule. Focus advocacy efforts on the most important 20 percent of stakeholders and customers for key initiatives. This might mean courting a few key legislators, influential business leaders, or directors of community programs, people with influence and connections who know how to get things done. On the other hand, "there are times when narrowly focused advocacy just isn't enough, and support at the grassroots level is indispensable."

Keep emphasizing the program's impact. "The advocacy can't be for your benefit—rather it must be about the needs of those advocating for you." Program staff and advocates seeking support need to emphasize the program's services. More resources will help the program do its important work better, save more historical material, and expand its services. Providing examples of what can be done—archives and artifacts saved, school students who could attend programs, examples of the sorts of exhibits that are contemplated—helps get across the message of the real beneficiaries of what is being sought.

USE MULTIPLE WAYS TO MAKE THE CASE

Many publications of the AASLH, the American Alliance of Museums, and other professional associations are useful sources for making the "case" for history programs: they are essential enterprises that link the past with the present and help us prepare for the future; study of history produces civic awareness and good citizenship in young people; historic preservation stabilizes and enhances neighborhoods; and heritage tourism boosts the economy. Every historical program needs a carefully composed "case" statement about what the program does and why it is important. It is the statement about the program's essentials and aspirations, the distillation of its value, and the point of departure for sustained advocacy. The case is like a brand, something succinct, easily understood, and readily explainable. The program's case needs three components:[2]

Differentiation. What is it that distinguishes your program? Is the mission "inspiring to enough people to attract a broad base of support to be sustainable for the long term? Do you have an achievable goal for success that will captivate people's imagination? . . . a compelling promise that captivates people's imagination and allows them to envision the mission being fulfilled."

Credibility. What is the assurance that the program will deliver on its promises? The program needs to demonstrate accountability—it can be trusted, has solid management practices, a track record of achievement, and funding and other resources will be put to good use.

Authenticity. Why should people care about your program and its cause? Successful organizations know that they need to go beyond the support from people who are directly affected by their programs and services. They need to impress and win over people not directly connected with the work by speaking authentically about the challenges they face as well as about the expertise they bring to the table.

The American Alliance of Museums notes that making the case when lobbying legislators is easy because the institutes we represent are so beneficial: "your museum is a community center where students come to learn, where families come to share a common educational experience and where citizens and visitors come to better understand their community and the world around them. As a valuable constituent, it is your right to speak up for your museum!"[3] The AAM's primer for 2014 national "Advocacy Day" presents multiple elements of the case for public support:[4]

Museums spend over $2 billion annually on education, and the typical museum devotes three-quarters of its budget to education.

Museums directly contribute $21 billion annually to the US economy and generate billions more through indirect spending by their visitors.

The "nonprofit arts and culture industry" annually generates over $135 billion in economic activity, supports over 4.1 million full-time jobs, and returns over $22 billion in local, state, and federal taxes.

Government support for arts organizations creates an annual return of over $7 for every dollar the government appropriates.

Seventy-six percent of all US leisure travelers participate in cultural or heritage activities.

About 22 percent of museums are located in rural areas and offer a wide range of programs in their communities.

"The state's diverse and vibrant museum community is central to the economic vitality of New York State and the education of its youth," noted an advocacy publication of the Museum Association of New York. It made the general case—museums are places of "awe and mystery . . . reflect the values of diverse communities . . . support lifelong learning" —and a more concrete appeal: museums generate over $1 billion into the state's economy each year, serve more than 6 million school children with educational programming, and had an annual attendance of 68 million people. "New Yorkers know what museums and heritage organizations do for their communities and want to help," says the document, adding another basis for appeal by noting that nearly 12,400 New Yorkers volunteer their time to serve as museum trustees and that museum volunteers contribute 9.6 million hours annually.[5]

History programs can learn from other groups that also carry out invaluable public services and constantly need to enhance their support base. Nonprofits, which include history programs but also encompass many other types of service organizations, emphasize extraordinary impact and return on investment. A recent statement on values explained that nonprofits are:[6]

Productive: Creating jobs and economic value; mobilizing assets to address public problems; enhancing local economic vitality

Empowering: Mobilizing and empowering citizens, contributing to public discourse; providing opportunities for civic engagement for the public good

Effective: Providing programs and services of the highest quality at reasonable cost; making a difference in the lives of individuals and the community

Enriching: Giving expression to central human values; providing opportunities for people to learn and grow; preserving culture and history, promoting creativity

Reliable: Resilient and demonstrating staying power both in good times and bad; operating in a trustworthy and accountable manner

Responsive: Responding to clients, patrons, and communities; meeting needs that the market and government don't meet; pursuing innovative approaches when needed

Caring: Serving underserved populations; providing services/programs at reduced or no cost to disadvantaged populations; community focused

The theoretical case for history's value in documenting and preserving the past and providing insights that we can use to shape the future can and often is made eloquently by people in our field. We are easily persuaded and tend to be incredulous when other people, such as newspaper editorial writers and budget analysts, don't seem convinced about the value of history. But what that actually means is that we need to go further. One strand of the advocacy theme should be the *business case* for history. That would include the points about the economic benefits of heritage tourism and historic preservation discussed earlier in this book. But it would also include:

Drawing on the past puts current problems into perspective. The Winthrop Group, a professional archival and history consulting firm, publishes essays that remind people about the historical origins of current issues. In April 2009, as the recession intensified, the firm published a white paper entitled "Leading in Uncertainty: Four Proven Principles from History," drawing on the experience of several Depression-era firms to suggest principles by which firms could re-assert control in the midst of economic crisis and lay the foundation for post-recession growth (including "take the long view," a perspective that historians often favor). A 2011 essay on "Medicine, Healthcare, and History: Past as Prologue" traced healthcare issues back to the early twentieth century. A 2013 essay "Government Shutdowns Have Happened Before" during a shutdown of the federal government over a budget impasse recalled that there had been seventeen full or partial shutdowns.[7]

Understanding an institution's past helps leaders address critical issues. Shared history is central to group identity, and past experiences can be summoned up in times of great challenge and change, told anew, and inspire people's commitment and energy. It can bring together groups that have been at odds by illustrating shared themes in their pasts. Decision making improves when leaders take the time to understand why actions were taken in the past, how decisions were implemented, and how assumptions have become deeply rooted in an organization's culture. "Great leaders don't talk about history only when planning their organization's next anniversary. They always think and talk about the past—in the present and in living color."[8]

Heeding past lessons helps get around impasses. In 2011, during an impasse in Washington over raising the federal debt ceiling, the editors of *American Heritage* wrote the president and congressional leaders, urging them to heed lessons of history and compromise on the issue. "Compromise is usually the only way out" of crises, noted the journal's editor-in-chief in the letter. Five historical examples were cited: compromises leading to the US Constitution, the Missouri Compromise of 1820, the Compromise of 1850, and the compromises that went into the making of the New Deal and Medicare. Leaders were urged to "think back over these examples in American history."[9]

Maintaining archival records helps citizens every day. The Council of State Archivists' advocacy publication explains that local government archival records such as birth certificates, land records, and building records "include information that is essential to sustain both government operations and the lives of individual citizens—like you." They "prove our identity and protect our rights . . . ensure government is efficient and accountable to its citizens . . . document our heritage and enhance our communities."[10]

Having a historian on the legal team can provide an edge. In complex litigation (e.g., involving environmental issues), historians can "employ specialized contextual knowledge and a disciplined methodology in their research and analysis . . . to effectively gather and synthesize the available historical evidence and to relate historical facts in a thorough and compelling manner. . . . The greater the scope of the historian's research, the more credible and reliable the historian's opinion." The historian's research skills and ability to synthesize reliable, impressive history from multiple sources can tip the verdict in favor of companies or government agencies who use their services.[11]

Starting an archival program can save you money. History Associates, a firm that provides historical research and archival services, made "the business case for archives" by pointing out that a sound archival program can reduce operation costs through efficient information retrieval and faster access, contribute to a sound risk management strategy, and generate added value for marketing and public relations activities.[12]

Historical parallels and insights can enlighten state policy. A series of historical essays in the Albany, New York, *Times Union* explained that many issues the state is facing are similar to what it addressed in the past. For instance, fiscal constraints during the recent recession resemble those of the Great Depression and economic downturns in the nineteenth century. State initiatives to broaden rail service were similar to policies pursued by state railroad regulators in the early twentieth century. Government reorganization proposed by Governor Andrew Cuomo, elected in 2010, had precedent in reforms carried out by Governor Al Smith, elected in 1918. The state's response to the devastation of Hurricane Irene in 2011 could draw guidance from public response to a blizzard that crippled New York City in 1888 and a hurricane that swept across Long Island in 1938.[13]

Archives provide perspective. The Vermont State Archives focused on high-visibility bills and researched legislative committee minutes on earlier bills or acts germane to the proposal and sent copies to sponsoring legislators, which helped shape bill drafting and debate. It also compiled a "Continuing Issues" series on key issues, identifying past proposals, linking to their text, and indicating what happened to them. It became a series legislators valued, demonstrating the Archives' institutional commitment.[14]

All of this reinforces a few key advocacy themes, namely that historical programs:

Are notably successful at the broad undertaking of selecting and preserving materials from the past and making them broadly available for people to use.

Are not just about "the past." In addition to preserving history, they have a role in discussions and debates of important contemporary issues.

Are operated efficiently and economically on modest resources and are therefore a good place to invest resources because there is a large return on investment.

Foster quality-of-life and community spirit by instilling understanding and pride.

International perspectives suggest added components for the case (See text-box, "Museums Change Lives: A British Perspective").

MUSEUMS CHANGE LIVES: A BRITISH PERSPECTIVE

History museums, and museums in general, can have an impact on the people who visit their exhibits, attend public events, or access them via the Internet. Several recent studies emphasize that we need to aim high, embrace patrons as partners, change people's insights and outlooks, and use that impact as a theme in promoting our programs. Some key points from the British Museums Association's report *Museums Change Lives: The MA's Vision for the Impact of Museums* (2013) are quoted below (http://www.museumsassociation.org/download?id=1001738).

> Audiences are creators as well as consumers of knowledge; their insights and expertise enrich and transform the museum experience for others.
>
> Museums foster questioning, debate and critical thinking.
>
> Museums are rooted in places and contribute to local distinctiveness.
>
> Museums . . . enrich the lives of individuals, contribute to strong and resilient communities, and help create a fair and just society.
>
> Museums can be ambitious about their role in society [and] can support positive social change.
>
> [Museums] have two-way relationships with communities, drawing on a wide range of skills, knowledge, experience and networks.
>
> Museums have a duty to be inclusive—to see their audience as everyone and to engage with the widest possible range of people, constantly seeking out new audiences.
>
> Active public participation changes museums for the better.
>
> People trust museums highly . . . and regard them as authoritative. However, museums are not neutral; the politics of the past and present shape collections, information and interpretation. The public expectations that museums are unbiased brings with it great responsibility. It means trying to be as honest as possible.
>
> Museums can present collections in ways that challenge assumptions and stimulate people to think about the world today and how it might be different in the future.

ENLIST A CORE OF ELITE, CAPABLE SUPPORTERS

Building and sustaining a dynamic program depends on having a core of committed and enthusiastic supporters with influence, resources, or both. These individuals understand the program's deepest values, mission, and potential; have confidence in the program's leadership; and are motivated through recognition for their association with a successful good cause. The book *The Generosity Network* explains fundraising strategies, but its insights are equally applicable to advocacy more generally. "People become dedicated to causes that . . . make their lives rich with meaning." The book explains that "people *want* to make a difference through their lives and their money. They *want* to work together to share their passions with like-minded individuals . . . philanthropy grows from deep-seated human needs." It's all about building a relationship, "a connection between people based on mutual commitment of resources to a shared future . . . an ever-growing, deepening reality based on mutual openness and on a shared willingness to follow mutual passions."[15]

Edie Hedlin, former director of a number of archival programs, summarizing the insights from a book on successful archival advocacy, identified the need to "stress a few key messages—such as the value of the records, the business case for the program, and the role of good records management in improving operations. Present the key points in your advocacy message in a variety of ways. Tailor your message to be meaningful to the person(s) you wish to influence."[16] Core supporters have several traits. They may have personal wealth of sufficient amount to provide substantial resources to the program and/or may have friends, business associates, or others with financial resources. More often, they are not personally wealthy but are leaders in their chosen field and have lots of experience with dynamic, successful enterprises. They have and know how to use influence with legislators and decision-makers whose actions are critical to the program's welfare. They are quietly persistent and know how to get things done, often behind-the-scenes and without calling attention to themselves. They are interested in the historical subject matter of the program, often because of a personal, heartfelt connection via ancestors and family, community, or things that intrigue them about some aspect of history or where they have a personal research interest. The program director involves them in a way that makes them feel invested but not intrusive (e.g., seeking their suggestions for, or review of drafts of, vision and mission statements and strategic plans). The director keeps them apprised of the status of key issues and progress or problems in areas of their particular interest or concern. They feel like valued insiders, and this heightens their emotional investment in the program's welfare. When the program succeeds and grows, their confidence intensifies and their pride increases because of their association with the successful enterprise. The program ac-

knowledges their generosity and tireless dedication, publically credits them
for effectiveness on successful initiatives, and, where appropriate, nominates
them (or gets others to nominate them) for honors and recognition by professional historical associations. The relationship is grounded in mutual respect
and admiration and a genuine concern for the cause of history.

BUILD ON ENGAGEMENT FOR A WIDE CIRCLE OF ADVOCATES

Historical programs need to build a second, and wider, circle of advocates,
beyond the corps of activists. Our programs are perceived as honest brokers,
presenting information in a balanced and objective way, enabling the visitor
to come to his or her own conclusions about the topic at hand. They are
exciting places where people can interact with artifacts, archives, and other
tangible manifestations of history. That sort of exciting interaction can be the
basis for building a wider circle of advocates. A conference of museum
professionals in New York State, struggling with how to explain the value of
museums, formulated a question:

> Why does New York's museum community struggle to make a case for itself
> that does not mimic Six Flags' list of exciting family fun, but rather one that
> speaks of museums as places filled with unexpected, unanticipated moments
> of revelation—the tiny piece of local history that sets a visitor thinking, the
> interactive exhibit that allows a quiet student to be successful for the first time,
> or the way the breath-taking beauty of a living exhibit ambushes visitors?

The conference concluded that advocacy work dovetails with engaging diverse stakeholders in shaping the program, collaborative work, and problem
solving. "Engage in learning. Engage in teaching both inside and outside the
museum. A staff needs to learn just like the audience it serves. Look for new
ways to tell the story and then ask people to take part. And find the story's
core: Is it about invention, parenting, revolutionary behavior? . . . those are
big umbrella topics to a 21st century audience." The New York meeting
found inspiration in the Matilda Joslyn Gage Center, profiled in chapter 8.
They learned that the director included on the sign that greets visitors: "Welcome to the Matilda Joslyn Gage Center. . . . Rules of the house: 1) Check
your dogma at the door. 2) Think for yourself. Please dialogue with us about
the challenging ideas you will find within these walls and together let us
envision the world we want to create. Please feel free to take photographs,
pick up books, play with the toys, sit on the furniture, and most of all write
on the walls!" The last request was not meant to be taken literally but rather
as an invitation for visitors to write reactions and suggestions on whiteboards
as they left.[17] That style of engagement makes for personal connections to

history and historical programs. As noted earlier in this book, a program is also likely to have a broader audience who connect via the Web.

Successful advocacy depends on being able to draw on the support of the informed, concerned, knowledgeable, and engaged people in this wide circle of advocates. They can be asked—occasionally—to lobby local officials, community groups, the news media, and local benefactors. They can be counted on to write state officials about the need for public funding for museums and historical programs and to show up at "Museums Day" at state capitols. The key is keeping their interest on a continuing basis and summoning them to take action when needed. The American Library Association's Office for Library Advocacy, one of the strongest in the cultural program field, recommends developing an "Action Plan" for advocacy.[18] It has developed a helpful planning worksheet with key questions:

> What is the goal of your campaign?
> What are your objectives?
> What are the key messages? (10–15 words)
> Who is the audience?
> Why is this important to them? (at least three reasons)
> What do we want the audience to (1) Think? (2) Feel? (3) Do?
> Three supporting points
> Examples, stories, and facts that support this message
> How will we determine the success of our campaign?

It has also developed a list of ten strategies for carrying out the plan. With a few modifications, they would support advocacy for history programs:

1. Start with an action plan and budget. Appoint a coordinator and assign tasks. A plan will help ensure a bigger bang for your buck by helping you use your resources strategically.
2. Get the whole library "family" involved—all staff, trustees and Friends. Make sure everyone understands the rationale and has an opportunity to give input.
3. Be enthusiastic and positive. Let those you are seeking to involve know they can help make a difference.
4. Talk about users' needs—not the library's . . .
5. Break tasks into bite-sized pieces. For those who are "too busy" but want to help, have a "to do" list to choose from such as attending one school board meeting, writing a letter to the editor or making one phone call to a key official.
6. Build a database of supporters with name, addresses, telephone number and e-mail addresses. Create an e-list to keep them informed of both successes and setbacks.
7. Support your supporters. Provide message sheets, tips and other materials to help them speak out. Train them in public speaking, media, and legislative skills.

8. Reach out to influential people in the community. Meet with key leaders and officials to educate them about library concerns and invite their support. Ask to speak to civic, campus and other organizations.
9. Distribute campaign information both in and outside the library—in the teacher's lounge, student union, bookstores, coffee shops, wherever people are likely to see and read it.
10. Thank and recognize your supporters at every opportunity!

CONTINUOUSLY REPORT ON THE PROGRAM'S IMPACT

Successful programs thrive on high visibility—they issue news releases, appeal for press coverage, invite the press to cover new exhibits and public programs, and prepare and issue reports even when they are not required. They make energetic use of their websites and social media to create "buzz" and get the word out. They give out awards for advocacy and support, use of their resources by teachers, historical essays by students, outstanding research projects, creative use of historical materials by the media, and other types of engagement. The awards recognize allies and users, but they also sustain the public profile of the program. This tireless push for attention reinforces other efforts to make their "case" and provides an opportunity to call attention not just to the program but to its impact and why it matters.

The Minnesota Historical Society, one of the nation's strongest and most successful history programs, is particularly adept at keeping its programs in the public eye. One of the best models is its reporting on projects funded under the "Legacy Amendment," an amendment to the state constitution approved by voters in 2008 that provides, among other things, for grants to preserve Minnesota's history and cultural heritage. The Society's reports provide details on projects that are funded. But they also point out the benefits to citizens and impact on the state. For instance, a recent report noted that the Society is investing Legacy history funds in projects in all Minnesota counties. The program costs $2.34 per person per year, less than the cost of a gallon of gas. The grants leveraged more than $1.4 million in outside sources to match the grants. Grants have provided educational tools for over ten thousand Minnesota teachers and programs benefitting more than half a million Minnesota students. The grants are made carefully in line with priorities suggested by the Minnesota History Coalition and with the advice of the Historical Resources Advisory Committee and approval of the MHS's Governing Board; the report emphasizes that there is broad input and review to assure funding of the strongest, most promising projects. An impressive section on "Accountability" explains that the Society holds down administrative costs and meets the requirement of the constitutional amendment that Legacy funds shall supplement and not substitute for traditional sources of funds. [19]

Its 2014 annual report profiled educational programs (helping educate hundreds of thousands of students in the classroom and through visits to historic sites and museums), historic preservation advisory services ("We help communities revitalize their business districts," says the program coordinator. "Through our program they discover they don't need to reinvent the wheel"), and leading-edge technology (for instance, a mobile app for users to find museums, plan itineraries, and make comments).[20]

The National Arts Marketing Project, an initiative of Americans for the Arts, notes that an *audience* is a body of listeners or spectators—passive recipients with unknown needs who receive products but have no impact on the product or its delivery. In marketing and promotional initiatives, power rests with the presenter. But *customers*—the main focus of advocacy and promotional campaigns—are active participants who want a two-way relationship with the program, want to be involved in product and delivery, and whose needs fulfillment is the key to success. Power rests with the customer rather than the presenter. The Project's publication on marketing the arts notes that marketing experts sell the "sizzle," not the steak. "They promote the features of a product that appeal to the prospect viscerally and emotionally, those that satisfy real, human, personal needs." It recommends four strategies for bringing the message to life:[21]

> Attention: The message needs to grab attention, make the individuals to whom it is directed say "This is important to me. This fills a need. I should pay attention to this message."
> Awareness: Generating awareness is "a building process. It starts with getting noticed. It moves through building interest. It culminates with being remembered—and being remembered for the right reasons."
> Attitude: "What people feel about your product is usually the result of an experience"—a personal visit, an ad, imagery, something they have heard by word of mouth.
> Action: "Your target acts—becomes a customer—buys a ticket, signs up for a class, sends for your brochure, becomes a subscriber" or member.

James Vaughan, executive director of the Pennsylvania Historical and Museum Commission (PHMC), testifying before a legislative committee after years of budget reductions, framed his message by noting that PMHC spends most of its time doing things that serve the citizens. He summarized the economic benefits of statewide historical and preservation efforts and explained that preservation work by the commission helps cities and towns keep up property values. Attuned to the economy-minded legislature, he described cutbacks, consolidation, and plans for finding cooperating partners to use space in "a number of facilities that exceed the needs of the commission." Vaughan noted the commission was ramping up its own fundraising.

He carefully answered questions from legislators about administrative practices, fiscal management, and technology. A legislator asked about visitation
to Pennsbury Manor and the first female governor of a colony, Hannah Penn.
Vaughan knew his history: he responded that Hannah Penn had administered
the colony for 14 years after William Penn had a stroke and that "she was a
better administrator than William Penn and helped the colony get out of a
number of financial and border issues."[22] There were five underlying but
unstated messages in Vaughan's impressive testimony: *We're on top of
things. We know our history. We run a tight ship. Our work helps all Penn-
sylvanians and communities throughout the state. If we had more resources,
we could do even more public good.* The testimony is a masterful blend of
information sharing, engagement, and advocacy.

PUT HISTORY TO WORK IN UNEXPECTED, IMAGINATIVE WAYS

History can intersect with public consciousness in many ways. Sometimes,
companies tie their commercial messages to heritage themes. For example:

- *Promoting business.* Bank of America produced a series of short, animated videos on historical events, including the Watt steam engine and the
  Louisiana Purchase, to illustrate the art of deal-making, the value of investment, and the bank's own loan offerings. http://promo-
  tions.bankofamerica.com/deal-hall-of-fame.
- *A moving adventure.* Pictures on the side of U-Haul trucks illustrate historical events and natural features in each of the US states and Canadian
  provinces. They constitute "a salute to the United States and Canada . . .
  our way of giving back to the communities we serve . . . carefully researched rare findings, little-known facts and mysteries that exist throughout the United States and Canada." The company's website provides additional information and links for teachers, students, and parents. http://
  www.uhaul.com/Articles/About/45/About-U-Haul-SuperGraphics.
- *A heritage of stewardship.* The Cape Cod Cranberry Growers' Association
  promotional brochure, *The Cranberry Heritage*, begins "Down on Cape
  Cod, a patch of wild cranberry vines traced the edge of a rolling stone. The
  wind gently blew sand over the vines, covering the runners. This tender
  act of nature, which caused the creeping plant to set down roots and send
  up shoots, was observed by Captain Henry Hall of East Dennis in 1816.
  The commercial cultivation of cranberries was born."

Another approach is to use a historical milestone as a basis for a public
commemoration. When planning a commemoration, it is useful to analyze

what place the organization being celebrated holds in the minds of patrons and communities, how you can use the event to call attention to the value of the institution and its history, and how to build on that to gain attention and support for the future of the program. "Milestones give an opportunity to look back and look forward," says Tara Lapointe, director of marketing and communication at the Canada Council for the Arts. "Find fun ways you can invite people to reflect on their histories and experiences and invest in being part of the organization's future."[23] A few examples:

> The Union Pacific Railroad, celebrating its 150th anniversary in 2012, noted that "with the stroke of a pen, President Lincoln signed the Pacific Railway Act and charged us with an extraordinary task—connecting the nation." A historical timeline chronicled the railroad's achievements and contributions. "Even though we've been at this since 1862, we're just getting started." Its website invited people who had worked on the railroad to upload stories and photos. ("In 1862, President Lincoln Said Start. He Never Said Stop," *Time*, July 21, 2012; http://www.up150.com.)

> CitiBank, celebrating its bicentennial in 2012, emphasized its investment in inventions and business innovations through photos, videos, and a Facebook app that could be downloaded from its website: "To celebrate our 200th anniversary, we're taking a retrospective through the last 20 decades. If you've ever wondered what life was like in 1862, or how you'd look in the 1940s, dive into '200 Years You' and find out. START THE APP." The company's CEO summarized its history: "The central mission of the company is to support economic progress." ("Citi Bank Celebrates 200 Years of Successful Banking," *Branding Magazine*, May 4, 2012; http://www.brandingmagazine.com/2012/04/05/citi-bank-celebrates-200-years-of-successful-banking)

> In 2013, Florida joyously celebrated "Viva Florida 500," commemorating the arrival of Spanish explorer Juan Ponce de León in 1513 and Florida's history since then. The kick-off press release defined the objective to "inspire an even greater pride in Florida heritage." The initiative's website lists over 800 commemorative events around the state. Creative advertising boosted heritage tourism and visitation to historic sites. There were special resources for teachers and students. The "Viva Florida 500" video is a model of blending history and promotional boosterism, emphasizing that Florida has always been "a state of firsts," describing growth in agriculture, business, and technology, and demonstrating Florida's upward historical trajectory (http://viva-florida.org).

It is important to keep making the case for the importance of history programs. A National Council of Nonprofits statement is a useful model.

> Nonprofits embody the best spirit and values of our nation. They help millions of individuals and families daily. They protect, feed, heal, shelter, educate, and nurture our bodies and spirits. Nonprofits also give shape to our boldest dreams, highest ideals, and noblest causes. They turn our beliefs into action— as promoters of democracy, champions of the common good, incubators of innovation, laboratories of leadership, protectors of taxpayers, responders in times of trouble, stimulators of the economy, and weavers of community fabric. . . . Nonprofits are all around us and touch millions of lives each day. [24]

LOBBYING PUBLIC OFFICIALS

Much of the support for historical programs comes, directly or indirectly, from government. It is important to cultivate key officials, including keeping them updated on activities and needs, inviting them to events, listening to their suggestions and requests, and thanking them for their support when appropriate. A good example is the partnership between the Mesa Historical Society and the city of Mesa. When the recession began in 2008, the city reduced its budget and was forced to cut some of the support it provided to the Society for heritage services. But the Society had built a strong case over the years for its value. The mayor recognized its role in making the city an attractive place to live. "We don't allow it to be called an amenity," he notes. "You can't succeed in the economic realm without creating a sense of who you are, and you need to use that to build upon so you know where you're going." The Society did its part by redefining its mission as community building, asking "In what way is the presence of heritage within the community required for building the future of the city/region? What is the museum's role in answering that question?" It began to work by "juxtaposing a historic overlay with contemporary examinations of our community." The Society's director kept highlighting the organization's evolving role and its value to the city and the community. The partnership worked and got stronger. The city provided space and covered some exhibit expenses and launched a bond issue for rehabilitation of an old post office and federal building into space for the Society. The Society came up with new exhibits to attract heritage tourists, including one on baseball, the "Cactus League Experience," that debuted during spring baseball professional training, one of the major drivers of the city's economy. It became more nimble and visible, mounting exhibits in city buildings, libraries, shopping malls, and the Phoenix International Airport. The Society came out of the recession stronger than ever as a result of its new image as "a significant partner in an effort to build a better community." [25]

Much of the direct lobbying with public officials is done in relatively brief meetings or on "Museum Day" or "History Day" lobbying visits while legislatures are in session. The Virginia Association of Museums provides pointers for getting your "message" across to busy public officials: [26]

- Introduce yourself and indicate what group (mention number of members) or institution you represent.
- Thank him/her—for SOMETHING: for past support of the arts and humanities, for past support of your museum, for past record of support for issues of concern to his/her constituents.
- Ask him/her—for something specific: i.e., favorable consideration on an issue, support for a budget amendment, and the like.
- Keep your message brief and to the point. Do not stay longer than 10–15 minutes. You should prepare a one-page fact sheet to leave behind with your main points and any additional information you think you might not have time to convey.
- Use anecdotes and real-life situations if possible—the impact of a VFH or VCA grant on your museum; the effect of your child's participation in a school/museum program; the uniqueness of an organization's cultural programming; the participation of an institution in vital research.
- Acknowledge the difficulty in stretching the state's resources to address all of its needs. Point out that support for museums and the arts should be considered an investment in an economic and educational resource which will provide a positive return.
- Offer to serve as a resource for information, contacts with the museum community, and so on. Leave your business card or other contact information.
- Thank him/her for his/her time and consideration. Ask for their support for your issue one more time.

LINK ADVOCACY AND PROGRAM DEVELOPMENT FOR THE LONG TERM

Advocacy and program development are intertwined; neither ever really stops for dynamic programs. They build success on success, momentum on momentum, and advocacy is the engine that drives much of their dynamic progress. The New York State Archives is an interesting example. New York was the last major state to establish a state archives, in 1975. Its program was later recognized as one of the strongest and best models in the nation, but it took two decades of leadership, advocacy, and work to reach that result. The program devoted considerable resources to advocacy, regarding it as a good investment even when it meant that other things, such as processing its holdings, might have moved faster if the resources were invested there. One of its programs, services to local governments, achieved several break-throughs, including a modern local records law and a law establishing a surcharge on local document filing fees which supported advisory staff in regional offices and a competitive grants program. Its strategies included: [27]

> *Operating from a vision of greatness.* The leaders of the program, particularly Larry J. Hackman, State Archivist from 1981 to 1995, who led the Archives' development and advocacy efforts, were not content with a program that would be under-resourced and generally accepting of the status quo. They were determined to build a model program distinguished by its engagement with both problems and opportunities. They had faith in such strategies as analysis and reporting, consultation to build networks and support, and building momentum resulting from early successes.
>
> *Articulating a clear agenda.* The Archives developed comprehensive, detailed analytical reports based on surveys and analysis, in consultation with its customer base, to develop an action agenda. A 1984 comprehensive report, *Toward a Usable Past: Historical Records in the Empire State*, carefully written and edited and illustrated to make it an eminently readable document, set forth an agenda for state and local government records and non-government historical records programs. A section on "Historical Records and Social Needs" discussed the multiple values of historical records.
>
> *Developing program services that meet or exceed customer needs.* The program was extremely customer-responsive. It superseded an emphasis on legal record preservation requirements with a program that was mostly advisory services and assistance with emphasis on developing comprehensive, adequately supported local programs. Staff in regional offices provided advice and assistance customized to local governments' priorities and needs.
>
> *Organizing customers as advocates.* A mutually respectful partnership was the key to successful advocacy. An expansionist State Archives allied with associations of local officials who valued the program's responsive services and had effective offices in Albany for lobbying the governor and legislature. Activist local officials were appointed to the Local Government Records Advisory Council, established in law to advise the Archives and approve grants. Politically astute Council members doubled as advocates for the program.
>
> *Securing the support of powerful leaders.* The Archives strengthened support of its parent agency, the State Education Department, through initiatives to encourage educational use of historical records, and careful consultation with department leadership and the state board of Regents, which oversees the department. It cultivated relationships with leaders in the legislature.
>
> *Providing continual information and publicity.* The Archives issued many reports and a quarterly newsletter, *For the Record*, which kept the archival and local government communities apprised on services, issues, and the status of legislative proposals. Each issue focused attention on a local government official or program that was doing exemplary work. The Local Records unit issued its own, more detailed

newsletter, *In the Field*, recognizing model programs in the regions. The Archives issued multiple press releases. It sent information to local government associations for their newsletters, and staff made presentations or presented workshops at every major association meeting.

A HIGH-VISIBILITY PUBLIC HISTORY ADVOCATE

Advocacy work at the institutional level is strengthened by overarching advocacy work at the state and national levels. Associations like AASLH, the Organization of American Historians, National Council on Public History, and the American Alliance of Museums, and state counterparts, issue advocacy materials and organize advocacy efforts for specific initiatives (e.g., lobbying for government grants programs). But more is needed to keep the benefits of history, and programs for its preservation, in the arena of public debate.

An excellent model, from an allied field, is the American Library Association's online "Advocacy University," with links to many advocacy tools and resources that can be easily modified and used for history programs. It emphasizes the development of tools and strategies in key areas such as demonstrating value, describing and dramatizing challenges, and building coalitions.[28]

Another useful model is *Historica Canada*, a nonprofit organization dedicated to creating informed, active citizens through greater knowledge, appreciation and pride in Canadian history.[29] The organization uses public opinion research and online and television resources to inspire Canadians to learn about their nation's past. It advocates for teaching Canadian history in public schools. Its "Encounters with Canada" program brings over a hundred Canadian youth to Ottawa each week during the school year to learn about Canadian history and identity. It is a chance for the students to "discover their country through each other, learn about Canadian institutions, meet famous and accomplished Canadians, explore exciting career options, develop their civic leadership skills and live an extraordinary bilingual experience." The "Citizenship Challenge" program lets classes answer questions that are based on the actual guide that immigrants use to study for their Canadian citizenship test. Its "Heritage Minutes" productions on television and online recall high points of Canadian history. It supports the online *Canadian Encyclopedia*, which it describes as "the most authoritative and comprehensive reference of all things Canadian." The ongoing "Memory Project" chronicles Canada's military history from World War I to the present through oral interviews and digitized versions of documents and artifacts. The personal stories reinforce the theme of Canadian identity and sacrifice. Other programs cover Canada's original peoples and the experience of minorities.

"Passages Canada" is a diverse group of immigrants and refugees who volunteer to share their experiences of coming to Canada with youth and community groups. *Historica Canada* has a patriotic, promotional agenda. "The qualities of what it means to be Canadian are at the heart of everything we do," said Anthony Wilson-Smith, president of the organization.[30] Its programs demonstrate the multiple values of history in charting the origin and evolution of political institutions, documenting shared sacrifice and collective will in building communities and a nation, and instilling young people with historical understanding that will help them become responsible citizens and participants in public affairs. The programs appeal broadly to the public, reinforcing the value of history and the role of historical programs.

A HISTORY BILL OF RIGHTS

As one strategic approach to advocacy, some public history programs have tried to develop statements that confirm government's minimum responsibilities to preserve and disseminate history on behalf of the people. The Pennsylvania Historical and Museum Commission developed and adopted this statement in 2010 and has arranged for its adoption by history programs around the state. (http://www.portal.state.pa.us/portal/server.pt/community/public_programs/1586/pa_history_bill_of_rights/694399)

THE PENNSYLVANIA HISTORY BILL OF RIGHTS

The Pennsylvania History Bill of Rights (PHBR) is based upon provisions of the Constitution of the Commonwealth of Pennsylvania and on the requirements of the History Code. During spring 2010 visitors to Pennsylvania historic sites and museums, thousands of Pennsylvania citizens, viewed the draft PHBR and ranked its provisions. The PHBR was formally adopted by the Pennsylvania Historical and Museum Commission on March 17, 2010.

A RESOLUTION TO ADOPT THE PENNSYLVANIA HISTORY BILL OF RIGHTS

Whereas understanding Pennsylvania's history is key to understanding America's history, and

Whereas Section 27 of Article I of the Constitution of Pennsylvania makes the Commonwealth trustee for the preservation of the historic values of the environment, and

Whereas, the irreplaceable historical, architectural, archaeological and cultural heritage of this Commonwealth should be preserved and protected for the benefit of all the people, including future generations, and

Whereas, the preservation and protection of historic resources in this Commonwealth promotes the public health, prosperity and general welfare, and

Whereas, it is in the public interest for the Commonwealth, its citizens and its political subdivisions to engage in comprehensive programs of historic preservation for the enjoyment, education and inspiration of all the people, including future generations, and

Whereas many individuals and organizations across the Commonwealth are working diligently to make sure that history is not lost, and

Therefore, be it resolved on this date _____ that we, _____ join with other heritage and cultural organizations across the Commonwealth to recognize and adopt the following Pennsylvania History Bill of Rights as guiding principles for our organization reflecting the needs and expectations of Pennsylvania's citizens in preserving and sharing Pennsylvania's heritage:

*Students in Pennsylvania schools understand Pennsylvania's history in the context of local, national and world events.

*Pennsylvania maintains a competitive position as a premier tourism destination for heritage travelers.

*Pennsylvania citizens have access to the current records of government and the permanently valuable documents which tell the history of the Commonwealth.

*Current and future generations are assured that Pennsylvania's historical resources are preserved for their enjoyment and use.

*Pennsylvania's museums, historical societies, and historic sites receive adequate public and private support to maintain high standards of stewardship and public access.

*Pennsylvania's communities retain the historic character and distinctiveness that are essential to attracting and retaining residents, businesses, and visitors.

NOTES

1. Lewis Bellardo, "Observations on Thirty Years of Advocacy," in Larry J. Hackman, ed., *Many Happy Returns: Advocacy and the Development of Archives* (Chicago: Society of American Archivists, 2011), 86–106.

2. Howard Adam Levy, "Branding Basics for Nonprofits" (November 30, 2009). http://npbrandit.com/articles/nonprofit-best-practices/branding-basics-for-nonprofits.

3. American Alliance of Museums, *Advocacy for Museum Matters* (2014). http://www.aam-us.org/advocacy/resources/advocacy-for-museums-matter.

4. American Alliance of Museums, *Did You Know?* (2014). http://www.aam-us.org/advocacy/museums-advocacy-day.

5. Museum Association of New York, *New York State's Museums: Building Community* (2010). http://manyonline.org/2010/11/new-york-states-museums-building-community.

6. Johns Hopkins Center for Civil Society Studies, *What Do Nonprofits Stand For? Renewing the Nonprofit Value Commitment* (2012). http://ccss.jhu.edu/wp-content/uploads/downloads/2012/12/What-Do-Nonprofits-Stand-For_JHUCCSS_12.2012.pdf.

7. The essays are available at http://www.winthropgroup.com.

8. John T. Seaman Jr. and George David Smith, "Your Company's History as a Leadership Tool," *Harvard Business Review* 90 (December 2012), 45–52.

9. "American Heritage Editors and Readers Urge Political Leaders to Heed Lessons of History and Compromise on Debt Ceiling" (July 25, 2011). http://www.americanheritage.com/about/press-releases/american-heritage-editors-readers-urge-political-leaders-heed-history-compromise-debt-ceiling-negotiations.

10. Council of State Archivists, *Valuing and Protecting Local Government Records* (2008). http://www.statearchivists.org/lga/LGA%20Case%20Stmt%20Aug%202010.pdf.

11. Michael C. Reis and David Weisman Jr., "The Historian's Valuable Role as Expert and Advisor in Environmental Litigation," *The Environmental Litigator* 22 (Spring 2011). http://www.historyassociates.com/wp-content/uploads/2012/06/199.pdf.

12. History Associates, *The Business Case for Archives: How History Can Bolster Your Bottom-Line* (2013). http://www.historyassociates.com/wp-content/uploads/2013/05/Business-Case-for-Archives.pdf.

13. Bruce W. Dearstyne essays in Albany *Times Union* Sunday "Perspective" section, 2009–2014. http://www.timesunion.com.

14. Gregory Sanford and Tanya Marshall, "Managing Change at the Vermont State Archives: A Continuing Issue," in Bruce W. Dearstyne, ed., *Leading and Managing Archives and Records Programs: Strategies for Success* (New York: Neal-Schuman, 2008), 207–226.

15. Jennifer McCrea and Jeffrey C. Walker, *The Generosity Network: New Transformational Tools for Successful Fund-Raising* (New York: Deepak Chopra Books, 2013), 11–71.

16. Edie Hedlin, "What the Case Studies Tell Us," in Hackman, ed., *Many Happy Returns,* 298.

17. Museum Association of New York and Museumwise, *The Challenge of "Value:" Engaging Communities in Why Museums Exist* (2011). http://manyonline.org/sites/default/files/pages/%3Cem%3EEdit%20Basic%20page%3C/em%3E%20Museums%20and%20the%20Economy/2011-The-Challenge-of-Value.pdf.

18. Workshop questions and strategies are quoted from ALA Office for Library Advocacy, *Developing Your Advocacy Plan* (2014). http://www.ala.org/advocacy/sites/ala.org.advocacy/files/content/advleg/advocacyuniversity/advclearinghouse/04-making_your_advocacy_plan.pdf.

19. Minnesota Historical Society, *Legacy Amendment* (2014). http://legacy.mnhs.org/legacy-amendment3.

20. *Minnesota History: Building a Legacy* (2014). http://legacy.mnhs.org/sites/legacy.mnhs.org/files/pdfs/mhs_legacy_report_2014.pdf.

21. Americans for the Arts—National Arts Marketing Project, "The Experts' Guide to Marketing the Arts" (2010), Practical Lesson 1 and Practical Lesson 8. http://www.artsmarketing.org/resources/practical-lessons/practical-lessons.

22. PA Museums, "PMHC Testifies at House Tourism and Recreation Committee Meeting" (Spring 2012). http://www.pamuseums.org/site/showpage.asp?page=24.

23. National Arts Marketing Project, "How to Market Milestones for Your Organization" (June 27, 2013). http://www.artsmarketing.org/resources/article/2013-06/how-market-milestones-your-organization.

24. National Council of Nonprofits, *The Faces of the Nonprofit Sector* (2013). http://www.councilofnonprofits.org/americas-nonprofits/faces-nonprofit-sector.

25. "On the Same Team: A Conversation with Mayor Scott Smith" and Lisa Anderson, President and CEO, Mesa Historical Museum, "Reinventing the Mesa Historical Museum," *Museum* (May/June 2014), 56–61.

26. Virginia Association of Museums, *Tools for Effective Advocacy* (2011). http://www.vamuseums.org/displaycommon.cfm?an=1&subarticlenbr=32.

27. Bruce W. Dearstyne, "Leadership, Advocacy, and Program Development: Transforming New York's Local Government Records Program, 1981–1995," in Hackman, ed., *Many Happy Returns: Advocacy and the Development of Archives*, 138–160. The author was one of the leaders of this effort.

28. American Library Association, *Advocacy University*. http://www.ala.org/advocacy/advocacy-university.

29. *Historica Canada.* https://www.historicacanada.ca.

30. Historica- Dominion Institute Renamed Historica Canada" (July 2, 2013). https://www.historicacanada.ca/node/3216.

Chapter Seven

Strategic Planning

PLANNING MEANS CHANGE

Conducting a strategic planning process can provide an opportunity for thinking about the status and future of the program. It can provide an assessment, identify what is working well and should continue, point out what is obsolete and should be dropped, and inspire new approaches. Strategy is more than just knowing *what* to do; it is also about deep understanding of *how* to do it. Undertaking a new strategic plan is advantageous when:

- The current plan is five or more years old and has not been revisited or revised since it was written.
- The program seems to be drifting without a clear enough sense of purpose or goals.
- There is a major change in leadership, for instance, a new director or a substantial number of new board members.
- The program is facing, or has just weathered, a crisis (e.g., a major reduction in its budget).
- Visitorship and other forms of public engagement are declining.
- The program is a department of an institution such as a corporation or university that has acquired new leadership and/or is branching out or moving into new areas or in new directions, and so the program also needs to change.
- The institution is in a geographic area where the economy is shifting, the demographics are changing, and the program seems out of touch with younger people or residents in the vicinity.

Strategic Planning Is Hard, Sometimes Stressful, Work

It requires energy, commitment, and confidence in the people involved with the program. It necessitates lots of conversations and discussions, some of them possibly uncomfortable because some good ideas just can't be accommodated because of the hard realities of resource and time constraints. It makes it necessary to involve a broad range of stakeholders, including trustees/boards of directors and staff, in a way that welcomes and values everyone's input, includes a process for sorting through ideas, and makes final decision-making authority—what actually makes it into the plan—clear. Planning of necessity often pushes people out of their comfort zones into new, unfamiliar territory. It means difficult decisions and choices—choosing to carry out one activity, for instance, the promotional and social media work discussed in chapter 5, which is very much in vogue these days, may mean postponing, curtailing, or even eliminating other activities which the program has long proudly supported.

Planning Needs to Include Asking Hard Questions

The planning process is an opportunity to discuss discomforting questions, including even whether the program has the leadership, will, resources, facilities, and mission to continue. The Museum Association of New York's museum planning guidelines suggest that there may be alternatives to starting up a new museum. Their suggestions might also be alternatives to consider at the beginning of a strategic planning process for an established program: [1]

> Becoming the programming committee for another museum or heritage organization. "You get to do all the fun stuff of research, creation and information sharing without the care and feeding of a legally incorporated organization to worry about."
>
> Focusing on important initiatives, such as documenting your community's history through oral histories, photos, and videos, and giving them to a local program or posting them online.
>
> Organizing public events such as history fairs or cultural festivals. This focuses the public's attention on the sources and excitement of history and may also encourage public support of other institutions and programs.
>
> Becoming advocates for heritage, preservation, and museum programs to help them achieve and maintain robust budgets—"cheerleaders who are ready and willing to press the case for support."
>
> Volunteering at other museums and heritage organizations. "You can do a lot to help these organizations stay strong or get healthy."
>
> Fundraising for museums and heritage organizations or for collections housed in them or at local libraries.

Developing a partnership (e.g., two programs sharing a common physical facility).
Merging with another program.

Only a few programs are likely to consider discontinuing operations or merging. But assuming a determination to continue, planning for any program needs to face the realities of the need for resources and clearly defined priorities. Recent plans that are useful as models reflect this in their goals. The Vermont Historical Society, for instance, in its "Statement of Values" includes among others:[2]

> *Ingenuity*: The Vermont Historical Society applies its limited resources in innovative ways to maximize the effectiveness of its programs and the efficiency of its operations.
> *Collaboration*: The Vermont Historical Society is a valued partner with cultural organizations, educational institutions and the State of Vermont.

The Oregon Historical Society's strategic plan, developed in 2011 after beginning to recover from several years of severe budget reductions, listed five goals. The first two related to programs. The other three related to resources:[3]

> 3. Create a stable, sustainable and secure financial condition through debt reduction, increased endowment, and revenue enhancement to ensure a balanced budget.
> 4. Create a plan for realizing the usage potential of OHS real estate holdings that anticipates needs and opportunities in using space to achieve organizational goals.
> 5. Align organizational resources to successfully implement the strategic plan.

Plans Should Be Bold and Grab Attention

Strategic planning is a high-visibility, high-stakes undertaking. Going through the process is evidence of the organization's earnest commitment to self-examination, keeping up with the times and strengthening its services. A plan is more than a roadmap—it needs to be a public relations document, a beacon for supporters, a convincing document for advocates, and a source of inspiration for staff. Jim Collins, co-author of *Built to Last: Successful Habits of Successful Companies* and author of *Good to Great and the Social Sectors*, contends that plans need to be attention-grabbing, vivid, even dramatic. He coined the term "BHAG's"—"Big, hairy, audacious goals"—to urge planners to move beyond thinking too small and use planning to create a sense of urgency. It's not about sloganeering or wordsmithing, which renders so many plans bland and uninspiring. "It is about picking a goal that will stimulate change and progress and make a resolute commitment to it. This is

not about writing a 'mission statement.' This is about going on a mission!"[4]
He recommends taking a moment to have everyone involved in a planning
session write an article that they would love to see published about the
program fifteen years from now; distill 3–5 of the most vivid snippets into
vivid descriptions that bring the envisioned future to life. Some tests that he
poses:

> Does the vivid description conjure up pictures and images to bring the
> vision to life, rather than bland platitudes?
> Does it express passion, intensity, and emotion?
> When reading the vivid description, do you think "Wow, it would be really
> fantastic to make all this happen. I would really want to be part of that,
> and I'm willing to put out significant effort to realize this vision!"?
> Is the BHAG clear, compelling, and easy to grasp?
> Will this BHAG be exciting to a broad base of people in the organization,
> not just those with executive responsibility?
> Will achieving the BHAG require a quantum step in the capabilities and
> characteristics of the organization?

Pushing for BHAG's "gets you out of thinking too small . . . and simultaneously creates a sense of urgency. . . . [I]t's a mechanism to stimulate
progress," Collins explains. Leaders enjoy pushing themselves and their organizations toward greatness even though sometimes it jars people's complacency. "You have to enjoy that sense of extended discomfort. It's the quest,
it's the training, it's the growth, it's pushing yourself."[5]

LEADING THE PLANNING PROCESS

Don't Go It Alone

There are lots of guidelines and models that can assist with strategic planning. Two widely used assessment tools can help. One is built around management pioneer Peter F. Drucker's list of "Five Most Important Questions,"
which are: *What Is Our Mission? Who Is Our Customer? What Does the
Customer Value? What Are Our Results? What Is Our Plan?* The "Five Most
Important Questions Assessment Tool" is available for purchase from the
Hesselbein Institute, a program dedicated to strengthening the management
of not-for-profit organizations.[6] A more extensive assessment tool, available
free online, is the McKinsey & Company's *Effective Capacity Building in
Nonprofit Organizations.*[7] It provides a framework for assessing and
strengthening in seven areas: aspirations, strategies, organizational skills,
human resources, systems and infrastructure, organizational structure, and
culture. Any strategic plan should be compiled with an intention to meeting
(and if possible exceeding) relevant professional standards and state accredi-

tation benchmarks.[8] Looking outside the United States and Canada can sometimes be helpful (see "Planning: Three Perspectives from Beyond the United States"). There are excellent publications with practical advice on developing effective plans.[9] Plans developed by other historical programs that are recognized for leadership and innovation can also be useful sources and models.

PLANNING: THREE PERSPECTIVES FROM BEYOND THE UNITED STATES

Sometimes we can gain fresh perspective on museum and history program planning from looking at how it is handled in other countries. Three examples:

- Te Papa National Services, *Developing a Strategic Plan.* 2001. Published by the National Museum of New Zealand, the document discusses how to achieve a vision but also manage through the steps required to develop a plan. (http://www.tepapa.govt.nz/sitecollectiondocuments/tepapa/nationalservices/pdfs/resourceguides/governance/stratplan.pdf)
- Museums Australia, *Strategic Planning Manual.* 1998. Particularly helpful for small to modest sized programs. (http://www.collectionsaustralia.net/sector_info_item/67)
- *National Standards for Australian Museums and Galleries.* 2013. Produced by a consortium of cultural organizations, the document sets forth overarching standards in three areas—Managing the Museum, Involving People, and Developing a Significant Collection—and describes detailed principles and "supporting standards" under each one. (http://www.mavic.asn.au/assets/NSFAMG_v1.3_2013.pdf)

Aim for Modest Timeframe

In the past, strategic plans were often long-term (5 years +), detailed, and long. That worked in some cases, but in this era where programs need to be more nimble, agile, and responsive, it is more useful to think of strategic plans as roadmaps rather than detailed blueprints. The plans cited below are good examples. Keeping them shorter-term (3 years or less) is a way of keeping them fresh. Making them more broad-brush and general provides the opportunity to flesh them out as you go along, in at least three ways. One, annual plans based on the strategic plan which lay out in a fair amount of detail what the program aims to accomplish in the next twelve months. Two, the sorts of ad hoc, opportunistic, iterative projects and initiatives described in chapter 3 are vehicles to probe and test new ideas consistent with the strategic plan but not necessarily spelled out in it. Three, a less detailed plan provides more opportunity (and hopefully more incentive) for individual staff to advance their own creative ideas, also described in chapter 3.

Broad Involvement but a Managed Process

Strategic planning needs to solicit input and suggestions for a broad range of stakeholders, including staff, customers, trustees, and others. But one person—almost always the director—needs to be clearly in charge with responsibility for making decisions about what goes into the plan (even if final approval rests, as it usually does, with trustees and directors). The director will also have the main responsibility for carrying out the plan. The information-gathering, analysis, and decision-making processes and responsibilities need to be spelled out, and clearly understood by everyone involved, before the process begins. Longstanding planning methodology advocates investigation and discussion of issues in four areas—*Strengths*, *Weaknesses*, *Opportunities*, and *Threats*, sometimes abbreviated as SWOT—as input into the strategic plan. A few potentially helpful questions:

Strengths:

- What advantages and outstanding capabilities does our program have?
- What does the program do particularly well?
- How can we make the best use of the experience, expertise, and know-how of long-time staff members and volunteers?
- How can we capitalize on the fresh experience/talents of the people we recently hired and those we intend to hire or volunteers we expect to recruit?
- How well developed is our capacity for fostering creativity and translating it into innovation and development of new services?
- How is our program regarded in our professional field?

Weaknesses:

- What does our program do badly or not at all?
- Where do the executives or resource allocators in the program's parent organization or key supporter (e.g., local government) seem least satisfied, most dissatisfied, or just not well informed?
- What are areas where its customers express dissatisfaction and/or ask for improvements?
- What are the gaps in our capabilities and how are they hurting us?

- How can we identify and make the best use of information technologies in our work?

Opportunities:

- What changes in lifestyle, demographics, social patterns, workers' expectations, and so on are likely to affect us?
- What unarticulated or unfulfilled customer needs can we help define, clarify, and address?
- What changes in technology are available that could enhance the program's capabilities?
- Are there upcoming events (e.g., commemorations, holidays, celebrations) that we can use to draw attention to the value of history and our program?
- What opportunities exist for partnerships and cooperative projects?

Threats:

- What obstacles does the program face; how serious are they?
- Are there any potential competitors—for collections, resources, or audience—on the horizon?
- Are changes in technology threatening our services (e.g., people bypass us and get their historical information from *Wikipedia* or other online sources)?
- Is the program overspending its budget or has it made commitments that it cannot afford?
- How will we deal with the impending retirement of key staff?
- Are there likely to be budget reductions in our parent organization or key financial source (e.g., local government) that may lead to downsizing of our program?

Elements in the Plan

Strategic plans come in many lengths, configurations, and varieties. But most plans should have these features:

A statement of purpose indicating why the plan was developed and what purposes it is intended to serve.

The process of development, including who worked on the plan, how input was sought, and who wrote and approved the final version.

The timeframe and monitoring should be spelled out—how long the plan covers, how often it will be revisited and evaluated (e.g., annually, when annual program and employee work plans are prepared), and what provision will be made for revising or superseding it as the period it covers ends.

The assumptions and guiding principles that guided its formulation. This might include selections, or a summary of key points, from the SWOT analysis referenced above. It should set forth the assumptions and principles that the plan's developers had in mind as they developed it.

The importance of the program's work should be summarized for two reasons: one, as a reminder to staff, trustees, and others how important the work (and therefore, the plan) is; two, as a message to an external audience, including resource providers and potential visitors and supporters, about what is at stake.

The program's mission, the fundamental purpose or reason that the program exists.

The vision—the endgame, what the program would look like if all its goals were achieved.

Goals—concrete, measurable, attainable milestones. Often, these are the most important part of a plan because they represent the bottom-line expression of what the program is committing to achieve. In general, the goals should be written in such a way that if the program achieved them, it would accomplish its vision. Goals have several characteristics: (1) relevance and criticality—obviously appropriate for the program and of sufficient scope and gravitas to merit being included as a goal; (2) results oriented—stated in terms of specific expected outcomes; (3) attainable—the program has the capability to achieve them even if they are aspirational or "stretch" goals; (4) timeframe—the time within which the results are to be obtained; and (5) measurable—means for measuring accomplishment.

Objectives—intermediate steps on the way to goals. The objectives need to be carefully aligned with goals; if all the objectives are accomplished, then in effect, the goal is reached.

Strategies—the "how we will get it done" part of the plan—may appear at the *Goals* or *Objectives* level or elsewhere in the plan. This reflects most directly the "strategic" part of the work, how the program expects to accomplish what is outlined in the plan.

Budget implications, a discussion of what the work is expected to cost and where the resources will come from.

Measurement and reporting provisions, including how outcomes or impacts will be measured and provision for reporting on progress on the plan.

PLANNING IN ACTION

Few strategic plans are likely to have every one of the elements described above. But the most successful ones convey a sense of thoughtful process, aspirations, and determined commitment to service. Several recent plans are described below. They have three things in common: (1) change was usually forced on the program, often by financial exigencies, but the program resiliently embraced change and put it to work; (2) effective leadership shaped the plan, sometimes taking a number of years to get it right, and provided for its execution; and (3) the institutions are determined to be visibly different, stronger, and more robust because of their plans.

Using Planning to Embrace the Community

Planning can be an opportunity to build broader or deeper connections with the community and audience the program serves and wishes to engage in the future. The Tolland (Connecticut) Historical Society's plan begins with a vision of making it a "vibrant, vital, and visible community organization" that will be a "must join" institution that "not only brings local history to life" for local residents "but [also] that intimately connects to them on a personal level." The plan has provision for creating "a more active membership and volunteer corps" for "embracing new ideas and concepts, developing inclusive history programming," and also supporting expanded fundraising and development initiatives.[10]

Using Planning to Bounce Back Resiliently from Hard Times

Hard times are good times to take stock, regroup, revisit mission, and brainstorm new ideas for moving ahead. Unquestioned assumptions about mission and priorities can be brought out into the open and debated. Options that were beyond consideration in the past can be examined anew for possible viability. The recession that began in 2008 diminished the budgets and programs of many historical programs. The budgetary shock led to something of a forced reconsideration of which programs to keep, which ones to scale back, and which ones might be discontinued altogether.

The Washington State Historical Society, for instance, entitled its 2009–2011 planning and budget document "Reflecting the New Reality" and set forth two striking goals: emerge as a more valuable organization, and use the crisis as an opportunity to reset and refocus. Broad strategies were developed, for instance leverage strengths, including its reputation and role as the state's flagship museum, its rich historical collections, its track record in women's history, the leadership experience and capacity of its senior staff, and the creativity of its workforce; "protect the brand" through statewide programs, in cooperation with other organizations where possible; shifting promotional emphasis to radio, cable TV, and trade publications; and developing social networking to expand "marketing" of the Society's programs. The plan focused resources on what the Society identified after analysis as "lines of business that have the greatest strategic value"—museum exhibits, Web presence, and statewide outreach.

It began to implement "strong cost-control mechanisms," including cutting back hours to "maximize audience capture rates" and "eliminate or repurpose fading programs." Internal management innovations including encouraging translation of creative ideas into innovative practices and empowering teams to move ahead expeditiously with exhibit design and development of the Society's website. The capstone strategy was identified as "keep the innovation pipeline full."[11] The Society instituted tighter management practices, including developing statistical performance measures. "Measuring our performance also demonstrates our relevance," said one report, a message intended for the governor, legislature, and beyond, to the people of the state to reinforce the theme of tighter, more efficient management. The Society provides "unparalleled cultural opportunities" but "it is [also] imperative that we make a difference in people's lives," says the Society, another reiteration of the theme of connecting individuals with history. The website's "performance measures" page provides data on multiple topics ranging from "percentage of artifact collections cataloged" through "number of attendees at traveling exhibits" and "good/excellent overall experience rating in the customer survey" to "good or excellent rating for cleanliness."[12]

Its strategic plan, developed in 2013, projected a vision of being the "constant champion for the value and utility of studying history" and a mission of collecting and presenting history that will make the Society "indispensable to the people of Washington and a vital part of state government." The goal for museum exhibits factored in partnerships and identified as performance measures "number of museum visitors; excellence ratings for exhibit quality, educational value, and entertainment value" in visitor surveys. The plan included a development and membership section that outlined a development plan intended to increase contributions 200 percent by 2017. Recognizing the prospect of continuing tight state budgets, it included as a performance measure "non-state income as a percentage of total operating budget and in absolute dollars. Marketing/public relations objectives included "establish and re-enforce organizational brand." Administrative objectives included more cooperative programs, stronger personnel management including employee performance plans, accountability expectations, and professional development.[13]

Using Planning to Reset Strategies

The Pennsylvania Historical and Museum Commission underwent a 50 percent reduction in state funding during the years 2008–2010. This shocking reduction jolted the Commission and its staff and occasioned, or forced, a thoroughgoing re-examination of programs and a shift in strategies. Jim Vaughan, hired as executive director in 2011, posed an uncomfortable question right after he arrived in Harrisburg: "What do we let go of and what do we hold onto?" He began making changes right away. Many of the state's historic sites had too many restrictive rules to be inviting venues for good learning experiences. "If you visit a site and the first things you are told are 'Don't touch' and 'Don't sit,' then all of our rules make the experience difficult to enjoy." We don't have to treat every object as though it were a Rembrandt, said Vaughan. Many of the sites were geared too much to the transient tourist trade. Vaughan said that the sites need to think more about servicing the communities where they were located. Many of the sites' employees, volunteers, and visitors came from the communities where the facilities were located, and so "we need to become more community-based resources." The Commission's emphasis shifted to more inviting, user-centric, visitor-friendly policies.[14]

Vaughan led a strategic planning process that determined to use hard economic realities as a springboard to a more vibrant future.[15] The plan set forth broad long-term goals to define a vision of the program for 2020 but matched the bold vision with carefully thought-out concrete strategies and tactics for 2012–2015. Under "Planning Assumptions," the plan noted an expectation of "predictable levels of state funding" but at well below the pre-2008 levels, necessitating a major push for private, foundation, and corporate support. The plan laid out activities to achieve tighter intellectual control over all collections and more careful, judicious collecting. It emphasized partnerships "to accomplish more with limited dollars" but also to gain new audiences and increase its appeal to potential donors. It committed to continued custody of sites with statewide significance but dramatically asserted an intention to transfer management or ownership of sites with more modest or local significance to local partners. The plan set forth a commitment to analyze current approaches to collection, stewardship, and interpretation and come up with new approaches "that differ fundamentally from the traditional practices of the past few decades."

Previewing a few of these, the plan identified improved electronic systems for collections management and interpretation, a more modular approach to exhibit production, and new ways of providing access including independent and user-centered learning experiences. Building on the plan as an advocacy document, Vaughan appeared before a legislative committee, as noted in chapter 6, to emphasize the value of investing in the Commission's programs. He noted that its budget was now one-tenth of one percent of the state's budget. The plan would ensure optimal use of those funds (e.g., asserting tighter control over holdings and reducing the collection by eliminating duplication). But he also described an initiative, based on the plan, to work with the Pennsylvania Heritage Foundation, the commission's not-for-profit fundraising partner, to get the non-state funds needed. [16] Planning did some heavy lifting in this case: make hard choices, drop some activities, strike out in new directions, and serve as a basis for appealing for resources.

A New Plan Dramatizes Relevance and Mission

Some historical programs use the strategic planning process to substantially expand their mission and alter the image they project. They aim for a transformation from a placid repository of artifacts and history exhibits to an exciting, visitor-focused dynamic center where people learn from the past, draw personal insights, interact with each other, and gain inspiration for how to change and shape their community's future. They position themselves as vital forums for discussion of community issues, including difficult contemporary problems. The planning documents read like more than just plans with goals and objectives; they are exciting, inspirational agendas reflecting bold aspirations for the future. They establish high, even soaring, expectations for the program and set the stage for garnering support from trustees, benefactors, and the community.

The Chicago Historical Society, for instance, expanded its public space and programs and rebranded itself the Chicago History Museum, a name change intended to convey a less elitist, more open and encompassing image. An extensive period of reflection by staff and a special Visioning Committee produced a dramatic new strategic plan, *Claiming Chicago, Shaping Our Future*, in 2008. [17] It identified these core values: discovery, creativity, empathy, authenticity, integrity, service, and collaboration. The planning document commits the program to encouraging creativity and translating new ideas into innovations—"the quality that allows us to take chances, try new things, and be original. Everything we do comes from a process of exploration, idea generation, and problem solving." The program will help people make personal connections: "We value the 'ah-hah' moment when a person makes a meaningful connection with the past, objects, ideas, Chicago, other people, and the world. . . . We will create experiences with history that are meaningful, memorable, and accessible—physically, cognitively, emotionally, culturally, and economically—to serve the diverse needs of our audiences."

Connecting with the past is not just for the traditional demographic and ethnic majority in the nation, another theme in the planning document and particularly appropriate for a vibrant, diverse city like Chicago. The document describes empathy as "the ability to see things from other people's perspectives and understand why that matters . . . work collaboratively and care about the stories of other people." The history needs to be "unembellished, unfiltered." A Museum staff member quoted in the plan said, "We help give voice to people's history. Telling their own story makes people see that they have some power." The museum's purpose is to "help people make meaningful and personal connections to history" and "add value and meaning to people's lives through history." Another dimension of the new mission is bringing perspectives from history to bear on civic issues, regarding "Chicago as an ongoing urban experiment."

Building on the values and commitments, the document boldly proclaims that "We claim Chicago." The Museum "will be fiercely Chicago" and "seek new ways to reflect the authentic voices of our communities." That assertion of relevance and deep connections within the city stakes out broad territory for the Museum. The plan also includes sections on resources, collaboration, staff development, and other aspects of the Museum's ongoing work. The plan has been the basis for an exciting series of public events and other initiatives over the past few years, for instance exhibits on:[18]

Lincoln's Chicago ("a dynamic young metropolis on the verge of greatness")

Unexpected Chicago ("reveals unexpected treasures of Chicago history a single artifact at a time")

Facing Freedom (the struggle for freedom in Chicago and elsewhere including civil rights, woman suffrage, and union activity)

Chicago: Crossroads of America ("Whether you are interested in Chicago's changing economy, challenging crises, diverse neighborhoods, groundbreaking innovations, or lively cultural scene, this exhibition is a must see!")

Planning to Make the Program More Inclusive and Inspire Historical Pride

A planning effort can be put to many uses, including transforming a moderately successful program into something more highly visible and putting it into the arena of promoting community identity and pride. The planning process needs to be managed to draw in lots of interested individuals and organizations, elicit good ideas, and shape something new and unprecedented. The government of Canada is using the countdown to the nation's 150th anniversary in 2017 to transform the Canadian Museum of Civilization to a new Canadian Museum of History. "Canadians deserve a national museum of history that tells our stories and presents our country's treasures to the world," said the Minister of Canadian Heritage and Official Languages in announcing the new initiative in 2012. The new museum will be much more

representative of the breadth and depth of Canadian history and life than the
current museum of civilization, he said. "Entire categories of endeavour—
politics, sports, culture and our contributions to the world, among others—
are poorly covered or not at all." The new museum would promote Canadian
unity and pride and strengthen its status as an international leader in culture
and history. "It's time for this country to think big," the Minister asserted.[19]

During 2012–2013, the Canadian Museum of Civilization, in cooperation
with the Canadian War Museum, held meetings around the country and also
mounted a crowdsourcing website, My History Museum, to stimulate conversations with Canadians and solicit feedback on how the new museum
should approach key issues—*What is the Canadian Story? Who has shaped
our country? Whose perspectives should be represented? What objects
should be included? What important historical events should be covered?
How can we make the museum work for everyone?* More than a thousand
people provided their ideas via the website.[20] In a related initiative, the
Parliamentary Standing Committee on Canadian Heritage launched "a
thorough and comprehensive review of significant aspects [of] Canadian
history" in 2013. The two initiatives provoked widespread, spirited discussion in the nation's historical community about the nature of Canadian history and the role of government in its interpretation. For instance, how would
the "first peoples," the original settlers, be treated? Would conflict and the
nation's participation in wars be used to promote nationalism? How would
the role of political parties be portrayed? The Canadian Historical Association called for "a balanced and non-partisan approach" to the parliamentary
study that would include consultation with professional historical associations.[21]

By early 2014, the Canadian Museum of Civilization had been renamed
the Canadian Museum of History but planning for its core program—the
Canadian History Hall—had just begun. Planners promised an exciting visitor experience built around exhibits and stories of seminal events, historically
important people, multiple perspectives on controversy and injustice, artifacts and documents, all adding up to "a journey through the Canadian experience." "Canada is a nation unlike any other," said the preliminary planning
document. "It is an inclusive, progressive, tolerant, multicultural nation
guided by principles of fairness and equality."[22] The new Museum's planning is geared toward conveying that perspective on Canadian history.

Plan to Tell a More Comprehensive Story

Some planning initiatives aim to broaden what the program covers, particularly in the area of neglected people or themes, and to make it more relevant
to current issues. The strategic plan of the National Museum of New Zealand
is a good example.[23] The plan committed the museum to innovation, "experi-

mentation that allows us to try new ideas and generate new knowledge, upon which we reflect and adapt our beliefs and actions, change behaviours, and enhance our performance." The plan tries to place the program at the center of public discussions, demonstrate its fairness, show its value, and establish it as a place for thoughtful deliberation about the past and contemporary issues. The plan committed to documenting diversity, "major traditions and cultural heritages" as a "statement of New Zealand's identity." It adopted a dramatic new vision: *Changing Hearts. Changing Minds. Changing Lives.* The document explains:

> In changing hearts, we provide experiences and encounters that are relevant, satisfying, emotional, and evoke a response.
> In changing minds, we provide experiences that provoke thought, reflection, and debate and facilitate social interaction.
> In changing lives, we provide experiences that improve the quality of life of individuals and communities and extend the impact of a visit beyond the Museum's doors.

The museum committed to exploring sensitive issues and the theme of conflict and its impact on people. It promised to become "a forum for the future. . . . As a cultural and intellectual leader, [the museum] will signpost pathways to the future by initiating, hosting, and engaging in debates that explore a wide range of contemporary issues." An important performance measure was stated as the "percentage of adult New Zealanders indicating they have learned something about New Zealand during their visits." At the same time, pursuing the plan, it shifted from being a site mostly intent on drawing visitors to its building in Wellington, the nation's capital, to one at the center of "a national collaborative network designed to meet the needs of multiple stakeholders."

Planning to Revitalize the Program

The New-York Historical Society, one of the nation's oldest and most prominent historical institutions, experienced severe financial problems in the 1990s and struggled to rebuild in the early years of the twenty-first century. [24] By 2004, when a new president and CEO, Louise Mirrer, took charge, the Society was still in the doldrums, its programs not widely known even in its home city, its research holdings underutilized, and its mission blurry. Mirrer undertook a fundraising and rehabilitation program to make the building's "forbidding exterior and inhospitable interior" much more inviting and user-friendly and, at the same time, led a strategic planning effort to forge a new future for the program. Its theme would be "New York in the nation"—American history as seen through the prism of New York City. The "Strategic Vision" plan described making the facility easier to navigate, adding an orientation film that would "recreate history and impart a sense of what it would have been like to participate in a given historical moment," expanding education programs and adding "Living History Days" for families, adding a new children's history museum in the facility, integrating technology, and changing exhibits designed to attract a broadened array of visitors.

The plan revitalized the Society's image, attracting a new and broader range of visitors though "extraordinary lectures, dynamic conversations and more." Its website notes that "the New-York Historical Society regularly plays host to the most eminent historians, writers and thinkers in the nation."[25]

Planning to Identify New Themes and Connections

Some planning efforts are undertaken to link history more imaginatively to heritage tourism and economic development, and to present history in a fresh way, different from the traditional era-by-era style. The New Jersey Heritage Tourism Task Force in 2010 derived a new vision: "enhance the image of New Jersey as a desirable destination with a rich history that played a vital role in our nation's growth; improve the state's economy through visitor spending, and contribute to the stewardship and sustainability of New Jersey's unique historic, cultural, and natural assets." Its mission included an intention to "offer compelling experiences that tell the stories of New Jersey's past, demonstrate the relevance and importance of the state's heritage today, and provide a foundation for future generations." The plan laid out imaginative strategies for managing state-owned heritage sites, initiating educational programs, developing heritage products, and building a strong marketing network.

The Task Force wanted a fresh view of state history to dovetail with heritage tourism. It commissioned a new essay on the history of the state from which themes could be created for use in historic site interpretations, the state historical marker program, heritage education curriculum, and tourism promotions. The essay presented six themes that captured the essence of the state's history but made ties to historic sites easy:[26]

> *New Jersey in Conflict*—New Jersey's pivotal role in the Revolutionary War began a military tradition that continues today
> *New Jersey at Work*—Industry and creative innovation shaped New Jersey and helped transform the world
> *New Jersey Land and Sea*—Making a living from the land and from the sea has long been part of life in the Garden State
> *New Jersey at Play*—New Jersey has a history of hosting vacationers seeking relaxation and inspiration

Many Faces of New Jersey—New Jersey's population has grown increasingly diverse from the first Native Americans to waves of immigrants from Europe and subsequently from all over the world

New Jersey by Design—New Jersey has a remarkable assembly of great design that is reflected in designed landscapes and planned communities, as well as in vernacular and high-style buildings of many architectural types

Planning to Connect with the New Demographics

The Valentine Richmond History Center underwent what its director, William Martin, called an "identity crisis" in the 1990s and early years of the twenty-first century. Founded in 1892, the program grew over the years to the point where it held over 1.5 million objects and substantial archival holdings. It had a large facility, encompassing a city block, and a superb location, just two blocks from Virginia's state capitol building. But its home city, Richmond, had changed from a placid place with a sense of nostalgia to a bustling urban center that was home to several Fortune 500 companies, robust cultural programs, and a population makeup of growing diversity. The History Center, with its traditional history exhibits, fell behind with "an aging donor base and a community that is radically changing generationally and ethnically." Attendance tapered off. In the early 1990s, a failed expansion program traumatized the Center. At one point, they were $10 million in debt, and the police were told to guard the collections because they might be needed as collateral to pay off the Center's creditors. Transformative change was needed.

The Center decided to use the guidance in the *Museums and Society 2034* report issued in 2008 by the Association of American Museums' Center for the Future of Museums. That report cautioned museums against clinging to traditional service models and defining audiences in the traditional mode of aging white visitors. Following the AAM's analysis produced some striking statistics for the History Center in a study it concluded in 2010. By 2025, 25 percent of Virginians will be over the age of 65, up from only 12 percent. But "Gen X'ers"—born from the early 1960s to the early 1980s—would become "the area's primary travelers, investors and decision makers," with different expectations for their cultural experiences from their older counterparts. Women will play an increasingly important role in both the family and civic life. By 2050, 1 in 4 Virginia residents will identify as Hispanic American. Within Richmond, while the majority of the population is aging, the youngest segment is growing rapidly and becoming more diverse. Housing values in Richmond were declining, leading to expectations of a population surge, but one that would make the demographic makeup even more diverse.

The demographic data raised difficult questions for the History Center about how to keep the program financially sound but meet scattered, inconsistent expectations that mirrored demographic, racial, and economic changes. "How do we serve our traditional donor base (the Greatest Generation) while developing new approaches for boomers and gen Xers and beginning to attract the attention, patronage and engagement of a younger and increasing non-white audience? Are there universal interests shared by these groups?" [27] The Center's plan, released in 2010, is striking for its determination to mirror the region's evolution. The introduction states its intention "to anticipate and engage changes in the area's culture and economy . . . a bridge for a museum, a community and a society in transition . . . recalibrate in order to remain viable, relevant, and proactive in a dynamic environment." [28] It aims to be appropriate for a future when a sizeable minority of the city's population has no personal connection to the city's history, a large part of the population is over 65, and a new generation of young professionals will be "active, diverse, technologically savvy and coming into their own as emerging leaders in the Richmond region."

The plan is up to the challenging task. Organized under four thematic headings—Campus (its facility), Collections, Community, and Connections—it projects continuing excellent history exhibits coupled with an expansive, high-visibility activist agenda. It sets forth its demographic analysis near the beginning of the plan, leaving no doubt of the change it is trying to fit. The plan envisions use of its facility as "a center for storytelling, civic conversations, community building and research" with an emphasis on "authentic experiences" based on the museum's collection of historical objects and documents. A highly interactive website was projected to allow broad access to the Center's holdings but also using "video and augmented reality" to allow people to experience the history of Richmond and its neighborhoods. An even bolder expectation was that the Center will "play an active role in community building throughout the region as it collaborates with local historical societies, strategically engaging the broader museum community and further establishes itself as a voice for Richmond's downtown and future growth." The plan envisions meeting everyone's expectations, within the limits of available resources:

> The wants and needs of the Richmond region will shift with its changing demographics: the Hispanic community, for example, will be interested in its own local history while the aging Boomer population will be concerned with accessibility. Generation X will seek family-friendly programming, and the Millennials will appreciate the ability to buy tickets, gift shop items and reproduction photographs online.

The plan is filled with activities to make the Center's programs responsive and relevant. It projects expanding digital conversion of paper archival documents, digital access to its collections, exploring third-party options such as *Flickr* and *Corbis* for broader dissemination. A development strategy was projected to particularly target baby boomers, a group with impressive financial resources and a desire to leave a legacy. A Public Awareness/Marketing Team will explore and develop appropriate partnerships and customize the Center's publicity to fit its various demographic segments. The whole plan is an embodiment of exciting aspirations, dynamic growth, and multiple initiatives to engage and partner with the community.

NOTES

1. Joan H. Baldwin, *What Comes First: Your Guide to Building a Strong, Sustainable Museum or Historical Organization (With Real Life Advice from Folks Who've Done It.)* Troy, NY: Museum Association of New York (2010). http://manyonline.org/2010/10/manys-latest-publication-what-comes-first.

2. Vermont Historical Society, *Towering Achievements: Vermont Historical Society Strategic Plan, 2013–2018* (2013). http://vermonthistory.org/images/stories/documents/VHS_Plan.pdf.

3. Oregon Historical Society, *Strategic Plan, 2011–2016* (2011). https://multco.us/file/15965/download.

4. Jim Collins, *Vision Framework.* http://www.jimcollins.com/tools/vision-framework.pdf.

5. Leigh Buchanan, "How to Achieve Big, Hairy, Audacious Goals," *Inc* (November 2012). http://www.inc.com/leigh-buchanan/big-ideas/jim-collins-big-hairy-audacious-goals.html.

6. http://www.hesselbeininstitute.org/tools/sat.

7. Venture Capacity Partners, *Effective Capacity Building in Nonprofit Organizations* (2001). http://www.vppartners.org/learning/reports/capacity/assessment.pdf.

8. For instance, the American Alliance of Museum's free online sources such as *Mission and Institutional Planning* and *Developing an Institutional Plan* and its publication *National Standards and Best Practices for U.S. Museums.*

9. For instance, Barry Lord et al eds., *Manual of Museum Planning: Sustainable Space, Facilities, and Operations* (Lanham, MD: Alta Mira Press, 2012), and Cinnamon Caitlin-Leguto, "DIY Strategic Planning for Small Museums," AASLH *Technical Leaflet* no. 242 (Spring 2008).

10. Tolland Historical Society, *Strategic Plan May 2012–May 2017* (2012). http://tolland-historical.org/about-us/strategic-plan.

11. Washington State Historical Society, *2009–2011 Budget: Reflecting the New Reality* (2009). http://www.washingtonhistory.org/files/library/Budget.pdf.

12. Washington State Historical Society, *Performance Measures* (2013). http://www.washingtonhistory.org/about/performance.

13. Washington State Historical Society, *2013–2017 Strategic Plan* (2013). http://www.washingtonhistory.org/files/library/Budget.pdf.

14. *Meet Jim Vaughan PHMC's New Executive Director* (January 19, 2012). http://www.portal.state.pa.us/portal/server.pt/community/about_the_phmc/1579/executive_director/259333.

15. Pennsylvania Historical and Museum Commission, *Summary of Strategic Plan, 2012-2015.* http://www.portal.state.pa.us/portal/server.pt/community/about_the_phmc/1579/strategic_plan_2012-2015/1249095.

16. *PHMC Testifies at House Tourism and Recreation Committee Meeting* (2013). http://www.pamuseums.org/site/showpage.asp?page=24.

17. Chicago History Museum, *Claiming Chicago, Shaping Our Future* (2008). http://www.chicagohs.org/documents/home/aboutus/CHM-ClaimingChicagoClaimingOurFuture.pdfIt.

18. Chicago History Museum, "Exhibitions" (2013). http://chicagohistory.org/planavisit/exhibitions.

19. Canadian Heritage, "Harper Government to Create the Canadian Museum of History" (October 16, 2012). http://www.pch.gc.ca/eng/1350400008284; "Former CEO Decries 'Parochial' Mandate for Renamed Museum," *Ottawa Citizen* (June 5, 2013). http://www.ottawacitizen.com/travel/proposed+history+mandate+rebranded+Canadian+Museum+Civilization/8484869/story.html.

20. "My History Museum" (2013). http://www.civilization.ca/myhistorymuseum.

21. Canadian Historical Association, "Canadian Historical Association Expresses Concerns, Insists on Professionalization of Commons Committee's Review of Canadian History" (May 10, 2013). http://www.cha-shc.ca/en/Advocacy_51/items/43.html.

22. Canadian Museum of History, *The Canadian History Hall Takes Shape* (Dec. 30, 2013). http://www.historymuseum.ca/newmuseum/the-canadian-history-hall-takes-shape.

23. Museum of New Zealand Te Papa Tongarewa, *Statement of Intent, 2013/14, 2014–15, 2015/16* (2012). http://www.tepapa.govt.nz/SiteCollectionDocuments/AboutTePapa/LegislationAccountability/Te.Papa.Statement.Of.Intent.2012-2015.pdf.

24. This discussion is based on Louise Mirrer, "Making History Matter: The New-York Historical Society's Vision for the Twenty-First Century," *Public Historian* 33 (August 2011), 90–98 and New-York Historical Society, *Strategic Vision* (2008). http://www.nyhistory.org/sites/default/files/N-YHS_Strategic_Plan.pdf.

25. New-York Historical Society, *Programs.* h ttp://www.nyhistory.org/programs.

26. New Jersey Heritage Tourism Task Force, *Linking Our Legacy to a New Vision: A Heritage Tourism Plan for New Jersey* (2010); and Howard L. Green, *The Contours of New Jersey History: An Essay for the Heritage Tourism Master Plan* (2010). http://www.njht.org/dca/njht/touring/master_plan_table_of_contents.html.

27. William Martin, "Practical Futurism: A Case Study," *Center for the Future of Museums* (June 14, 2011). http://futureofmuseums.blogspot.com/2011/06/practical-futurism-case-study.html. The *Museums and Society 2034* report is available at http://www.aam-us.org/docs/center-for-the-future-of-museums/museumssociety2034.pdf.

28. Valentine Richmond History Center, *Strategic Plan 2010.* http://www.richmondhistorycenter.com/sites/richmondhistorycenter.com/files/pictures/VRHCSP10StrategicPlanFINALdesigned.pdf.

Chapter Eight

The Historical Enterprise in Action

Previous chapters assessed conditions and discussed leadership, planning, and innovation. This one describes examples of notably dynamic programs that exemplify application of those strategies. These programs represent excellent models of the historical enterprise in action.

HISTORY MADE ENTERTAINING AND EDUCATIONAL

Some programs, particularly outdoor "living history" museums, go beyond engagement to make history positively entertaining, even fun, for visitors. They blend appeals as family vacation designations with in-depth presentations about history. They invite local school groups, actively solicit visitation from the surrounding geographical community, and also bring in heritage tourism. The Jamestown Settlement and Yorktown Victory Center in Virginia host a combined website, Historyisfun.org. "History is fun!" is their slogan.[1] They advertise "old fashioned fun and games" and assert that "historical summer themes [and] hands-on programs make history fun." The two sites are actually adjacent to the history they present—one is a few miles up the James River from where the original Virginia colony was established in 1607 and the other is near the site of the decisive victory that ensured American independence in 1781, Yorktown Battlefield, administered by the National Park Service—but the history they present is authentic and engaging. Located about 20 miles apart, they cooperate to present programs based around the theme "Experience the Beginning and End of Colonial America in a Single Day." It is exciting hands-on history with particular appeal for families and young people. "MAKE SOME HISTORY OF YOUR OWN" says the visitor brochure:

Step into the boots of ordinary soldiers and witness the Revolution from their perspective at the re-created Continental Army encampment [at Yorktown]. You can try on a military coat and hat, step into soldiers' quarters, visit the camp surgeon, and examine the quartermaster's area to discover the importance of managing supplies. You may even be recruited to join the artillery crew as they load—and fire—a replica weapon.

Costumed interpreters also explain what it was like to cross the Atlantic on a ship in the colonial period, demonstrate the realities of subsistence farming, and illustrate relations between European settlers and native Americans. The interpreters "not only share their stories, they also invite you to participate in their chores, explore their ships, try on their armor, cultivate their crops . . . get ready for some hands-on fun . . . History doesn't get more active than this!" Seasonal events include "Foods & Feasts of Colonial Virginia" in November and "A Colonial Christmas" in December. There are more traditional exhibits and learning experiences such as the "Jamestown's Legacy to the American Revolution" in 2013–2014. A few other features:

- A "History is Fun" video channel with videos welcoming visitors, a "Curator's Corner" describing interesting artifacts, and "videos that offer a glimpse back in time to Colonial customs, triumphs, and hardships."
- An *All about the Revolution* blog by staff members. Among the interesting recent entries: "Rosie the Riveter's Great-Great-Great Grandmother," "Revolutionary War Military Attire Was Less Than Uniform," "Jefferson's 'Wall of Separation' Between Church and State," and "Breaking News from Virginia: Colony Declares Itself Independent of Great Britain."
- Both sites have educational programs (e.g., Summer Teacher Institute for educators; curriculum materials tied to state and national standards including "Discovering Jamestown: An Electronic Classroom Adventure" which includes lesson plans, images and videos; on-site programs for student group visits; and staff who visit schools with "hands-on, inquiry-oriented outreach programs that bring history to life in your Virginia classroom").
- Both locations offer dramatic spaces that can be rented for private events, meetings, weddings, receptions, and special occasions and special "History-Is-Fun-For-Kids" events that include a themed hands-on presentation in a classroom, tour of the museum with your own guide, and then return to a private party room for a box lunch.
- The programs cooperate to manage a very active Facebook site where staff and visitors can post comments and photos. They keep changing technical applications with the evolution of technology (e.g., a pared-down version of the website for mobile phones).

Visitors are enthusiastic. "A series of artifact-packed rooms . . . delves into the lifestyles and traditions of the English, the Powhatan Indians and African cultures," noted a *Washington Post* columnist. "You can . . . stroll down a mock English land complete with tenements and barking dogs."[2]

The programs are administered by a foundation chartered by state government and governed by a board of trustees that includes the governor, other state officials, and private citizens. About 43 percent of its $15 million budget comes from state appropriations, the rest from admissions, sales at the gift shop, and other sources. The foundation's annual report emphasizes its value to the state. It reported 560,519 visitors in 2012, including 75 percent from out of state, who spent an estimated $107 million in the region. The two sites hosted visits by 269,718 Virginia students, and staff made presentations at 106 schools. Political leaders used the sites to showcase Virginia pride and history. The National Governors Association annual meeting included an event at Jamestown where Governor Robert F. McDonnell addressed his fellow governors from the deck of a replica of the *Susan Constant*, one of the ships that brought English colonists to Virginia in 1607.[3]

The program is dynamic, with strategic ambitions for the future. The Yorktown site is being transformed to become the American Revolution Museum, scheduled to open in 2016, with exhibits, videos, touch-screen computers, and other interactive presentations on the coming of the war, major battles, the homefront, and the early years of the new nation. The goal is for visitors to make a personal connection to the momentous events of the era. "These artifacts, when coupled with multisensory exhibits and hands-on, living-history programs, broaden each visitor's understanding of the past," said Foundation Executive Director Philip Emerson. They "create a physical and emotional link between the visitor and the men and women of 18th century America." The expansion is an excellent example of a public-private partnership. State funds are supporting most of the construction, but gifts and grants from individuals, corporations, and foundations are supporting much of the other costs, such as acquisition of artifacts, production of films, and educational programs.[4]

HISTORY AS DRAMATIC ADVENTURE

There are many ways of connecting people with history. At Conner Prairie Interactive History Park in Fishers, Indiana, visitors are promised that "look, don't touch" becomes "look, touch, smell, taste and hear." Conner Prairie is recognized as one of the most successful and engaging outdoor history sites in the nation. But it wasn't always that way. In 2000, after years of repetitious programs and declining enrollment, staff embarked on a series of in-depth, anthropological research studies to discover how much visitors were actually learning. They conducted post-visit interviews and surveys and analyzed comment cards, but also went much further, recording guest visits with audio and video recorders for analysis of how guests were actually interacting with interpreters. It became apparent that guests were not engaging museum staff and vice versa and that guests were experiencing minimal learning in most cases. Management began a massive change, borrowing good ideas from wherever they could find them, including theme parks, science museums, and even retail clothing operations. They developed new training programs, restructured how staff were deployed, and conducted extensive conversations about putting guests at the center.

The initiative developed into a new philosophy, called "Opening Doors," and a new vision: "Conner Prairie will set a new standard for living history interpretation. We will do this by establishing engagement as an essential component of good interpretation." Front-line staff became "ambassadors to the past and facilitators of learning experience," active engagers of "guests"—as visitors were now called—rather than just lecturers of information. The focus shifted from provider of education and conveyer of facts to provider of exceptional experiences to guests. Interpreters were trained in communications skills as well as content expertise. Attendance climbed. Guests felt welcome and engaged, and they learned history through talking with staff and engaging in activities as they strolled through "Prairietown," a restored village, the "Lenape Indian Camp" to learn about the area's first settlers, and the "Animal Encounters Barn" where they could get close to the animals. One guest noted in 2005 how much had changed since an earlier visit. "The last time we only watched everyone work but this time we were allowed to participate in everything."[5]

Conner Prairie goes even further in the area of dramatic re-enactments. In its "Follow the North Star" events, guests are invited to play the role of runaway slaves before the Civil War. "Become a runaway on the Underground Railroad, fleeing from captivity, risking everything for freedom," says the program description.

> *Follow the North Star* plays out as an intense, living drama where guests become actors on a 200-acre stage, running from slave hunters and working together to navigate the Underground Railroad to freedom. This powerful program brings to life a pivotal period of our nations' history, and shines a light on issues of social injustice that we still struggle with today in schools and workplaces across the country. . . . *Follow the North Star* is not for everyone. You should be prepared to take on the role of a runaway slave; you'll be walking outside on rough terrain in all kinds of weather, told to keep your eyes focused downward and spoken to in an abrupt manner. . . . You'll walk away with a lot to think about.[6]

The experience is realistic, vivid, moving. Equally as engaging is "1863 Civil War Journey: Raid on Indiana." It is based on an attack by Confederate general John Hunt Morgan on southern Indiana; Confederate soldiers destroyed rail lines, burned bridges, and plundered civilians' farms and horses. Guests walk into the recreated town of Dupont just after the raid and witness the destruction first-hand. They experience the raid through the experiences of a sixteen-year-old teenager who wrote of the raid as it happened and volunteered to join a militia unit which aided Union forces who repelled the invaders. Through engaging re-enactors who treat guests like potential recruits for the militia force, presentations that use audio, visual, and special effects technology, they explore a soldier's camp, participate in military drills, gather supplies for a local Soldier's Aid Society, and talk with average citizens who were experiencing the privations of war every day. A companion website provides extensive information on the historical raid and Indiana's role in the Civil War. "It's fun. It's flashy. It's a modern, hip way to learn history," said the *Indiana Business Journal.*[7]

New York Times museum expert Edward Rothstein called Conner Prairie "this endearingly strange place . . . a hybrid of historical society, amusement park, 19th century village, and high-tech theater" that "tries to tell history in a different way: not as fact but as experience." One outstanding feature, he noted, was the interpreters' attentiveness to the varied ages of visitors, an attempt to engage families in conversations and interactions, and an eagerness to share experiences. The park attempts to convey history not as a recitation of facts but as something lived, something that is reflected by people's experiences and understanding.[8]

ENGAGE THE COMMUNITY AND SCALE BACK TO ESSENTIALS

Some historical programs, caught between diminishing resources and overextended commitments to maintain historic structures, have made strategic, carefully considered retreats to sustainable core functions. The Southern Oregon Historical Society in Medford, Oregon, founded in the 1940s to save an endangered courthouse, grew over the next six decades to become the second-largest historical society in the state.[9] Programs grew to include facilities in three cities, including a farm with ten permanent structures, a large library and archives; 42 paid staff administered the programs; and the budget included $2.2 million annually from the county. But county support diminished and then stopped in 2007. Austerity measures, staff reductions, and closing facilities kept the program afloat temporarily, but by September 2009, the society was broke and had to suspend public operations. Society trustees and staff began an intensive community outreach campaign which revealed that lack of community engagement and support were the underlying reasons for the program's difficulties. There was a long list of complaints: the Society seldom sought community input, squandered county resources, spurned offers to volunteer, seldom changed exhibits in its historic house museums, and kept interesting collections in storage, out of view of visitors.

The society underwent a transformative process:

- New board members were recruited, people who were entrepreneurial, business-oriented, and experienced in leading large, complex organizations. The board worked hard at rebuilding relations with the county, including outlining plans to make the program a going concern. The county was supportive, short of restoring the past operating funds.
- The research library was reorganized and initially staffed by a corps of volunteers managed by an unpaid volunteer coordinator. A few months after it opened, the Society hired a professional librarian who built on the progress by making archives more accessible to visitors and launching a system for people to access them online.
- The Society moved to deaccession artifacts that did not fit within the museum's mission, and to develop a new collections policy to guide and focus future collections efforts.
- The Society leased the farmland to a local farmer and a seed company and diversified its offerings at the farm site to include a community garden, self-guided tours, special events, and a draft horse farming program, all staffed by volunteers.
- It reduced the size of its administrative offices and leased the extra space, first to an automobile dealership, and later to a children's hands-on activity center that had been looking for a new home.
- Some of the other buildings were leased, including one to a newly formed historical society in one of the cities which garnered local support, and the board decided to keep others closed to avoid operating expenses.
- The Society initiated a unique traveling exhibit, *History: Made by You*, with community participation in every phase of exhibit development, including selecting the topic, conducting the research, identifying the artifacts, and planning programs for public viewing and discussions.

As the partnerships broadened and deepened, the society built and improved its relationships with government entities, universities, businesses, nonprofits, and other organizations, creating "positive interdependence and new sources of earned income."

"We focus on services that are most relevant to the community," the society's director wrote in 2012. "We tailor opportunities to community interests." The momentum has continued, for instance, through programs for teachers and students and "History: Made by You" public forums that engage participants in discussions about changes in their community and how people have dealt with them. Through a contract with the Oregon Heritage Commission, the Society offers technical support ranging from cataloging and handling artifacts through marketing and board development, to heritage-based nonprofits in southern Oregon.[10]

NEW USES FOR A HISTORIC HOUSE

Alexander Ramsey was Minnesota's first territorial governor, its second state governor, a US Senator, and Secretary of State under President Rutherford B. Hayes. A capable businessman, he spent subsequent years in business pursuits and made a sizeable fortune in real estate development. He built a grand mansion in St. Paul in 1872, which passed down through his heirs and was deeded by his granddaughters upon their deaths in 1964, to the Minnesota Historical Society, which Ramsey had helped establish in 1849.[11] The splendid house had many furnishings dating back to the time of its construction and rich documentation from Ramsey's long career. The site operated on the traditional historic house model of guided tours and don't-touch exhibits for many years, with heavy funding from the state.

But from 1997 to 2007, the site experienced a 22 percent drop in attendance, and this decline, coupled with reductions in state funding during the recession, forced the MHS to close the site for all but seven weeks out of the year.[12] The building was structurally sound, its location in the city of St. Paul gave it proximity to other historical and cultural attractions, and there was plenty of parking nearby. But the Minnesota Historical Society, one of the most progressive and innovative in the nation, recognized that the site as it had been administered was no longer relevant or sustainable. Staff set out to reconceptualize and redevelop the site based largely on public input about historical themes and operational issues, determined to consider opinions from "both its biggest critics and its biggest fans." With a modest amount of state funding, they hired a team of consultants and established a steering committee that included representatives of the site's board of governors, but also a tourism expert and individuals representing St. Paul public schools, the city's African American and American Indian communities, and the site's neighbors.

The project developed robust audience evaluation tactics, including an online survey, shareholder interviews, and visitor panels that included some people who had visited the site and others who reflected the demographics of the site's potential audience in the region. The steering committee met regularly to sift through ideas and identify potential initiatives. "The process was iterative with next steps and testable prototype programs developed based on front-end evaluation results." Prototypes were tested via online surveys. The steering committee poured over the reactions to sharpen proposals into specific, usable ideas. Through this intense analytical, discussion, and consensus-forming process, the committee developed proposals in three areas: interpretation and programs, new revenue streams, and community engagement. Implementation began right away in the same spirit that had characterized the development of the recommendations: try several things, keep what works, modify or discontinue what does not.

The changes transformed the site:

- Ramsey House's schedule shifted from a "regular open hours" to primarily an "events only" operating model. Each event focuses on a different historical topic with a different guest speaker. A bar is set up in the mansion's kitchen, staffed with an outside bartending service, and snacks and two drinks are included with the price of admission. "This program was designed to allow people to engage with history inside the mansion in a social and informal way." It also helps build partnerships and, through the variety of topics covered, attracts new audiences. In addition, it generated "buzz:" *Minnesota Monthly's* "Best of the Twin Cities" 2012 issue called the "History Happy Hour" events the "Best Nerdy Nosh."
- The site is open to the public during the Christmas season, but it hosts student field trips and will schedule group tours, with costumed guides, upon request. People can also arrange for group self-guided tours. The stanchions and velvet ropes that used to guard the furniture are gone; the "do not touch" signs much rarer. Some of the most sensitive and fragile items have been moved to safe storage, and the furniture has been rearranged to facilitate traffic patterns approximating what the people who lived there experienced, helping visitors make a more direct connection with the past. The whole place is meant to be friendly and inviting.
- The exhibits were broadened to include more national events and contentious historical themes, including good and not-so-good aspects of Ramsey's political career, such as his controversial policies in dealing with Minnesota's American Indian tribes.
- The site instituted online ticketing and broadened its rental offerings for special events such as wedding receptions, receptions, and meetings of local groups, thereby strengthening its community connections.

Attendance at Ramsey House events kept climbing, including "old fans" who found enough of the traditional historical exhibits and programs to keep them coming and new audiences who realized there were changes and fresh perspectives. The Minnesota Historical Society drew several conclusions from the experiment:

Get to know the audience—both current visitors and the potential audi-
    ence—and determine what they really want, need, and expect. Don't
    assume you know without analysis and discussion.
Approach critics, not just fans, for feedback and suggestions.
Ask people outside the organization to help through partnerships, spon-
    sorships, promotion, and continuing evaluation.
Provide access to history but also consider what else the facility can offer:
    space, community, socialization, or even "quiet, almost spiritual expe-
    riences."
"We should be confident that every historic site has something to offer
    new, diverse, twenty-first-century audiences—we just need to take the
    time and have the humility to listen and find out what it is."

AN EXCITING NEW WAY TO EXPERIENCE HISTORY

The Indiana Historical Society in Indianapolis, which calls itself *Indiana's
Storyteller*, launched "The Indiana Experience" in 2010 after several years of
planning, fundraising, and internal reconfiguration of public space. John
Herbst, who became president and CEO in 2006 after extensive leadership
experience elsewhere, including as president of Conner Prairie, believed the
Society's building was under-utilized and its program stuck in time.[13] They
had archival and photographic collections but no artifacts, unlike their Indianapolis neighbor, the State Museum, but they were mainly used by researchers, and public visitation, even for archival exhibits, was low. They
had an adequate endowment, but not enough to mount major new initiatives,
and for years their engagement of the public in their region, and across the
state, had not been extensive.

Herbst led a planning process to change all of that, asking strategic questions. The Society was "artifact-free," which ruled out traditional museum
exhibits but also meant the program did not have to worry about having
artifacts behind ropes where no one can touch them. How can we turn that to
advantage, Herbst wondered? He challenged the staff: "Let's do a time travel
program where you can travel to a place or explore a topic in the past and use
our collections to do that." As ideas and concepts developed for what came to
be called *The Indiana Experience*, Herbst tested and refined them though
public awareness studies. He launched a successful campaign for individual
support and corporate sponsorship to get behind the new ideas. Appealing to
Indiana pride, he was able to secure a major gift from Eugene and Marilyn H.
Glick, who had built one of the largest real estate development firms in the
nation and were known for generous support of arts, education, public health,
and other programs in Indiana. The building was renamed the Eugene and

Marilyn Glick Indiana History Center, and "The Indiana Experience," with a tagline "a new way to live history" opened in 2010.

It has two main features:[14]

> *You Are There.* Visitors step into a three dimensional recreation of one of the society's photographs to find first-person interpreters playing the people in, and around, the images. For instance, in "You Are There, 1924," the visitor can step into a Ford car repair shop in Hartford City, look around the garage, ask questions of the mechanics, the owner's daughters, and other people who happen by. In "You Are There, 1939: Healing Bodies, Changing Minds," visitors enter the 1939 Indianapolis office of African American physician Dr. Harvey Middletown for a discussion and demonstration of electrocardiographic technology. Indicative of the Society's strategy of seeking outside funding for particular exhibits, this one was supported by a local hospital, a local healthcare benefits and care management provider, the county public health department, and the Indiana State Medical Association.
>
> *Destination Indiana.* Using innovative technology, touch screens, and immersive displays of historical images, groups of visitors can explore stories from all regions of the state "about African-Americans, the Civil War, the Ohio River, mapping the state, social justice and reform, rail transportation and agriculture. You decide where you want to travel and what you want to know more about."

The Indiana Experience won a 2011 AASLH Award of Merit for innovation. A reviewer in the *Journal of American History* noted that it "emphasizes the extraordinary personal connections that visitors can make to ordinary people in everyday moments from the past." Recent visitors commented that it was "surprisingly informative and innovative," "a museum for adults," a "fun experience," and that "the interactive exhibits were fantastic."[15]

CONFRONT AND DISCUSS THE CONTROVERSIAL PAST

The Levine Museum of the New South in Charlotte, North Carolina, has won awards from the Institute of Museum and Library Services and other groups for its open, frank portrayal of controversial historical events, with a view toward deepening public understanding and shedding light on current issues. The museum covers the period since the Civil War, and the emphasis is on people—"The New South continuously reinvents itself as newcomers, natives, immigrants, visitors, and residents change the composition and direction of the region." Its centerpiece exhibit, *Cotton Fields to Skyscapers: Charlotte and the Carolina Piedmont in the New South*, offers an interactive, hands-on experience to help people understand both the glories and triumphs and the setbacks and disappointments of the "New South."[16] It uses artifacts, photographs, video clips, and oral histories to present history from the perspective of the people who actually lived through it. Visitors are invited to:

- Step inside a one-room tenant farmer's house
- Run a hand through a pile of seed cotton
- Listen to the churning of the cotton mill
- Play checkers on the front porch of a mill house
- Sit in Good Samaritans Hospital Chapel, one of the first African-American hospitals in the South
- Walk down Main Street and try on a hat in an early Belk department store
- Sit at a lunch counter and hear personal accounts from local sit-in leaders during the Civil Rights movement

In 2009–2010, the museum offered an ambitious multi-part project to explore how the people in the Charlotte region are dealing with the growing cultural diversity and changes created by the influx of newcomers from across the United States and around the world—*Changing Places: From Black and White to Technicolor.*[17] The Charlotte-Mechlenburg County region had been among the fastest growing and most rapidly diversifying areas in the nation, with a 600 percent increase in the number of Latino immigrants in the previous decade, among other changes. *Changing Places* included a museum exhibit, public programming, dialogues for groups of teens and adults, a public television documentary, and an interactive website that encouraged video responses and personal narratives for inclusion in the exhibit. The exhibit included a feature called "video-talkback," where visitors could record their responses to questions based around the exhibit and those responses became part of the exhibit. The questions in the exhibit and discussions were provocative, intended to get people talking about tough issues: *Who judges you without knowing you? Who do you judge? What parts of your cultural heritage have you kept? Let go of? What cultural aspects of the South most surprised you?* In the center of the exhibit space, a park-like setting included benches, a break dance area, a community bulletin board, and a picnic table with "recipes for conversation," inviting visitors to sit down and share stories with each other.

The Levine's programs explore both comfortable and uncomfortable aspects of history, inviting and deepening reflection. "The theme of the exhibition [is that] cross-cultural encounters lead to misunderstanding and divisions," wrote one reviewer. "The show is meant to be an educational corrective. . . . There is an appealing integrity in the way the museum takes on its subjects . . . [a] mixture of the traditional and the iconoclastic."[18] Much of the information from the exhibit, documentary videos, and teacher resources were captured and made available on a website.[19]

The Levine Museum continues to explore local history but also features a regular "New South for the New Southerner" series by a local historian on "Charlotte's History and Its Future;" "Civic by Design" (a monthly forum exploring growth issues, presented in partnership with the American Institute of Architects); and an annual "A Woman's Place" event in recognition of Women's History Month to explore the evolving roles of women in the New South and to celebrate their accomplishments.[20] Sharing its expertise and experience, the Levine Museum has also formed partnerships with museums in Atlanta and Birmingham in the "Latino New South Project." The project aims to help Latino communities to become full partners with museums in the work of community-building in their cities.

HISTORY PROGRAMS ARE ABOUT THE PRESENT AND FUTURE

Historical programs can discuss history but also serve as forums for exploring current issues and future directions. For instance, the Chesapeake Bay Maritime Museum, situated on eighteen waterfront acres in the historic town of St. Michaels, Maryland, offers exhibits, demonstrations, boat rides, and annual festivals that celebrate Chesapeake Bay culture, boats, seafood, and history. Visitors can take a guided tour, hear historical accounts about the Bay, and even learn the rudiments of boatbuilding. "Find out why the Chesapeake Bay plays an important role in our nation's story through our interactive, educationally rich exhibits," says the Museum's promotional material. "Discover through stories and oral histories how the Bay provided an avenue for trade, a plentiful food source for a growing country, a site for the fight for independence, as well as a popular recreation destination."[21]

But the Museum has also organized and sponsored meetings and conversations about the Bay region's future. "The Chesapeake Bay region faces tremendous pressures to its environment, cultures and ways of life. The health of the Bay region is now more than ever dependent on human decisions and actions." The Museum began programs to "inspire people to connect with the Bay region as a place and to envision its future." It hosted "Bay Day" to call attention to these issues and organized exhibits to include messages about the future of Bay communities, fisheries, forests, and land use. To hone its new, interpretive messages, the Museum created a multi-disciplinary team of advisors and regional leaders, including scientists, ecologists, and land use experts that it had never worked with before and reached out to other regional institutions including the Eastern Shore Land Conservancy and a nearby campus of the University of Maryland. An exhibit on "A Rising Tide in the Heart of the Chesapeake" tied environmental concerns to global climate change.[22] Its public forums on "The State of the Oyster" explored the status of the oyster fishing industry and its past, present, and future significance to various Bay communities. [23]

Another example is the Harriet Beecher Stowe Center, located in the historic Hartford, Connecticut, home of the famed author of the book *Uncle Tom's Cabin*. [24] The Center's exhibits and programs highlight the work of Stowe and the influence of the momentous novel. But it identifies as "a 21st Century museum" that explores "the contemporary face of race relations, class and gender issues, economic justice and education equity." Public forums and discussions, called "Salons at Stowe," have dealt with such sharp and contemporary social issues as "Walking in My Shoes: How Can We Teach Empathy?," "Mental Health: Stigmas, Stereotypes and Solutions," "Cultural Diversity Awareness," and "Pollution Is Harmful to Your Health." The annual Stowe Prize is awarded for outstanding writings to advance social justice. School programs cover Stowe's life and work but also include "*Her Words Changed the World*: Using the activism of the 19th century's most famous American woman as a model, your class will discuss Hartford history, the Civil War, and the roles of women and African Americans and consider strategies for positive change today." The Stowe Center shows how iconoclastic ideas from the mid-nineteenth century can still provide guidance and incentive to continue progressive change.

The Jane Addams Hull House Museum in Chicago mounted an exhibit entitled "Unfinished Business: 21st Century Home Economics." It connected the work of the first generation of progressive home economists, who were concerned with the impact of domestic work on women and the need for clean, wholesome food for children a century ago, with contemporary issues about working conditions for domestic workers, house cleaners, and school lunch workers. The museum turned to the Chicago Coalition for Household Workers for insights into domestic work in the city and connections in the community. The Coalition was advocating state legislation to improve the wages and working conditions of domestic workers. The museum discovered "an exciting new blend of collaboration—one that blended the missions of two very different organizations and allowed the museum to become a partner in social change by creating avenues for empathy, education and cultural activism." The exhibit and accompanying public programs "situated the domestic worker rights' movement in a long historical narrative, bridging and blending contemporary and historical activism." Domestic workers donated artifacts, helped shape the exhibit, and collaborated on exhibit labels. The museum got the benefit of authentic, first-hand experience which helped show historical developments and connections. The domestic workers and their organization wanted to change attitudes and pass legislation. They "hoped the exhibition would do the difficult work of transforming the public understanding of domestic work: highlighting the labor struggle while demonstrating the dignity and love inherent in the work itself." The work "transformed a historic house museum into a vibrant space of inquiry about a contemporary issue."[25]

In an unusual innovation, the museum launched an experimental "slow museum" program, providing opportunities for visitors to experience the museum as a site of "leisure, recreation, reflection and respite from the busyness of life." Visitors can engage in unguided tours, relax in an artist-made "reflection room" with musical components, enjoy poetry writing and communal games and meals, and at the end fill out playful visitor evaluations. The concept has two sets or roots at the museum. It has long supported the "slow foods" movement which encourages farming using plants and seeds characteristic of the local ecosystem and enjoyment of traditional and regional cuisine. Jane Addams and other reformers who lived at Hull House defined leisure as a basis for culture and therefore essential to socialization and learning.[26]

Matilda Joslyn Gage (1826–1898) was a nineteenth-century suffragist, abolitionist, Native American rights activist, freethinker, and prolific author. The Matilda Joslyn Gage Foundation, which maintains her home in Fayetteville, New York, near Syracuse, invites visitors to "meet the woman who was ahead of the women who were ahead of their time."[27] Gage, "born with a hatred of oppression," devoted her life to crusading against injustice, and the Foundation's mission is "educating current and future generations about Gage's work and its power to drive contemporary social change." The program is slanted toward activism. The modest-size historic house features several innovations. Instead of the usual recreation of the home's interior with contemporary furnishings, each of the rooms is devoted to a different theme: women's rights ("Gage worked for rights women still seek to attain today"), the Underground Railroad (the home was a "stop" on the road to freedom for escaping slaves), Native American rights (one theme is the government's history of breaking treaties), religious freedom (her 1893 book *Woman, Church and State* railed against religious oppression of women), local history, and a teachers' room with educational resources.

The biggest surprise is the "Family Parlor & Oz Room." (Gage was the mother-in-law of L. Frank Baum, author of *The Wonderful Wizard of Oz.* "Matilda gave Frank the blueprint for the land of social justice he created," the Foundation's description explains. "The vision that his mother-in-law created in *Woman, Church and State* found its practical application in Oz . . . the matriarchal world Gage spent her life trying to create, where women are equal to men; everyone has what they need and gives what they can; morality exists outside the walls of a church; diversity is celebrated and war is not allowed.") The Foundation's website has information on the continuing historical significance of the themes in each room. It is a very visitor-friendly place where people can sit on the furniture, eat and drink, take photos, touch the exhibits, and even "play the piano and sing abolition and women's rights songs that Matilda sang." Visitors are invited to "Write on Our Walls!"—there are large whiteboards for comments on each of the rooms for visitors' reactions and reflections, comments are posted on the website, and visitors to the site are invited to add their own thoughts about Gage's ideas about indigenous rights, women's rights, abolition, or religious freedom as part of a "respectful dialogue" on her continuing influence. Guest lectures and public events explore such issues as voting rights, women's issues, and religious freedom.

OLD TIMERS AND NEWCOMERS

Many progressive historical programs are positioning themselves as the links between past and present, connecting families with venerable, deep roots in the community and newcomers, and helping to put what is sometimes wrenching social and economic change into historical context. In some cases, this means substantial interpretive exhibits; in others, just adding a new dimension to bring the historical themes and stories down to present-day. The Morrison County Historical Society, located in Little Falls, Minnesota, had for many years tried to compile oral histories using the traditional approaches of taping people's reminiscences and transcribing the tapes, but few people were interested and the work proved very time consuming.[28]

The idea of recording contemporary history had strong appeal, so the Society decided to try something else, a new participatory approach that could engage many people and could be conducted mostly via the Society's Web page. They developed a project to document people's life experiences by writing short (200–1,000 word) essays on "What's It Like [. . .] in Morrison County?" Individuals could fill in their own topics ("Come up with your own essay idea. The topics are limited only by your imagination. Feel free to be creative!"), but the Society provided multiple suggestions, for instance to be a teacher, farmer, writer, musician, student, or actor, as well as some edgier suggestions: to be poor/wealthy/middle class, to be black/white/brown, to be an immigrant, to speak a language other than English, and to be a crime victim. "We want snippets of history that, taken together, will provide a picture of the complexity of living in Morrison County," said the description on the program's website.

A "Getting Started" section on the website provided suggestions, guidelines, and encouragement. But the guidelines were general, anyone could participate, and it was meant to be broad and inclusive. The Society asked for basic demographic information on each person who submitted an essay, including name, date of birth date, birth place, gender, contact info, and dates residing in Morrison County. Society staff offered to help with editing and grammar. Writers could simply e-mail their essays to the society though handwritten versions were also accepted. The Society plans to release the essays online, and to deposit written copies with the Charles A. Weyerhaeuser Memorial Museum, which the Society owns and operates, for research, but only after obtaining written releases and approval from the writers. "We want to collect the histories of people who don't have their histories collected that often—to have a representative sample that's not just the famous people or the rich people," explained museum manager Mary Warner. It took a while for the idea to take flight. "You have to remind people, keep reaching out," said Warner. "We are constantly educating people that current history is history too." As essays started to come in, the Society took a further step and began building exhibits around some of the historical events and experiences described in them.

VENTURING OUT, BUILDING MOMENTUM

The Johnson County Museum in Shawnee, Kansas, exemplifies many positive traits. It is a unit of county government with an Advisory Council, appointed by the county government, to oversee its operations and budget. The Johnson County Museum Foundation, a not-for-profit organization, raises private funds to support the museum's operation. A staff of six full-time and four part-time employees is supplemented by over fifty community volunteers.[29] A 2006 "strategic vision" document, developed with a great deal of community input and advice, set out a vision for fresh ways of telling the county's history, expanded and stronger partnerships and collaboration, more work with teachers and students, more online material, raising public awareness, and expanding the museum to make it "a community gathering place."[30]

The Museum secured a grant from the Institute for Museum and Library Services to cooperate with the Johnson County Library to create a web-accessible online collection containing about 30,000 photographs from the mid-1850s to the present, historic atlases, and aerial and architectural photographs. Each photo was carefully described, but, in an adaption of "crowd-sourcing," each online description also had a place for "Can you tell us more about this image?" and space for comments. The IMLS designated it as a model project and made a video about it. Museum director Mindi Love emphasized cooperation with the library, noting that the Museum drew on the library's experience in putting information online. She cited as its most innovative feature the involvement of the community in providing information about the photos, describing it as letting members of the community "create content that is important to them. . . . [I]f we [are going to] be relevant in our communities, we need to be doing more of that as museums." The online photo collection is widely accessed, averaging 5 to 8 million hits per year, local teachers use it in their teaching, and in the video, students also endorse it. "I want to know what was here before me," said one middle school student. "I like knowing where I live and I like to be proud of it."[31]

The museum was justly proud of its many awards, including recognition from AASLH and the Institute for Museum and Library Services. Its space became cramped as it added new collections and hosted more student programs and other events, but its aspirations were large. In 2011, it proposed to expand its programs and create a National Museum of Suburbia and Suburban Policy Forum. "As an exemplary American suburb, Johnson County is an ideal location for a museum about suburbia," said an impressive strategic planning document that it presented to county government. "No other museum in the nation presents the story of the American suburbs." A professor of urban planning was quoted in the document:

> Johnson County is a perfect location for a museum of suburbia. In the middle of the country, part of an archtypical American urban area with a very rich suburban history and with a Museum that has long had an interest in explaining suburban history, as well as a dynamic vision of its place in the community—I see all the ingredients for a successful new institution.

A plan projected sixty thousand visitors annually. The county legislature voted funds to purchase a historic building that could be rehabilitated to house the new museum. But the museum and county government then decided to pause, taking time to consider all the implications of the plan, including financial support. Whether the grand vision for a museum of suburbia can be realized depends on substantial fundraising from sources beyond county government.[32]

BRINGING OUT THE WHOLE TRUTH

Cliveden was an estate in the Philadelphia suburb of Germantown during colonial times; now a bustling urban neighborhood has grown up around it. Its builder, attorney and colonial government official Benjamin Chew, was a loyalist during the Revolution, quartered British troops in his home, and the Battle of Germantown was fought near the site, resulting in heavy losses on both sides and an American retreat. The Philadelphia tourist website calls the estate "the suburban scene of a bloody revolutionary battle" and adds "one of the most lavish mansions of its era, Cliveden is stocked with furniture and artifacts designed to evoke colonial times."[33] It is a site of the National Trust for Historic Preservation. But Cliveden had another side: Chew was a slaveholder, the grand home had been staffed by the indentured and the enslaved, but the slaveholding past of the estate was largely undocumented or overlooked.

With grant support from the Pew Center for Arts & Heritage, Cliveden staff began a project they called *Emancipating Cliveden*, a reinterpretation based on evidence of the Chew family's slaveholding history. The project included a year-long planning process that involved extensive community discussion and outreach. New exhibits and programs were developed to explore the relationship among wealth, privilege, race, and slavery in early American culture.[34] When the rehabilitated museum opened on July 4, 2012, visitors could learn about Charity Castle, an enslaved servant brought to the estate by Harriet Chew in 1814, resulting in a protracted legal case when Chew separated from her husband and Castle resisted being returned to him. They could learn about the family's plantations in Maryland and Delaware, all staffed by slave labor whose hard work made the Chews wealthy. David Young, Cliveden's executive director, said the goal of the new approach was "tell the truth. . . . This changes what this historic site means. It extends its significance beyond the battle and the Chews"[35] An ongoing series of public events, *Cliveden Conversations*, explore issues of race, enslavement, and memory. Each event includes a presentation by a scholar (educators, poets, historians) followed by an audience conversation about the issues raised and their connection to contemporary issues. "At Cliveden, expect to be *challenged* to understand the struggles and contradictions that comprise American history," says David Young. "Cliveden is a place that tells the truth: that American history is difficult."[36]

The site is using its new open, outward-oriented mission to help revitalize its area of the city. "Cliveden plays a lead role in a challenged, yet historic neighborhood—one where History can really play an important part in understanding the present," Young explains. The estate's grounds host scores of community events, concerts, and neighborhood festivals. It serves as an anchor for different kinds of community organizations, including a consortium of fifteen historic sites in the Germantown area. The consortium operates a literacy-based field trip program that accommodates two thousand students annually. Cliveden co-founded a local commercial corridor revitalization corporation. It is committed to continued community engagement, Young explains.

> We consider it our mission to make Cliveden's history useful and to help build vibrant communities in Greater Germantown. That so many neighbors and community stakeholders had a voice in how we program our new interpretation came as a revelation—that people from different backgrounds can come together to discuss the past in ways that celebrate what is good while honestly facing what is not. Historic sites can be a place for people to have civil dialogue about how to address contemporary problems.[37]

BRINGING HISTORY DOWN TO THE PRESENT

Waterbury, Connecticut, had a long history as an industrial center manufacturing watches, clocks, and brassware, including castings and fittings. The brass industry was so central to the city's identity that its informal name is "Brass City" and its motto is *Quid Aere Perennius?* ("What Is More Lasting Than Brass?"). The Mattatuck Museum, an art and history museum in the city, had excellent exhibits documenting history from the early rural days through industrialization. But the brass industry declined after World War II, and the city's economy and demographic makeup also changed. Curators realized that "the brass industry is history now, too. But that's not the end of Waterbury. . . . [N]ow we're a different city than we were. How are we going to bring it up to date. . . . [H]ow do we show Waterbury now, as a very different city than it was 50 years ago? And whose story do we tell, and do we tell a story of decline or of change? Is it the collapse of the city, or is it the story about how people create different ways of living—one group moves out of a neighborhood and another group moves in?"[38] After consulting with local community leaders, scholars, and museum experts, the museum developed an entirely new exhibit, *Coming Home: Building Community in a Changing World*, a permanent exhibit of regional history with changing displays.[39]

The history stretches back to the earliest years but also has major themes for 1950–present, "telling stories that are relevant to those who live here today." The exhibit is lively, engaging, and uses touch-screen monitors and other modern technology to draw the visitor into the story:

> This exhibit is packed with hands-on activities designed to entertain while educating. Build a village and decide where to place your home, mill, church or shop on Waterbury's rugged but swampy terrain. Move a lever and see how Waterbury changes from a farming community to an industrial city to a city divided by highways. Work the production line, and realize the stress of making a button in 30 seconds. Play Risky Business, a pinball game based on the risks and rewards of starting a factory in 19th century Waterbury.

Visitors can dial up oral histories for first-hand accounts of Waterbury, past and present. On one wall, there is a screen that runs a looped mash-up of local home movies, newsreel-like footage, and other images. Perhaps the most notable feature is "The Conversation Table" that features a digital map where, with the wave of a hand, a visitor can display data on housing density, population, manufacturing jobs, income levels, and other features of the Waterbury area. At the "Election Game" exhibit, visitors can "run for election" by creating a personal campaign platform by answering questions relating to local issues, including education, immigration, and economic development. The exhibit's computer system collects the data and decides if the visitor gets "elected" or not, based on the votes of other visitors. The exhibit opened to rave reviews, which the Museum very creatively highlighted in its promotional material. Eric Foner, a history professor at Columbia University and a sometime critic of museums for avoiding the controversial aspects of history, wrote that "The Mattatuck Museum is a national leader in placing the experience of a local community in a national context." A reviewer for *Connecticut History* asserted that "this is public history at its best . . . particularly strong in its ability to engage different kinds of learners." The newspaper *New Haven Independent* commended both the exhibit development process—"a great deal of listening, learning, and feeling the pulse of their environment" —and the result—"one of the most indispensable teaching environments in Connecticut. . . . It's hard to imagine a higher and better use for museums." [40] As part of its continuing campaign to stay fresh and relevant, the museum conducted periodic visitor surveys via Facebook.

NOTES

1. Jamestown Settlement & Yorktown Victory Center, *History Is Fun*. http://www.historyisfun.org.

2. Andrea Sachs, "At Williamsburg, History Does Not Repeat Itself," *Washington Post* (April 25, 2013). (The article covered Williamsburg, Jamestown and several other regional attractions.) http://img2.wpdigital.net/lifestyle/travel/at-williamsburg-history-does-not-repeat-itself/2013/04/25/19a81dce-a7ad-11e2-b029-8fb7e977ef71_story.html.

3. Jamestown-Yorktown Foundation, *2013 Facts*. http://historyisfun.org/pdf/fact-sheet/JYF_Fact%20Sheet_Aug_2013.pdf.

4. Yorktown Settlement & Yorktown Victory Center, "Yorktown Victory Center to Become *American Revolution Museum at Yorktown*." http://historyisfun.org/yorktown-museum-overview.htm.

5. Ken Bubp and Dave Allison, "Opening Doors to Great Experiences," *History News* (Spring 2007), 20–23. http://www.connerprairie.org/About-Us/Who-We-Are/Opening-Doors-to-Great-Guest-Experiences.aspx#Opening.

6. Conner Prairie, *Follow the North Star*. http://www.connerprairie.org/plan-your-visit/special-events/follow-the-north-star.aspx.

7. Conner Prairie, *1863 Civil War Journey: Raid on Indiana*. http://civil-war.connerprairie.org.

8. Edward Rothstein, "Where Park Visitors Answer a Call to Battle," *New York Times*, June 21, 2011.

9. This discussion is based on Allison Weiss, "Relevance, Relationships and Resources: The 3R's of Museum Management," *History News* (Summer 2012), 7–16.

10. Southern Oregon Historical Society, *Welcome!* http://www.sohs.org.

11. Alexander Ramsey House, *History*. http://sites.mnhs.org/historic-sites/alexander-ramsey-house/history.

12. The rest of the account of Ramsey House is from Rachel Abbott, "New Ideas, Same Old House: Public Feedback, Change and the Alexander Ramsey House" (2012). American Alliance of Museums. http://www.aam-us.org/about-us/grants-awards-and-competitions/brooking-paper/past-recipients/new-ideas-same-old-house.

13. "A Life in Public History: A Conversation with John Herbst," *Indiana Magazine of History* 107 (June 2011), 153–169, is the source for the discussion in this paragraph.

14. Indiana Historical Society, *Indiana Experience*. http://www.indianahistory.org/indiana-experience#.UoLXpXYo4qQ.

15. John Dicthl, "The Indiana Experience: You Are There," *Journal of American History,* 98 (June 2011), 129–134; Trip Advisor, *Indiana Historical Society.* http://www.tripadvisor.com/Attraction_Review-g37209-d110138-Reviews-Indiana_Historical_Society-Indianapolis_Indiana.html.

16. Levine Museum of the New South, *Cotton Fields to Skyscrapers.* http://www.museumofthenewsouth.org/exhibits/detail/?ExhibitId=1.

17. Levine Museum of the New South, *Changing Places: From Black and White to Technicolor.* http://www.museumofthenewsouth.org/exhibits/detail/?ExhibitId=94; "Case Study: Cultivating Cross-Racial and Ethnic Experiences and Understanding," American Association for Museums, Center for the Future of Museums, *Demographic Transformation and the Future of Museums* (2010), 21. http://www.aam-us.org/docs/center-for-the-future-of-museums/demotransaam2010.pdf.

18. Edward Rothstein, "An Enigmatic Land of Great Expectations," *New York Times,* Feb. 13, 2010.

19. *Changing Places: From Black and White to Technicolor.* http://www.changingplacesproject.org.

20. Levine Museum of the New South, *Programs & Events.* http://www.museumofthenewsouth.org/programs_events.

21. Chesapeake Bay Maritime Museum, *Adult Learning at the Chesapeake Bay Maritime Museum,* http://www.cbmm.org/l_adults.htm.

22. "Can a Regional History Museum Be a Place to Think about the Future?," Mid Atlantic Regional Center for the Humanities, *Crossties* 3 (Fall 2009). http://march.rutgers.edu/wp-content/uploads/CrossTiesFa09.pdf.

23. http://cbmm.org/stateoftheoyster.

24. Harriett Beecher Stowe Center, *Welcome, Program Events* and *School Programs/Resources.* http://www.harrietbeecherstowecenter.org.

25. Heather Radke, "Unfinished Business," American Alliance of Museums, *Museum* (May/June 2013). http://www.aam-us.org/resources/publications/museum-magazine/unfinished-business. The exhibit is described in Jane Addams-Hull House Museum, *Unfinished Business: 21st Century Home Economics.* http://www.uic.edu/jaddams/hull/_museum/_exhibits/_Unfinished-Business/_21stcenthomec/21stcenturyhomeecon.html.

26. Anne Brooks Ranallo, "Hull-House Turns to 'Slow Museum' Programs" (September 17, 2013). http://news.uic.edu/hull-house-slow.

27. The Matilda Joslyn Gage Foundation, *The Gage Home—Ideas in Action.* http://www.matildajoslyngage.org.

28. Morrison County Historical Society, *What's It Like [. . .] in Morrison County, Minnesota?* http://morrisoncountyhistory.org/whatsitlike; "Developing a Participatory, Provocative History Project at a Small Museum in Minnesota: Interview with Mary Warner," *Museum 2.0 blog* (January 30, 2013). http://museumtwo.blogspot.com/2013/01/developing-participatory-provocative.html.

29. Johnson County Museum, *About Us.* http://www.jocomuseum.org/about.shtml.

30. Johnson County Museum, *Strategic Vision 2006–2011.* http://www.jocomuseum.org/docs/JohnsonCountyMuseumStrategicVision2006-2011.pdf2006-2011.

31. Institute of Museum and Library Services, *Johnson County Museum, Shawnee, KS: "Johnson County's Photographic History on the Web"* (September 2011). http://www.imls.gov/research/mfa_evaluation.aspx.

32. Johnson County Museum, *National Museum of Suburbia and Suburban Policy Forum* (September 2011). http://www.jocomuseum.org/docs/2011InterpretiveMasterPlan.pdf; Steve Volkrodt, "Johnson County Got a Deal on King Louie; Turning it into a National Suburbia Museum Won't Be a Bargain," *The Pitch* (June 18, 2013). http://www.pitch.com/kansascity/king-louie-west-museum-of-suburbia-johnson-county-commission/Content?oid=3256283.

33. *Philadelphia and the Countryside: Cliveden.* http://www.visitphilly.com/museums-attractions/philadelphia/cliveden.

34. The Pew Center for Arts & Heritage, *Cliveden of the National Trust.* http://www.pcah.us/dance/grants-awarded/heritage-philadelphia-program-2011-grantee-cliveden-of-the-national-trust.

35. Stephan Salisbury, "Cliveden 'Emancipates' Its History in New Exhibition," *Philly.Com* (July 4, 2012). http://articles.philly.com/2012-07-04/entertainment/32524365_1_chews-germantown-avenue-carriage-house.

36. "Cliveden: Who Was Benjamin Chew? An Interview with David Young." *The Ultimate History Project* (2013). http://www.ultimatehistoryproject.com/interview-with-david-young-about-cliveden.html.

37. "Cliveden: Home to Many Americans. Part II of an Interview with David Young." *The Ultimate History Project* (2013). http://www.ultimatehistoryproject.com/cliveden-and-battle-of-germantown-part-ii.html.

38. Leah Arroyo, "The Historian in the Museum: An Interview with Eric Foner," Guillin + Merrell (April 2006). http://www.guillinmerrell.com/pdfs/mn_arroyo.pdf.

39. Charles Monagan, "Making History," *Connecticut Magazine* (November 2008). Available at Guillin + Merrill, http://www.guillinmerrell.com/pdfs/cm_monagan.pdf; Mattatuck Museum, *Orton P. Camp Gallery—Coming Home: Building Community in a Changing World.* http://www.mattatuckmuseum.org/orton.

40. Mattatuck Museum, *Exhibit Reviews: Coming Home: Building Community in a Changing World.* https://www.mattatuckmuseum.org/mattatuckmuseum/HistoryExhibit_Reviews.pdf.

Bibliography

Ackerson, Anne W. and Joan H. Baldwin. *Leadership Matters.* Lanham, MD: Alta Mira, 2014.

Adair, Bill et al, eds. *Letting Go?: Sharing Historical Authority in a User-Generated World.* Walnut Creek, CA: Left Coast Press, 2011.

Alexander, Edward P. and Mary Alexander. *Museums in Motion: An Introduction to the History and Functions of Museums.* Lanham, MD: Alta Mira, 2007.

Allison, Eric and Lauren Peters. *Historic Preservation and the Livable City.* New York: Wiley, 2011.

American Association of Museums, *Mastering Civic Engagement: A Challenge for Museums.* Washington: AAM, 2002.

———. *National Standards & Best Practices.* Washington: AAM, 2008.

———. *Slaying the Financial Dragon.* Washington: AAM, 2003.

Amabile, Teresa and Steven Kramer. *The Progress Principle: Using Small Wins to Ignite Joy, Engagement and Creativity at Work.* Boston: Harvard Business Review Press, 2011.

Anderson, Erika. *Leading so People Will Follow.* New York: Jossey Bass, 2012.

Anderson, Gail, ed. *Reinventing the Museum: The Evolving Conversation on the Paradigm Shift.* Revised edition, Lanham, MD: Alta Mira, 2012.

Baldwin, Joan H. *What Comes First: Your Guide to Building a Strong, Sustainable Museum or Historical Organization (With Real Life Advice from Folks Who've Done It).* Troy, NY: Museum Association of New York, 2010.

Baldoni, John. *Lead With Purpose: Giving Your Organization a Reason to Believe in Itself.* New York: AMACOM, 2012.

Bennis, Warren. *On Becoming a Leader.* Boston: Perseus Books, 1989.

Bennis, Warren and Robert Thomas. *Leading for a Lifetime: How Defining Moments Shape the Leaders of Today and Tomorrow.* Boston: Harvard Business School Press, 2007.

Bergeron, Anne and Beth Tuttle. *Magnetic: The Art and Science of Engagement.* Washington: American Alliance of Museums, 2013.

Bitgood, Stephen. *Attention and Value: Keys to Understanding Museum Visitors.* Walnut Creek, CA: Left Coast Press, 2013.

Brown, Tom. *Change by Design: How Design Thinking Transforms Organizations and Inspires Innovation.* New York: Harper Collins, 2009.

Bryson, John M. *Strategic Planning for Public and Nonprofit Organizations: A Guide to Strengthening and Sustaining Organizational Achievement.* San Francisco: Jossey Bass, 2011.

Buckingham, Marcus. *The One Thing You Need to Know about Great Managing, Great Leading, and Sustained Individual Success.* New York: Free Press, 2005.

Cohn, Steven. *Do Museums Still Need Objects?* Philadelphia: University of Pennsylvania Press, 2010.

Collins, Jim. *Good to Great.* New York: Harper Collins, 2001.

Collins, Jim and Morten T. Hansen. *Great by Choice: Uncertainty, Chaos, and Luck: Why Some Thrive Despite Them All.* New York: Harper Business, 2011.

Connors, Roger and Tom Smith. *Change the Culture, Change the Game: The Breakthrough Strategy for Energizing Your Organization and Creating Accountability for Results.* New York: Portfolio Trade, 2012.

Cuno, James. *Museums Matter: In Praise of the Encyclopedic Museum.* Chicago: University of Chicago Press, 2012.

Daft, Richard L. *Management.* 6th edition, Mason, OH: Thompson Southwestern, 2003.

Davenport, Tom and Brook Manville, *Judgment Calls: Twelve Stories of Big Decisions and the Teams That Got Them Right.* Boston: Harvard Business School Press, 2012.

Dearstyne, Bruce, ed. *Leading and Managing Archives and Records Programs: Strategies for Success.* New York: Neal-Schuman, 2008.

deBrabandere, Luc and Alan Ivy. *Thinking in New Boxes: A New Paradigm for Business Creativity.* New York: Random House, 2013.

Deering, Anne and Anne Murphy. *The Partnering Imperative: Making Business Partnerships Work.* New York: Wiley, 2003.

DeGroot, Jerome. *Consuming History: Historians and Heritage in Contemporary Popular Culture.* New York: Routledge, 2009.

Drotner, Kirsten and Kim Christian Schroeder, eds., *Museum Communication and Social Media: The Connected Museum.* New York: Routledge, 2013.

Dubberly, Sarah, ed. *Organizing Your Museum.* Washington: AAM, 2001.

Dudley, Sandra, ed. *Museum Materialities: Objects, Engagements, Interpretations.* London: Routledge, 2010.

Duggan, William. *Creative Strategy: A Guide for Innovation.* New York: Columbia Business School, 2013.

Durel, John. *Building a Sustainable Nonprofit Organization.* Washington: American Association of Museums, 2013.

Genoways, Hugh M. and Lynne M. Ireland. *Museum Administration: An Introduction.* Lanham, MD: Alta Mira, 2003.

George, Gerald and Carol Maryan-George. *Starting Right: A Basic Guide to Museum Planning.* 3rd edition, Lanham, MD: Alta Mira, 2012.

Falk, John H. and Lynn D. Dierking. *The Museum Experience Revisited.* Walnut Creek, CA: Left Coast Press, 2012.

Falk, John H. and Beverly K. Shepard. *Thriving in the Knowledge Age: New Business Models for Museums and Other Cultural Institutions.* Lanham, MD: Alta Mira, 2006.

Farrell, Betty and Maria Medvedeva. *Demographic Transformation and the Future of Museums.* Washington: Center for the Future of Museums/Association of Museums Press, 2010.

Fortney, Kim and Beverly Sheppard, eds. *An Alliance of Spirit: Museum and School Partnerships.* Washington: American Alliance of Museums, 2010.

Gerstner, Louis. *Who Says Elephants Can't Dance? Leading a Great Enterprise through Dramatic Change.* New York: Harper Business, 2002.

Gostick, Adrian and Chester Elton. *All In: How the Best Managers Create a Culture of Belief and Drive Big Results.* New York: Free Press, 2012.

Gratton, Lynda. *The Shift: The Future of Work Is Already Here.* New York: Collins, 2011.

Hackman, Larry, ed. *Many Happy Returns: Advocacy and the Development of Archives.* Chicago: Society of American Archivists, 2011.

Hamm, John. *Unusually Excellent: The Necessary Nine Skills Required for the Practice of Great Leadership.* New York: Jossey Bass, 2011.

Harris, Donna Ann. *New Solutions for House Museums: Ensuring the Long-Term Preservation of America's Historic Houses.* Lanham, MD: Alta Mira, 2007.

Hesselbein, Frances. *Hesselbein on Leadership.* San Francisco: Jossey Bass, 2013.

Hesselbein, Frances and Marshall Goldsmith, eds. *The Organization of the Future II: Visions, Strategies and Insights for Managing in a New Era.* San Francisco: Jossey Bass, 2009.

Hill, Linda A. and Kent Lineback. *Being the Boss: The Three Imperatives for Becoming a Great Leader.* Boston: Harvard Business Review Press, 2011.

Hincliffe, Dion and Peter Kim. *Social Business by Design: Transformative Social Media Strategies for the Connected Company.* San Francisco: Jossey-Bass, 2012.

Holo, Selma et al. *Beyond the Turnstile: Making the Case for Museums and Sustainable Values.* Washington: American Association of Museums, 2009.

Janes, Robert R. *Museums in a Troubled World: Renewal, Irrelevance or Collapse?* London: Routledge, 2009.

———. *Museums and the Paradox of Change.* 3rd edition, London: Routledge, 2013.

Keeley, Larry et al. *Ten Types of Innovation: The Discipline of Building Breakthroughs.* New York: Wiley, 2013.

Kelley, Tom and David Kelley. *Creative Confidence: Unleashing the Creative Potential within All of Us.* New York: Crown Business, 2014.

Kotler, Neil et al. *Museum Marketing and Strategy.* San Francisco: Jossey Bass, 2008.

Kurtzman, Joel. *Common Purpose: How Great Leaders Get Organizations to Achieve the Extraordinary.* New York: Jossey Bass, 2010.

Lafley, A. G. and Ram Charan. *The Game Changer: How You Can Drive Revenue and Profit Growth with Innovation.* New York: Crown Business, 2008.

Lafley, A. G. and Roger L. Martin. *Playing to Win: How Strategy Really Works.* Boston: Harvard Business Review Press, 2013.

Leavitt, Mike Leavitt and Rich McKeown. *Finding Allies, Building Alliances.* San Francisco: Jossey-Bass, 2013.

Leonard, Dorothy and Walter Swap. *When Sparks Fly: Igniting Creativity in Groups.* Boston: Harvard University Press, 2009.

Li, Charlene and Josh Bernoff. *Groundswell: Winning in a World Transformed by Social Technologies.* Boston: Harvard Business Press, 2008.

Liedtka, Jeanne and Tim Ogilvie. *Designing for Growth: A Design Thinking Toolkit for Managers.* New York: Columbia Business School, 2011.

Lord, Barry et al, eds. *Manual of Museum Planning: Sustainable Space, Facilities and Operations.* Lanham, MD: Alta Mira, 2012.

Lord, Gail Dexter and Barry Lord, *The Manual of Museum Management.* 2nd edition, Lanham, MD: Alta Mira, 2009.

Mansfield, Heather. *Social Media for Social Good.* New York: McGraw Hill, 2012.

Martin, Roger. *The Opposable Mind: Winning through Integrative Thinking.* Boston: Harvard Business Press, 2009.

McCrea, Jennifer and Jeffrey C. Walker. *The Generosity Network: New Transformational Tools for Successful Fund-Raising.* New York: Deepak Chopra Books, 2013.

McLean, Kathleen and Wendy Pollock. *The Convivial Museum.* Washington: Association of Science Technology Centers, 2011.

———, eds. *Visitor Voices in Museum Exhibitions.* Washington: Association of Science Technology Centers, 2011.

Mellon, Liz, *Inside the Leader's Mind: Five Ways to Act Like a Leader.* New York: Prentice Hall, 2011.

Menkes, Justin. *Better under Pressure: How Great Leaders Bring Out the Best in Themselves and Others.* Boston: Harvard Business Press, 2011.

Merritt, Elizabeth E. and Victoria Garvin, eds. *Secrets of Institutional Planning.* Washington: American Association of Museums, 2007.

Michelli, Joseph A. *Leading the Starbucks Way: 5 Principles for Connecting With Your Customers, Your Products and Your People.* New York: McGraw-Hill, 2014.

Mims, Carlson and Margaret Donohue, *The Executive Director's Guide to Thriving as a Nonprofit Leader.* San Francisco: Jossey-Bass, 2010.

Nussbaum, Bruce. *Creative Intelligence: Harnessing the Power to Create, Connect, and Inspire.* New York: Harper Business, 2013.

Norris, Linda and Rainey Tisdale. *Creativity in Museum Practice.* Walnut Creek, CA: Left Coast Press, 2014.

Page, Scott E. *The Difference: How the Power of Diversity Creates Better Groups, Firms, Schools and Societies.* Princeton: Princeton University Press, 2008.

Pontefract, Dan. *Flat Army: Creating a Connected and Engaged Organization.* San Francisco: Jossey-Bass, 2013.

Potter, Ned. *The Library Marketing Toolkit.* London: Facet, 2012.

Ramaswamy, Venkat and Francis Gouillart. *The Power of Co-Creation.* New York: Free Press, 2010.

Renz, David O. *The Jossey-Bass Handbook of Nonprofit Leadership and Management.* San Francisco: Jossey-Bass, 2010.

Ries, Eric. *The Lean Startup: How Today's Business Entrepreneurs Use Continuous Innovation to Create Radically Successful Businesses.* New York: Crown Business, 2011.

Rosenzweig, Roy and David Thelen. *The Presence of the Past: Popular Uses of History in American Life.* New York: Columbia University Press, 1998.

Ruynyard, Sue and Ylva French. *Marketing and Public Relations for Museums, Galleries, Cultural and, Heritage Attractions.* New York: Routlege, 2011.

Rypkema, Donovan. *The Economics of Historic Preservation: A Community Leader's Guide.* Washington: National Trust for Historic Preservation, 2005.

Schein, Edgar H. *Organizational Culture and Leadership.* 4th edition, San Francisco: Jossey Bass, 2010.

Schultz, Howard. *Onward: How Starbucks Fought for Its Life without Losing Its Soul.* New York: Rodale, 2011.

Sheehan, Robert M., Jr. *Mission Impact: Breakthrough Strategies for Nonprofits* (The AFP/Wiley Fund Development Series). New York: Wiley, 2010.

Skramstad, Harold and Susan Skramstad. *A Handbook for Museum Trustees.* New York: American Association of Museums, 2003.

Sims, Peter. *Little Bets: How Breakthrough Ideas Emerge from Small Discoveries.* New York: Free Press, 2011.

Silberglied, Gail Ravintzky. Speak Up for Museums: The AAM Guide to Advocacy. Washington: American Association of Museums, 2011.

Silverman, Lois H. *The Social Work of Museums.* London: Routledge, 2010.

Simon, Nina. *The Participatory Museum.* Santa Cruz, CA: Museum 2.0, 2010.

Speck, Jeff. *Walkable City: How Downtown Can Save America, One Step at a Time.* New York: Farrar, Straus and Giroux, 2012.

Suchy, Serene. *Leading with Passion: Change Management in the 21st Century Museum.* Lanham, MD: Alta Mira, 2004.

Thomas, David and John Seely Brown. *A New Culture of Learning: Creating the Imagination for a World of Constant Change.* New York: Createspace, 2011.

Trautlein, Barbara A. *Change Intelligence: Using the Power of CQ to Lead Change That Works.* New York: Greenleaf Book Group Press, 2013.

Wagner, Rodd and Gale Muller. *Power of 2: How to Make the Most of Your Partnerships at Work and In Life.* New York: Gallup Press, 2009.

Wallace, Margot. *Museum Branding.* Lanham, MD: Alta Mira, 2006.

Weaver, Stephanie. *Creating Great Visitor Experiences: A Guide for Museums, Parks, Zoos, Gardens & Libraries.* Walnut Creek, CA: Left Coast Press, 2007.

Weil, Stephen E. *Making Museums Matter.* Washington: Smithsonian Institution Press, 2002.

Weinberger, David. *Too Big to Know.* New York: Basic Books, 2012.

Wells, Marcella et al. *Interpretive Planning for Museums: Integrating Visitor Perspectives in Decision Making.* Walnut Creek, CA: Left Coast Press, 2013.

Williams, Dean. *Real Leadership: Helping People and Organizations Face Their Toughest Challenges.* San Francisco: Berrett-Koehler, 2005.

Wiseman, Liz and Greg McKeown, *Multipliers: How the Best Leaders Make Everyone Smarter.* New York: Harper Collins, 2010.

Woodward, Walter et al. *Teaching History with Museums: Strategies for K–12 Social Studies.* New York: Routledge, 2012.

Worth, Michael J. *Nonprofit Management: Principles and Practice*. New York: Sage, 2011.
Zolli, Andrew and Ann Marie Healy, *Resilience: Why Things Bounce Back.* New York: Free Press, 2012.

Index

AARP, 69

Ackerson, Anne, 11, 25, 34

advertising. *See* Marketing

advocacy, 54, 69, 70, 107, 125; "Advocacy Day," 110; audience, 116, 117, 119, 126–127; campaign goals, 55, 59, 60, 117, 119; engagement building, 111, 116–118; *History Bill of Rights*, 126–127; lobbying, 110, 122–123, 124, 125; long term, 123–125; making the case, 109–114; participatory historical program initiatives, 56–58; program development and, 107–109, 123–125; promoting history, 120–122; reporting, 118–120; social media and, 87–90; supporters, enlisting of, 115–116; visibility, 125

American Alliance of Museums, 12, 29, 49, 53, 92, 102, 109, 125; "Advocacy Day," 110; *Museum Assessment Program*, 68; *Museums and Society*, 147

American Association of Museums (AAM), 16, 69, 100; Center for the Future of Museums, 20, 49, 53, 147; *Excellence*award, 29; "Innovation lab for Museums," 122

American Association for State and Local History (AASLH), 17, 109; advocacy and, 125; Award of merit for innovation, 160, 167; *Developing History Leaders*, 25, 29, 53; *Standards and Excellence Program for History Organizations*(StEPs), 67

American Heritage, 112

American Historical Association, 12

American Library Association's Office for Library Advocacy, 117–118; "action plan," 116; Advocacy University, 125

American Museum of Natural History, 92

Americans for the Arts, 118; National Arts Marketing Project, 118

Anderson, Maxwell, 90

audience, 10, 11–12, 14, 15–16, 19, 54, 73; advocacy and, 116, 117, 119, 123–124, 126–127. *See also* digital information and technology

Australia, 8, 94, 98; Museums Australia, *Strategic Planning Manual*, 135; *National Standards for Australian Museums and Galleries*, 135

Baldwin, Joan, 25, 34

Bank of America, 120

Bellardo, Lewis, 108

Bennis, Warren, 26, 38, 63

Bernstein, Shelley, 91

Berry, Steve, 5

Bezos, Jeff, 52

brand engagement, 103, 103–104

British Museums Association, 8; *Museums Change Lives: The MA's Vision for the*

Impact of Museums, 126–127
Brooklyn Museum, 91, 93
Buckingham, Marcus, 37
Built to Last(Collins and Porras), 37, 133
BYOD (Bring Your Own Device), 86

California History-Social Science Project,
    80
Canada: Canadian Centre for the Study of
    Historical Consciousness, 81; Canadian
    Museum of Civilization, 143–144;
    Canadian Museum of History, 143,
    144; *Historica Canada*, 125; *Historical
    Thinking Project*, 81
Canada Council for the Arts, 120
Canadian Encyclopedia, 125, 144
Canadian Historical Association, 5, 125,
    144
Cape Cod Cranberry Growers'
    Association, 120
Chesapeake Bay Maritime Museum, 162
Chicago Historical Society, 142
Chicago History Museum, 142–143;
    *Claiming Chicago, Shaping Our
    Future*, 142
CitiBank, 121
Civic Participation Index, 7
Civic Ventures, 69
Civil War, 58, 79, 81, 88, 154–155, 160,
    163; re-enactments, 154
Clough, G. Wayne, 86
Coca-Cola Archives, 40
Collins, Jim, 37, 133, 134
Colonial Williamsburg, 93
Common Core Standards, 10, 80
Community participation, 21, 91, 94, 98,
    102, 156; *History: Made by You*, 156
Connecticut: Mattatuck Museum, 169;
    Tolland Historical Society, 139
Conner Prairie Interactive History Park,
    153–155, 159
*Cotton Fields to Skyscrapers: Charlotte
    and the Carolina Piedmont in the New
    South*, 160
Council of State Archivists, 112
Creative Confidence(Kelley and Kelley),
    62
Creativity in Museum Practice (Norris and
    Tisdale), 47

decision making, 7, 31, 32, 68, 73, 107,
    108, 112, 132
Deerfield, MA, 88
demographics, 9, 12, 15, 16–17, 18, 19, 31,
    48, 72, 131, 147–148
design thinking, 54, 59–61, 63
Developing History Leaders (AASLH), 25,
    53
"Digital Engagement Framework," 97, 99
digital information and technology:
    audience, 85, 86, 88, 89, 91, 94, 95,
    97–98; brand engagement, 86,
    103–104; BYOD (Bring Your Own
    Device), 86; communication, 87–92;
    development, 87, 93, 97–98; "Digital
    Engagement Framework," 97, 99;
    framework, 97, 99; models, 50–53,
    92–94; opportunities, 85–86;
    organization, 97, 100; platforms, 89, 94,
    95, 96, 101, 102; policy development,
    98–100; skills, 94–96; social media
    and, 92–94; "Social Media Strategy
    Worksheet," 100; strategy, 97–98;
    trends, 90
Drucker, Peter, 35, 42, 51, 134
Durel, Anita Nowery, 21
Durel, John, 21

*Effective Capacity Building in Nonprofit
    Organizations*(McKinsey & Company),
    134
Encyclopedia of Local History (Kammen),
    20
Eugene and Marilyn Glick Indiana History
    Center, 159–160
experiencing history, 6–7, 9, 15–16, 17,
    19–20

Facebook, 15, 53, 83, 88, 89, 91, 92,
    92–94; as a platform, 96, 121; brand
    engagement, 103–104; followers and,
    101–103, 169; skills and, 94–96
The First 90 Days(Watkins), 29
Flickr, 12, 89, 94, 103, 148
Florida, "Viva Florida 500," 121
Fogerty, James, 98
Foner, Eric, 170
Fordham Foundation, 78

Gage, Matilda Joslyn, 116, 164
The Generosity Network (McCrea and Walker), 115
George Mason University, 82, 88; Center for History and the New Media, 101
Gerstner, Lou, 52
Good to Great and the Social Sectors(Collins), 133
Google, 12, 101

Harriet Beecher Stowe Center, 163
Hedlin, Edie, 26, 115
Herbst, John, 159
heritage tourism, 67, 76–78
historical houses, 5, 17, 67, 77, 85, 157–159
historic preservation, 11, 17, 18, 49, 57. *See also* strategic management
Historic Preservation and the Livable City (Allison and Peters), 77
Historica Canada, 125
historical program models: adventure, 153–155; community engagement, 155–156; contemporary and past history, 165–166; controversial past, 160–162; educational, 151–153; entertainment, 151–153; experiencing history, 159–160; future trends, 162–164; homes, historic, 157–159; innovation and, 166–167; interpreting past, 152, 153–154, 155, 157, 160, 162, 165, 168; present day and, 162–164, 169; truth and history, 167–169
historical programs, 5–8; challenges, 8–15; demographic shift, 13, 15, 16, 16–17, 19, 21; individual-centric engagement, 18–19; learning styles, 15–16; proactive, 19–21; reinterpretation, 13–15; resources, 11–12; trends, 14, 16; value of, 6–7. *See also* innovation
Historical Society of Pennsylvania, 58, 68, 93
Historical Thinking Matters, 82
history and public education, 78–82
History Associates, 113
History Bill of Rights, 126–127
"History Day," 123
History: Made by You, 156
History News, 53, 58, 99

Historyisfun.org, 151
Historypin, 93
Honeysett, Nik, 97

IBM, 42, 46, 52, 54
identity museums, 14
Indiana: Conner Prairie Interactive History Park, 153–155, 159; Eugene and Marilyn Glick Indiana History Center, 159–160; Historical Society, 68, 159; "The Indiana Experience," 159; *Indiana's Storyteller*, 160; Local History Services Team, 68
innovation: action plan, 51, 117; advancement of, 58–62; creativity, 46–49; design thinking, 54, 59, 60–61, 63; models, 50–53, 92–94; participatory initiatives, 56–58; using, 49, 62–63
"Innovation Lab for Museums," 49
Instagram, 89
Institute of Museum and Library Services (IMLS), 15, 100, 160; *National Medal for Museum and Library Service*, 29, 160
Iowa, 58, 76; *Museum Week*, 76

J. Paul Getty Museum, 97
Jamestown Settlement, 76, 151–152, 152, 153
Jane Addams Hull House Museum, 163–164
Johnson County Museum, 166–167; National Museum of Suburbia and Suburban Policy Forum, 167
Johnson, Steven, 48

Kammen, Carol, 20
Kelley, David, 62
Kelley, Tom, 62

Lafley, A.G., 51
Lapointe, Tara, 121
leadership: approaches, 25–29, 68–69; culture, 33, 35–37, 39, 41; decisions, 7, 31, 32–33, 68, 73, 107, 108, 112, 132; elements of, 29–30; issues, 42; making connections, 40; models of, 31, 33, 34, 36; purpose , common, 37–39; skills, 40–41; styles and traits, 30–32, 33–34;

traits, 34–35
Leadership Matters (Ackerson and Baldwin), 25
Leading for a Lifetime (Bennis and Thomas), 38
The Lean Startup (Reis), 59
Levine Museum of the New South, 160, 162
"Libraries and Museums in an Era of Participatory Culture," 21
LinkedIn, 89
linking, 90, 102, 113. *See also* social media
lobbying, 110, 122–123, 124, 125
London, 87

Maine Memory Network, 88
Mansfield, Heather, 103
marketing : "action plan," 51, 117; "Advocacy Day," 110; audience, 116, 117, 119, 126–127; campaign goals, 55, 59, 60, 117, 119; engagement building, 111, 116–118; lobbying, 110, 122–123, 124, 125; making the case, 109–114; program planning and, 107–109, 123–125; promoting history, 120–122; supporters, enlisting of, 115–116; social media, 89–90
Matilda Joslyn Gage Center, 116, 164
Mattatuck Museum, 169
Mesa Historical Society, 122
McCullough, David, 7
McKinsey & Company, 134
Minnesota Historical Society, 7, 57, 68, 93; Enterprise Technology, 97; History Coalition, 157–158; Legacy Amendment, 118; Local History Services Office, 100; Minnesota's Greatest Generation, 88; *Northern lights*, 81; St. Paul public schools and, 80; "Social Media Strategy Worksheet," 100
Mirrer, Louise, 145
models of historical organizations, 29, 50–53; digital, 50–53, 92–94
Mooney, Philip, 40
Morrison County (Minnesota) Historical Society, 165
Mount Vernon, 93

Museum Association of New York: advocacy and, 11, 110, 116, 132–133; guidelines, 132–133
"Museum Day," 122
Museum 2.0 (blog), 54, 55, 94
Museums and Society 2034, 147
Museums Change Lives: The MA's Vision for the Impact of Museums, 8, 114, 126–127

National Archives and Records Administration (NARA), 93
National Arts Marketing Project, 119
National Council for History Education, 6–7
National Council on Public History, 125
National Museum of American History, 7, 94
National Museum of New Zealand Te Papa Tongarewa, 94, 135, 144; *Changing Minds, Changing Lives*, 144
National Park Service's (NPS), 70, 93; Organization of American Historians study and, 13–14; Yorktown Battlefield, 14, 151
New England Museum Association, 9
New Jersey Heritage Tourism Task Force, 146–147
New Media Consortium (NMC), *Horizon Report 2013*, 86
New-York Historical Society, 145–146
New York State, 113; museums and, 11, 110, 116, 132–133; "Path Through History," 76
New York State Archives, 75, 81; advocacy and program development, 123–124; Archives Partnership Trust, 81; Documentary Heritage Program, 68; Local Government Records Advisory Council, 124
Norris, Linda, 18, 47
North Carolina, Levine Museum of the New South, 160–162

Ohio, 17; *Citizen's Guide*, 5; Historical Society, 20; survey by University of Toledo, 7; *Toledo's Attic*, 88
Oregon Heritage Commission, 9–10

Organization of American Historians, 13, 125

P & G, 51
P.T. Barnum's American Museum (1841-1865), 88
"participatory museum," 14, 94
participatory program initiatives 56–58
Pennsylvania, 88; Cliveden, 167–168; Pennsbury Manor, 119
Pennsylvania Historical and Museum Commission, 58, 68, 75, 93, 119, 126, 141; *History Bill of Rights*, 126–127
Peters, Lauren, 77
Pew Research Center, "Millennial Generation," 85
photos, 85, 89–90, 103–104; Instagram, 89; sharing applications, 92, 101, 102–103
Pinterest, 89
placemaking, 78
platforms, 89, 94, 95, 96, 101, 102
policy development, 98–100, 107–109, 123–125
program planning and development, 107–109, 123–125
promotion: campaign, 55, 59, 60, 117, 119. *See also* marketing
public education and history, 78–82
Public Historian, 93
public radio, *Backstory with the American History Guys*, 83

Ramsey House, 157–159
re-enactments, Conner Prairie Interactive History Park 153–155, 159
Report on the State of U.S. History Education, 10, 78
Retired Public Employees Association, 69
Richardson, Jim, 97
Richmond, Virginia, 147–148
Ries, Eric, 59
Roth, Darlene, 7
Rothstein, Edward, 14, 155

San Francisco Museum of Modern Art, 94
Santa Cruz Museum of Art and History, 55, 94
Scheinfeldt, Tom, 101

Schultz, Howard, 52
Service Core of Retired Executives, 69
Simon, Nina, 14, 54, 55, 59, 94
Sims, Peter, 59
slavery, 154, 164, 167–168
Smithsonian Institution, 86, 94; digital policy, 100
social media, 89–90; digital-native generation, 19; New Media Consortium (NMC), *Horizon Report 2013*, 86; policies, 98–100; program engagement and, 15, 82, 90–92, 111, 116–118; skills and, 94–95; "Social Media Strategy Worksheet," 100; strategy development, 97–98; trends, 90; web and, 74, 87–92. *See also* digital information and technology
Social Media for Social Good (Mansfield), 103
"Social Media Strategy Worksheet," 100
South Carolina: Historic preservation and, 77; public education and history, 78–79; U.S. History educational standards report and, 10
Southern Oregon Historical Society, 133, 155, 156; *History: Made by You*, 156
Spock, Dan, 7–8
Standards and Excellence Program for History Organizations (StEPs), 67
Starbucks, 52–53
Stowe, Harriet Beecher, 163
strategic management: advisory, 67–69; capacity building, 69–70; cooperation, 73–75; engagement, 70–73; heritage tourism, 67, 76–77; historic preservation, 67, 77–78; heritage tourism, 67, 76–78; placemaking, 78; public education and history, 78–83; strategic planning ; change and, 131–132; demographics, 9, 131, 137, 142, 147–148; elements, 132–134, 137–139; future of organization, 139, 142, 145–146, 147–148; inclusion and, 136–137, 143–145; leadership, 134, 139, 145; process, 134–135; strategies, 139–143; themes, 145–147
statistics, 7, 26, 61, 140, 147
support for programs, 8, 15, 76, 110, 115–116, 120, 122–123

surveys, 7, 124, 140, 153, 157, 169; creativity and, 46, 56, 85; Minnesota Historical Society, 16, 17; Oregon Heritage Commission, 9; North Carolina, 11

Tisdale, Rainey, 47
Toward a Usable Past: Historical Records in the Empire State, 124
Trends, 26–28, 33, 41, 42, 46, 61, 68, 85, 86, 90
Twitter, 19, 90, 91, 94, 95, 96, 102

U-Haul trucks, 120
Uncle Tom's Cabin (Stowe), 163
Underground railroad, 93, 154, 164
Union Pacific Railroad, 121

Vaughan, James, 119, 141
Vermont Historical Society, 133
Vermont State Archives, 113
Virginia, 151–153; *Historyisfun.org*, 151; Valentine Richmond History Center, 147–148
The Virginia Association of Museums, 100, 123
Virginia Center for Digital History: *The Valley of the Shadow: Two Communities in the Civil War*, 88
Virginia Foundation for the Humanities, 83; American Revolution Museum, 153; *Backstory with the American History Guys*, 83
Visser, Jasper, 97

Washington State Historical Society, 17, 139
Washita Battlefield National Historic Site, 14
Watkins, Michael D., 29
Weinberger, David, 12
Wikipedia, 12, 54, 90, 96, 137
Winthrop Group, 111

Yorktown Victory Center, 151–152, 153
YouTube, 12, 90, 92, 93, 94, 96, 103

About the Author

Bruce W. Dearstyne holds a BA in History from Hartwick College and a PhD in History from Syracuse University. He has taught American and New York State history at SUNY Albany, SUNY Potsdam, and Russell Sage College.

Books include *Railroads and Railroad Regulation in New York State, 1903–1913* (1986), co-author of *New York: Yesterday, Today, and Tomorrow* (1990), *Managing Historical Records Programs* (2000), *The Management of Local Government Records* (1988), and *Managing Records and Information Programs: Principles, Techniques, & Tools*. He was the editor and contributed two chapters to *Leading and Managing Archives and Records Programs: Strategies for Success* (2008). His book *The Spirit of New York: Defining Events in the Empire State's History* is being published in 2015.

He has also written dozens of articles on history, archives, libraries, historical programs, and related topics, including two articles for the American Association for State and Local History's *History News* and three AASLH *Technical Leaflets*, including "The Nature of Leadership: Strategies for Leading Historical Programs," *Technical Leaflet* no. 258 (Spring 2012).

He served on the staff of the Office of State History, 1973–1976, and was a program director at the State Archives, 1976–1997.

Dr. Dearstyne was Associate Professor at the College of Information Studies, University of Maryland, 1997–2000, and Professor, 2000–2005, where he still serves as an Adjunct Professor, teaching graduate courses on management. He also directed the University's joint HiLS (History/Library Science) graduate program, 1997–2005.

He was the guest editor and writer of two articles in a special issue of the journal *The Public Historian*, August 2011, "Strengthening the Management of State History: Issues, Perspectives, and Insights from New York." He also published forty articles on New York State history in the Sunday "Perspective" Section of the Albany *Times Union*, 2009–2014.